THE IRON DICE OF BATTLE

THE
IRON DICE
— OF —
BATTLE

ALBERT SIDNEY JOHNSTON
AND THE CIVIL WAR IN THE WEST

TIMOTHY B. SMITH

Louisiana State University Press

Baton Rouge

Published by Louisiana State University Press
lsupress.org

Manufactured in the United States of America
First printing

Designer: Michelle A. Neustrom
Typeface: Sentinel
Printer and binder: Sheridan Books, Inc.

Jacket illustration: Albert Sidney Johnston, ca. 1860.
Courtesy of the Library Congress, Prints and Photographs Division.

All maps created by the author.

Portions of chapter 6 first appeared "To Conquer or Perish: The Last Hours of Albert Sidney
Johnston." In *Confederate Generals in the Western Theater: An Anthology, Volume 3,* edited
by Larry Hewitt and Art Bergeron. Knoxville: University of Tennessee Press, 2011.

Library of Congress Cataloging-in-Publication Data
Names: Smith, Timothy B., 1974– author.
Title: The iron dice of battle : Albert Sidney Johnston and the Civil War in the West
    / Timothy B. Smith.
Other titles: Albert Sidney Johnston and the Civil War in the West
Description: Baton Rouge : Louisiana State University Press, [2023] | Includes
    bibliographical references and index.
Identifiers: LCCN 2023012376 (print) | LCCN 2023012377 (ebook) | ISBN
    978-0-8071-8048-8 (cloth) | ISBN 978-0-8071-8084-6 (pdf) | ISBN
    978-0-8071-8083-9 (epub)
Subjects: LCSH: Johnston, Albert Sidney, 1803–1862. | Generals—Confederate
    States of America—Biography. | Confederate States of America. Army—
    Biography. | United States—History—Civil War, 1861–1865—Campaigns. | Shiloh,
    Battle of, Tenn., 1862.
Classification: LCC E467.1.J73 S65 2023 (print) | LCC E467.1.J73 (ebook) | DDC
    973.7092 [B]—dc23/eng/20230425
LC record available at https://lccn.loc.gov/2023012376
LC ebook record available at https://lccn.loc.gov/2023012377

TO TERRY WINSCHEL

CONTENTS

•———•

Illustrations follow page 104.

MAPS

—•——•—

PREFACE

—•——•—

Albert Sidney Johnston sat on the bold bluff along Locust Grove Branch watching his brigades maneuver toward the Union lines in the distance. The day was April 6, 1862, and the Battle of Shiloh had been raging now for some seven or eight hours. "We sat on our horses, side by side, watching that brigade [James R. Chalmers's] as it swept over the ridge," Johnston's staff officer Major Edward W. Munford explained. "And, as the colors dipped out of sight, the general said to me, 'That checkmates them.'" Munford "told him I was glad to hear him announce 'checkmate,' but that 'he must excuse so poor a player for saying he could not see it.' Johnston laughed and said, 'Yes, sir, that mates them.'"[1]

A slow, methodical contest of chess was Johnston's game of choice, not the faster-moving and often injurious gambling games of poker or dice. At one point early in his military career, when Johnston was home in Kentucky on leave, he met a younger friend who was just coming out of a gambling hall and obviously distraught. The boy admitted that he was caught up in more than he could handle at the time, and Johnston calmly proposed they take a walk, during which he "introduced the subject of games and gaming." Johnston did not lecture his colleague but gave evidence of the vice and calmly recommended, "come, my friend, I wish to teach you a game more intellectual than whist or any game of cards. It needs no betting to make it interesting; and, indeed, the interest would be spoiled by a bet." The two went to Johnston's father's residence and, "for the first time, he introduced me to the chess-board, and taught me the game," the grateful friend recalled.

He added, "I shall never forget the patience with which he, an accomplished player, instructed me in the moves and principles of the game; and frequently in after-life I have felt that nothing but a desire to save and reform me, which to a great extent was effectual, could have promoted his action."[2]

Johnston's passion for chess does not reduce the fact that gambling was occasionally a part of his life, lived primarily on the frontier of America. Gaming and even taking acceptable chances in life were common and expected of a Southern gentleman. In one episode, Johnston even lost "a suit of clothes" in a wager over the 1840 presidential election. But he quickly learned the evils of gambling and opted for the slower-paced and mentally satisfying—and much less dangerous—game of chess. One friend later wrote: "We often played chess together—his knowledge of the game was very thorough. Whenever I was so fortunate as to be the winner, he would fight on to the last, though perhaps the fate of the game might have been long decided, saying, 'While I have a man left I will not despair.'"[3]

Chess certainly seemed to fit Johnston's personality and mindset more than the gambling games of chance like poker or dice. Johnston was a large man (over six feet tall) who could have used force to impose mastery on others, but instead he had a calm and easygoing personality containing few egotistical components. In fact, fitting his methodical personality, he would sometimes play chess via the mail, a slow but sure way of play. One friend gave insights into these personality traits that would become major factors during Johnston's Confederate command. For instance, she wrote that "in the smallest as in the greatest affairs of his life, he took time to deliberate before acting. I was struck with an observation of his (which goes to prove this), when I remarked that he took a good while to write a letter. 'Yes,' said he, 'I do, for I never put on paper what I am not willing to answer for with my life." She added, "so also, in conversation, he considered well before he spoke."[4]

Deliberation is fine in chess and praiseworthy in normal life, but once matters become fast paced and uncertain in war, which is often much more like a game of chance, such a personality of deliberation and calm can prove to be a detriment rather than an attribute. That is especially the case when calm and thorough chess players are suddenly forced into situations where they must seemingly play fast and high-stakes poker, something to which they are not accustomed and to which they do not respond well. Unfortunately, in these life-or-death situations for all involved, many thoughtful and cerebral people grasp at long odds to stay relevant. They try to gain a quick fortune through gambling or risk their lives needlessly in the short move across the fine line between "calculated risk"—famously used by Admiral Chester Nimitz—and all-out habitual gambling to win back everything in one hand. Historian Rhys Isaac has described this action as "a concept of irrationality . . . gambling for stakes so high that the possible returns from winning cannot outweigh the destructive consequences that flow from losing the play."[5]

Ironically, though made up originally of a meek and evenhanded personality that preferred deliberation, which at times put him at odds with his peers and certainly affected him negatively as a military commander, Johnston also occasionally, when forced by desperate situations, lived his life as that of a gambling card player rather than a careful chess player; once life's events began to spiral out of his control, he often took drastic gambles just to keep up, much less to get ahead. It was not so much a lust for the thrill of the chance but rather the occasional need to gamble everything, even life itself, out of desperation. Essentially, Johnston the methodical and restrained chess player was far too lenient in military command, unable to gamble and bluff quickly and effectively enough to win, while sometimes overreaching in the other direction and risking too much when his original meekness brought about desperation. Tottering to the extreme in both directions, Johnston is thus a classic example of historian James Broomall's concept of the emotional life of Southern men, who were often thrust into situations they did not understand.[6]

Albert Sidney Johnston was thus an anomaly of his time, in many ways stalwart, nonegotistical, and solid—attributes that caused him to not always fit into the social norms of Southerners. His adverseness to gambling and even more so his meekness, which often showed restraint against wrongs and caution in personal relationships, are clear examples. He essentially had his own concept of malleable honor that, while incorporating many of the tenets of Southern manhood that historian Bertram Wyatt-Brown has described as the "ancient ethic [that] was the cement that held regional culture together," nevertheless kept him out of step with his contemporaries. Most Southerners viewed honor as affirmation by peers, but Johnston did not always fit the mold of self-aggrandizement and self-promotion, which often came at the expense of others and frequently included laying blame elsewhere for failures. While many Civil War generals or politicians lie in the middle of the pack as far as character is concerned (some generals such as P. G. T. Beauregard, George B. McClellan, and Joseph E. Johnston seem overly flawed and frankly phony), certain others come across as overly genuine and solid, men such as Abraham Lincoln and Robert E. Lee. Among this latter group is Johnston as well, and his calmness in many situations and refusal to react harshly or negatively when normal definitions of his honor were tested put him at odds with the contemporary notions of mastery on all levels as a Southern gentleman. But these restrained reactions would not serve him well as a military commander when, on the other extreme, he also had his moments of loss of self-control. Whether it was when life's circumstances forced him to part with the normal notions of honor and Southern manhood and embrace risky endeavors because of desperation or military situations that he could not overcome, Johnston ultimately strayed across the thin line between calculated risk taking and foolish gambling to win it all back in a figuratively reckless hand of cards or roll of the dice. He certainly rose to those occasions, his blood boiling inside of him when he worked himself and others up to the point of recklessness. "In repose his eyes were as blue as the sky," one contemporary wrote, "but in excitement they flashed to a steel-gray, and exerted a wonderful power over men." Jefferson Davis agreed, writing that "in combat he had the most inspiring presence he ever saw." Johnston was, as a result, a complicated individual who was flexible in his use of the contemporary notions of honor, sometimes being the meek, passive, and kindhearted benefactor while at others being the forceful, determined, and even hardheaded shaper of events.[7]

Obviously, the times Johnston acted forcefully and took those huge risks, which shaped events much more than his typical passiveness, concern historians the most. Certainly, his passiveness as a commander was at the root of many of his and the Confederacy's problems in the western theater that led to the need for those eventual risks, but the actual acts of desperation that led to crossing the line between logical risk taking and careless abandon decided his future. Many of these tendencies had appeared in Johnston's earlier life, including his involvement in dueling as well as in bad economic decisions, not to mention his bold and often too-risky military gambles. Ironically, it was his original desire for the basic honor that Southern manhood provided that led him to many of these episodes, unfortunately at times when life's circumstances had spiraled out of hand and Johnston had to take long, desperate risks to regain control and secure or retain that honor he craved. For example, there was one report of a duel while at the U.S. Military Academy; it is unsubstantiated, however, the cadets preferring to keep it out of official reports. There were also reports that Johnston acted as a second in another duel. Then the famous duel in Texas with Felix Huston nearly cost Johnston his life at that time and may have contributed to his death later. Certainly, the quickness to offer his life on the altar of honor was noble then if questionable now, but Johnston insisted, "I would maintain my honor at the risk of my life." Historian Wyatt-Brown perfectly described dueling as mostly done by "the upper ranks of Southern society," to which Johnston aspired. In fact, death seemingly was no real deterrent to Johnston, another attribute of gentlemanly Southern manhood: "I look to the end with more concern than to the length of life. If that be decorous and honorable, I feel that I can encounter the grim monster unflinchingly whenever he may present himself." Even if it was honorable within the Southern code of manhood, such frivolity with life and death is certainly more of a gambler's mentality than a sophisticated chess player's mindset.[8]

The Iron Dice of Battle: Albert Sidney Johnston and the Civil War in the West is an attempt to take a fresh look at Johnston's preferred command mentality, much like the methodical game of chess, juxtaposed against his alternate gambling character and personality that defined much of his life due to the desperation in which he so often found himself embroiled. Obviously, these dual forces at work in his mind influenced his command in the western theater of the Civil War.[9]

But do we need another examination of Albert Sidney Johnston? There is already a wonderful biography by revered historian Charles P. Roland, *Albert Sidney Johnston: Soldier of Three Republics* (1964). Roland also wrote a small monograph for the McWhiney Series, *Albert Sidney Johnston: Jefferson Davis' Greatest General* (2000). The only other biography of Johnston appeared in 1879 by his son William Preston Johnston, *The Life of General Albert Sidney Johnston*. While the son's work is understandably heavily prejudiced in favor of his father, Roland's full biography, perhaps not as biased but still positively slanted, is the only modern, academic treatment, one of many biographies that the centennial era produced of leading Civil War figures. Newer research has replaced many of these works, with biographies of William T. Sherman, Ulysses S. Grant, and Robert E. Lee rolling off the presses frequently. Yet other centennial studies that remain the seminal works on their subjects need to be replaced. For example, many have called for new biographies of William S. Rosecrans or P. G. T. Beauregard. Few calls for a new biography of Johnston have emerged, however, simply because of the quality of Roland's 1964 book. Indeed, there is no pressing need for a new full biography of Albert Sidney Johnston.[10]

Yet in examining Johnston's life, the Civil War years consume less than a third of Roland's book, fewer than one hundred pages. More importantly, the strongest portions of that volume discuss Johnston's early life before the war, negating a need for new exploration in that area. Roland expresses his opinions on Johnston the Civil War general, but historians have challenged them, and some have even wondered if there might have been some hero-worship involved in his assessment, especially in the later monograph subtitled *Jefferson Davis' Greatest General*. Certainly, much work on the early war in the West has been done in the years since the centennial, and much new thinking has been produced since Roland's biography appeared. In fact, all three major studies of the Forts Henry and Donelson Campaign (by Frank Cooling, Kendall Gott, and Timothy Smith) and all five of the major studies of Shiloh (by Wiley Sword, James Lee McDonough, Larry Daniel, Edward Cunningham, and Timothy Smith) were all published after Roland's biography appeared. Roland did not have the benefit of this modern scholarship when writing his biography. As it has been almost sixty years since he published that volume, there is definitely room—and need—for a new examination of Johnston's role in the Civil War. One historian, in fact, has concluded that "the Shiloh Campaign is so important to the outcome of the Civil War and the debate over Johnston so heated that periodically it is necessary to reevaluate the issue in light of current scholarship and what is now known about the campaign."[11]

The major thrust of this volume is an examination of Johnston's Civil War activity by looking at the flexible ways he commanded, at times with passive moderation such as the self-professed methodical chess player he thought he was, while at other times as a risk-taking gambler. Despite his claims to the contrary, Johnston's early life demonstrated such risky gambling when life-or-death or life-altering decisions confronted him; similarly, there were times when he put his family or army organizations at risk out of desperation to remain master of his situation. Johnston certainly gambled during his tenure as Confederate western theater commander as well, and much like a gambler, he had to bluff and deceive. He also ultimately had to call his opponent's hand, which he did at Shiloh, where he declared he must "roll the iron dice of battle." It was a gamble to be sure, but it had to be done—or as he stated it, he and the Confederate army must "conquer or perish." That much was well-considered risk-taking, but his death was an act of pure desperation to achieve the goal of victory that, by 2:30 on the afternoon of April 6, had almost slipped from the realm of possibility. He perished in taking that enormous risk of leading a charge himself, and his defeat on top of the setbacks earlier in 1862 led to a terribly dismal situation for the western Confederacy. The key for Johnston, of course, was the nuance between gambling acceptably and gambling irresponsibly, the difference in which the methodical chess player was not well versed.

Examination of what it all meant in the bigger picture accompanies the details of Johnston's command tenure. A baseball pennant or presidential nomination cannot be won in April and May of a baseball season or in Iowa or New Hampshire in presidential caucuses and primaries. But a hole can be dug so deep at that time that it is hard in either analogy to recover. The Confederacy was not out of the war by any means when Johnston died at Shiloh, as it obviously continued on for three more years, but his tenure dug such a deep hole that the Confederacy was hard pressed to ever get itself out. And that effect did not stop with Johnston's death at Shiloh. His fall left the western Confederacy woefully lacking a major commander who was both acceptable to the Davis administration and head and shoulders above all other generals in ability. The result was constant infighting and backstabbing among the Confederate high command for the remainder of the war in the West.

Divided into six chapters, this book is not a traditional biography but rather a "think-piece" on Johnston's command in the West. Much shorter than a traditional biography, only the first two chapters deal with his prewar life. These synthetic chapters have a two-fold purpose: first, to lay the foundations for his life for readers who may not have read Roland's or William Preston Johnston's biographies and, second, to delineate and emphasize the major dual patterns of caution and irresponsible gambling in Johnston's early life that later so shaped his Confederate command. Chapter 1 accordingly covers the first thirty years of Johnston's life, when all was well and he found himself enjoying a good living. Unfortunately, within the span of two years in the mid-1830s, that idyllic existence came crashing down around him and almost everyone dear to him, as well as his chosen profession, were lost. Indeed, all the attributes of a Southern gentleman's life were quickly gone and he found himself in crisis mode, adrift in a loss of identity.

Chapter 2 deals with Johnston's next thirty or so years and his effort to regain control of his life and situation, often through wild gambles out of desperation. Although he gained high rank by the late 1850s, Johnston's experience after the mid-1830s was about catching up and reacting rather than the formation of circumstances.

While only two chapters cover Johnston's pre–Civil War life, four chapters examine his Confederate command. Chapter 3 discusses his gambles and bluffs after assuming control of the Confederacy's Department No. 2, the western theater of operations, in September 1861. Johnston faced innumerable problems that shaped his course rather than he shaping it, and his gambles, admittedly at times the only options he had, proved surprisingly successful in 1861. Chapter 4 shows his gambles catching up with him as his genial personality and methodical thinking exacerbated an enemy invasion that turned into a disaster. The loss of Forts Henry and Donelson was in large part the result of Johnston's paltry circumstances, but it was made worse by his passive command decisions, most notably putting too much faith in abysmal subordinates and not taking command himself at critical points. Chapter 5 examines the Confederate retreat from Nashville to a concentration with other forces and Johnston's critical decision to offer battle at Shiloh while the enemy was separated into two forces. That was an acceptable risk because it was the only real option he had, but it was largely brought about because of his earlier gambles and passive command style. Chapter 6 focuses on Johnston's last day on earth, April 6, 1862, and examines his command decisions amid the fog of battle. One of those decisions was his final, desperate, and fatal gamble to guide the fighting personally, which led to his mortal wounding early that afternoon.

Such a reexamination is needed because, if for no other reason, the standard historiographical treatment is growing quite old. Since Roland's biography appeared, historians have had a hard time understanding Johnston and his role in the western theater. Some historians, Larry J. Daniel has argued, have been "strangely bedazzled" with Johnston; Thomas Connelly has called the phenomenon's cause "the Johnston mystique." Certainly, Roland fits into this school of thought, backed by other first-rate historians such as Albert Castel who remarked that "Johnston should not be blamed too much for failing to do what would have been difficult under the best circumstances and which, under the actual circumstances, was nearly impossible." On the other hand, the leading critic of Johnston's tenure in the West is Connelly, who called him "a military failure in the Civil War." While many consider Connelly's *Army of the Heartland* (and a second volume on the later war—*Autumn of Glory*) as the last word on the Confederacy's western army—eventually named the Army of Tennessee—it is not and, in fact, is full of overblown statements that his admittedly concise and analytical narrative does not fully support. For instance, he claimed without support, "Johnston seemed to live in a world to himself. He was never able to establish rapport with his sub-commanders." Daniel has taken up the anti-Johnston mantle from Connelly and also sees the general as a total failure. He argues that the final tally is evidence enough: Johnston lost the iron and copper region of the Confederacy, vast agricultural areas, the gunpowder works at Nashville along with the city itself, and a large chunk of his army in losing Kentucky and Tennessee to the Confederacy.[12]

So which was it? Was Johnston the Confederacy's greatest general as described by Roland and Castel, one who was unfortunately plagued by mitigating circumstances beyond his control? Was he Connelly's and Daniel's incompetent commander who never should have been elevated to that level in the first place? Or, as in most cases, did Johnston's performance fall somewhere in the middle? Perhaps Johnston's failure in the West was simply the result of a methodical chess player who suddenly found himself in a high-stakes poker game of war that quickly forced him to take excessive gambles instead of calculated risks to win back all that had been lost.

ACKNOWLEDGMENTS

———•———

Many people have helped me along the way of analyzing Albert Sidney Johnston's Civil War command. Discussions with fellow members of the Historians of the Civil War Western Theater, particularly at the 2021 yearly meeting revolving around Forts Henry and Donelson in Murray, Kentucky, helped mold my thoughts. Other interactions did as well, including time spent with Charlie Roland on several occasions, most memorably when we led a tour of Shiloh during the sesquicentennial.

This book has benefited from others reading the manuscript. Two friends in particular read the chapters and offered sage advice. John Marszalek, who also helped lead the tour at Shiloh with Roland, as well as Larry Daniel each read the manuscript and provided wonderful suggestions that made the argument and the book stronger. The peer-review process was enlightening as well, and working with LSU Press, especially Rand Dotson, has been a pleasure. Copyeditor Kevin Brock polished the entire manuscript and caught many nagging issues.

Thanks also go to Derek Dees and Mike Beara of Bonney, Texas, who gave me access to Johnston's ranch, China Grove. They allowed me to explore the grounds leading all the way back toward Oyster Creek all I wanted to. It was a special experience; I could almost feel the aura of Albert Sidney Johnston in that open prairie.

Most thanks go to my wonderful ladies, Kelly, Mary Kate, and Leah Grace. Life would be nothing without them, and I thank God for them and his providential care and salvation.

This book is dedicated to my friend of many years Terry Winschel, the retired historian at Vicksburg National Military Park. I have long desired to dedicate a book to him to publicly show my appreciation for everything he has done for me over the past twenty-five years. I originally intended to do so with one of my Vicksburg volumes, but he has been so involved with those, reading the manuscripts and kindly offering promotional blurbs, that I did not want to create a conflict of interest. Being out of the Vicksburg realm, this book is the perfect place to publicly say thank you to Terry for his very generous work on my behalf and on behalf of the American people during his long tenure with the National Park Service and the U.S. Army Corps of Engineers.

THE IRON DICE OF BATTLE

— 1 —

TO A GENTLEMAN THIS TASTE IS ESSENTIAL

THE MAKING OF A MAN

The first decade of the 1800s produced many of the leading statesmen and generals who would conduct the Civil War fifty years later. Robert E. Lee and Joseph E. Johnston were both born in 1807 in Virginia. Abraham Lincoln and Jefferson Davis were born in 1809 and 1807 respectively, not far from one another in Kentucky. Just a state for a mere decade or so, Kentucky also saw one of its most famed sons of this conflict born in 1803, the same year that the vast Louisiana lands became part of the United States and Lewis and Clark set off on their whirlwind trek across a continent. Albert Sidney Johnston came from sound New England stock, both sets of grandparents hailing from the Northeast. His father's parents had grown up in Salisbury, Connecticut, where his grandfather Archibald Johnston was a physician of note in the town. Archibald's son John Johnston likewise became a physician and married a New England native, Mary Stoddard. The couple had three sons but moved west to the barrens of Kentucky in 1788, even before it was a state. Times were tough in the wilderness despite John's thriving medical practice, and Mary died in 1793. John then married Abigail Harris the next year. Having emigrated to Kentucky from New England, her parents were from Newburyport, Massachusetts, where her father, Edward Harris, was a prominent Presbyterian minister.[1]

The whole mixture wound up in Washington, Kentucky, in then Mason County, where Reverend Harris preached the gospel and Dr. Johnston tended to the people's physical needs. Their children continued the family presence in Kentucky as well, the union of John and Abigail producing six more children in addition to the three sons born from John's first marriage. The second from the youngest of the six was named Albert Sidney, born on February 3, 1803.[2]

Comparatively little is known about Albert Sidney Johnston's early childhood, and only a few family stories and recollections of stories told by himself remain. It seems young Sidney, as he was known, grew up in a safe and loving environment and received a good education, something that would be expected from the son and grandson of medical doctors and ministers. By all accounts, he developed into a courteous and mild-mannered boy, although with an inpatient and volatile temper he had to continually learn to control. One account from those who knew the future general as a boy related that he grew up "handsome, proud, manly, earnest, and self-reliant . . . and as far from being a bully as any boy in the world." In fact, Johnston seemed to relish taking up for the underdog, whether it be runt animals or small children. The tales were numerous that he would stand up for those weaker and would confront the bullies himself.[3]

Johnston thus quickly assumed a leadership position among friends and acquaintances, though not through harshness. One observer noted he was not the bully, "yet he was one whom the bullies left undisturbed." Another even described how there was "one fellow about Washington who was proud of playing the bully, but who, to the amusement of the town, always skipped Albert Johnston and Black Dan Marshall." It did not hurt, of course, that young Sidney was growing fast, ultimately to a height of over six feet tall. Yet he used his strength as a force for good and not ill. In fact, the same observer noted his "reserved and quiet manners . . . and his habitual interference for the protection of the smaller and weaker boys." Sidney's sister likewise noted his care for even animals that could not protect themselves, a trait shared by his opponent of decades later, Ulysses S. Grant: "His dog and his horse he always treated with the kindest consideration. I have often known him to walk, and lead his horse, when it had become fatigued."[4]

That said, Johnston could at times let others or his emotions get the best of him. One story, actually told on himself, related how he was a champion marble player and collected everyone's marbles in town, which he would then place for safekeeping in a buried jar. He soon met an antagonist who could never beat him but seemed to have an inexhaustible supply of marbles; later, he realized that the other boy had found his stash of marbles and was taking from it at the same rate Johnston was winning them. Another story related Johnston's temper as a teenager. When trying to get on a smaller-than-required boot, he became exasperated and threw it out the window in a rage. His sister called him on it, and he went and retrieved the boot and simply set it in its place. Years later, when he was a soldier and trying to fire a musket that continually misfired, the same sister related that she would have guessed he would have broken it over a fence by this time. Johnston retorted, "you remember the boot." He added that he had not forgotten the lesson and that he had "learned that a soldier should have perfect control of himself, to be able to control others."[5]

Johnston's boyhood education also seemed befitting that of a prominent son of social leaders of Washington, Kentucky. He studied with some of the best local teachers, including Mann Butler and James Grant, as well as for a time at a school in western Virginia at age fifteen. Later, he attended Transylvania University in Kentucky with some of the generation's most famous figures, including Jefferson Davis. He learned a solid basis of the classics and mathematics, which he excelled in, as well as medical preparation, everyone assuming he would become a third-generation doctor. Johnston had other ideas, however, and mostly desired to join the U.S. Navy. His parents and presumably the grandparents as well were less than thrilled and tried to talk him out of it, but this brought forth another attribute of Johnston: stubbornness. He would not give in but, in an effort to figure out his destiny, agreed to go to Louisiana to confer with his brother who had reached prominence there by this time.[6]

Thus appeared in Johnston's life one of the hallmarks of a young man seeking to rise in prominence as a Southern gentleman: kinship. By the time Johnston reached manhood, he had about him, although through no work of his own, vast kinship ties of leading family members who helped pave his way forward toward the elite of Southern society. His father and both grandfathers, of course, had been prominent citizens in both New England and then in their corner of Kentucky, two as physicians and one as a minister. Those were beloved and honored positions in Southern society.[7]

Similarly, his brothers by this time were well established in honorable positions all across the South, and they provided a large network for young Sidney Johnston to feed from and seek to follow. Johnston being the second to youngest child of his father's second marriage, many of these brothers were much older and had entered adult life well before Sidney came of age. For example, his half-brothers from his father's first marriage were well off by this time. Darius Johnston was a lawyer of note, having studied with a future member of a presidential cabinet. Orramel Johnston chose to continue his lineage in medicine, studying in New Orleans. Both of these brothers fought in the Mexican War, which unfortunately broke their health, one dying soon thereafter and the other later on. Of Sidney's full brothers, Harris Johnston also became a prominent lawyer. Death also affected his full brothers, however, with Lucius Johnston dying of yellow fever in his mid-twenties after migrating to Louisiana to become a planter. His brother John also moved to Louisiana and became a prominent lawyer and politician, serving in the Louisiana legislature and as a judge.[8]

Yet none of the brothers or half-brothers, excluding Sidney himself, became as prominent as the eldest of John Johnston's sons, Sidney's half-brother Josiah Stoddard Johnston. He was actually born in Connecticut but moved very early with the family to Kentucky, although his father sent him back there for school. Known as Stoddard, he later attended Transylvania University in Lexington, as would many of the brothers including Sidney, and studied law under prominent lawyers of the area. He moved to the wilds of Louisiana in 1805, just two years after his last half-brother's birth, and quickly rose to prominence as a plantation owner, legislator, soldier, and judge. His district elected him to Congress in 1821, and the state legislature sent him back to Washington as one of Louisiana's two U.S. senators in an 1823 special election. He gained a full term in the Senate in 1825 and a second one in 1831, even though he and the state legislature's majority were of opposing parties—such was the esteem felt for Josiah Stoddard Johnston at the time.[9]

Stoddard became a major player in Washington in the 1820s and 1830s, the volatile era of Andrew Jackson. He rose to the chairmanship of the Committee on Commerce in the Nineteenth Congress. Stoddard was a close friend of Henry Clay, which put him at odds with Jackson, of course, as well as many in his state. He opposed nullification but backed a high protective tariff. Still, he was revered by most in Louisiana.[10]

Stoddard took heavy interest in his brothers, both full and half, and wielded considerable influence on them, especially after their father's death in 1832. He was something of a father figure to them even before that, as evidenced by several siblings moving to and starting to make their own names in Louisiana. But Stoddard's youngest brother was a special cause, as Sidney himself later reflected: "I am more indebted to my brother Stoddard for whatever I am, than to any other man." Significantly, Sidney would go to Stoddard when he was grappling with the larger issues of life, particularly his vocation. His desire to join the navy brought something of an intervention by the rest of the family, whose consensus was to send him to Louisiana so that his revered politician-planter brother could hopefully talk some sense into him. It worked, as after a few months Sidney agreed to return to his studies at Transylvania. Perhaps in doing so, the navy missed an admiral in this future general.[11]

Amid this vast and growing network of kinship at his disposal, Sidney was nevertheless very desirous—in fact, somewhat stubborn—to make his own mark. He accordingly began to develop a second major trait as he grew to maturity. A major tenet of Southern manhood was honor, and Sidney Johnston seemed to, more than perhaps others, define a code for his life even from the earliest years as a boy. Numerous acquaintances and family members spoke of his ethical code, perhaps acquired from his minister grandfather who once threatened to resign as Washington's postmaster because new regulations required him to deal with the mail on Sunday, which went against his convictions. Sidney early on grew quite frank and straightforward, which some determined also came from his father, who one acquaintance described as "bold and blunt to a remarkable degree." Sidney certainly gained from his parents his lifelong favor of "Spartan simplicity," as his own son later described it, although even in such modesty he always strove to look neat.[12]

Albert Sidney Johnston thus had a wide network of kinship and a strong self-bred character already formed by the time he neared his twenties and began to cast out into life. And here it was necessary to acquire a third set of attributes that led to manhood. Southern gentlemen of the time were expected to have an honorable career, a large and successful family of wife and children, and own land and slaves. In essence, the Southern gentleman was master of his domain, whether it be in the facets of family, slaves, or his own self. Certainly, that is the route many of Sidney's lineage and brothers had taken, the offices of minister, physician, lawyer, and certainly politician and slaveowner being much revered in the Old South. Any of these vocations could lead to wealth, which more often than not was quickly invested into the ultimate goal of planting and slaveowning. If that was successful, it allowed for retiring at a comparatively young age from many of those professions as well as experimenting, for those not already involved, in political office. Thus, it was critical what Sidney chose to do with his life, whom he chose to marry, and how he spent his livelihood, control being the common denominator in the slaveholding class.[13]

For his career path, Sidney Johnston made the fateful decision to join the U.S. Army, which would have wide-ranging ramifications throughout his life. He decided against the medical field of his father and grandfather as well as the law and politics that his brothers were so immersed in. Also spurned was a career in the ministry such as his grandfather had selected, and despite a life of humility and good deeds, especially to those less fortunate than he, there never seemed to be a major concern for religious matters on Sidney's part. There was on the other hand some family history of military service, his preacher grandfather having fought in the Revolutionary War and his half-brother Stoddard in the War of 1812.[14]

Not all careers in the military were suited for a potential Southern gentleman, however, certainly not as a common foot soldier. In fact, those positions were often filled with rogues or those who were down on their luck and had no other option. That was perhaps the family's concern with Johnston's intention to join the navy, there being no formalized path to officer status at the time (the U.S. Naval Academy would not be established until 1845) except through years of grueling commoner work on ships. But there was such a mechanism within the army, another outgrowth of President Thomas Jefferson's first decade of the nineteenth century, the U.S. Military Academy. An officer in the army was well looked upon socially as well as politically and economically. Even better, a West Point–trained officer was at the top of those status-oriented hierarchies. In contrast to the family's concern for Johnston joining the navy, there was great rejoicing at his decision to enter the noble and manly realm of an army officer.[15]

And even better, there was family support for that process. West Point cadets had to be appointed by federal politicians such as representatives, senators, cabinet officials, or even the president. Johnston had just such a connection at that time in his eldest half-brother, Representative Josiah Stoddard Johnston, and soon received his appointment to the military academy in 1822 for the class that would graduate in 1826. Johnston made his way to New York in the summer of 1822, a mere nineteen years old but tall and strong already. On the steamboat trip northward, he not surprisingly met and befriended another future cadet, Nathaniel J. Eaton, who described Johnston as "a full-grown man, of commanding figure and imposing presence." Conversely, Eaton described himself as "a stripling of a boy, not quite fifteen years old, and as green as I was young." Significantly, Johnston treated Eaton with the same courtesy and respect he showed everyone else, although at one point after arriving and watching the current corps of cadets march on the drill field, "he laid his hand on my head and said kindly, 'Well, my young friend, what do you think of that?'" Eaton continued to enjoy a friendship with Johnston as the two advanced through the army's ranks.[16]

The appointment was obviously the doing of his politician-brother, something the strong-willed and honorable Sidney Johnston would seethe at later in life as he worked to make his own way. Stoddard was certainly the main mover, Sidney's appointment actually coming from a Louisiana slot rather than his native Kentucky. The young man nevertheless accepted it: "I have the honor to acknowledge the receipt of your letter of admission to the military school . . . & to apprise you of my acceptance. I shall report myself to the superintendent at West Point early in June." He added, "I hand you enclosed a declaration from my Father giving his consent to my engagement to serve five years." His father wrote below that notification: "Whereas my son Albert S. Johnston has been admitted into the military academy I authorize him to enter into articles binding himself to serve five years or until discharged or to make any other engagement which the laws of the institution require as if he was of full age."[17]

Johnston arrived at West Point in early summer and went through the indoctrination program before starting classes in the fall. Throughout his four years there, he was among the top performers. He moved little in his class ranking from year to year, finishing at ninth of 80 cadets in his first year and moving up to eighth of 62 his second year. He remained eighth of 52 his third year and finished eighth of 42 cadets in his final year. Johnston, while not a perfect student in terms of deportment, was far above average. In his senior year, for instance, he accumulated a total of only 19 demerits. That same year, freshman cadet Robert E. Lee and six others received no demerits at all, and 27 cadets had fewer marks than Johnston. But the other 179 cadets had more than him and his best friend, Bennett Henderson, who was tied with Johnston at 19. Junior-year cadet Jonathan C. Clark accumulated a whopping 621 demerits that year, while sophomore Jefferson Davis had 120.[18]

Numerous colleagues and acquaintances remarked on Johnston's values exhibited at the military academy. One classmate described him as "a high-minded, honorable gentleman and soldier." Others described his fairness as well as his aloofness; one remarked how Johnston "commanded the respect of all who knew him," while another described his "reticence and dignity of manners." Classmate and close friend Jefferson Davis later wrote, "we belonged to the same 'set,' a name well understood by those who have been ground in the Academy mill," and described how Johnston "did not have an enemy in the corps, or an unkind feeling to any one, though he was select in his associates." He probably rarely, if ever, snuck out to the famed Benny Havens; in fact, he soon became the adjutant of the corps, a position of highest esteem. Johnston apparently also had the choice of a captaincy, which he declined.[19]

The stubborn cadet stood up for himself when necessary. His son William later recorded the story of his father being competent in all math problems except two, which happened to be the two the instructor gave him. He explained his predicament, to which the superintendent sternly ordered him to be quiet and be seated. Johnston objected and later wrote a letter challenging the outcome. The school gave him another examination, which he passed easily.[20]

Johnston emerged from his four-year West Point odyssey with an honorable and sufficient path in life. He was a military officer, a vocation acceptable for the purposes of manhood and honor. Likewise, Johnston also added to his network of kinship, if not through strictly familial connections then certainly in his associations with friends made at the academy. Apart from his "most intimate friend" Henderson, others of his class of 1826 were such future luminaries as Silas Casey and Samuel P. Heintzelman. Relative upperclassmen through Johnston's four years included such cadets as Charles F. Smith, Robert Anderson, and Lorenzo Thomas. Junior to him were Davis (two years behind), with whom he established a warm friendship (much to Johnston's later benefit), and his roommate Leonidas Polk, one year behind him. Polk wrote home of his "good fortune as to roommates." Entering as freshmen the year Johnston graduated were Robert E. Lee and Joseph E. Johnston.[21]

After a long furlough, Johnston's work in life began, serving first in the 2nd U.S. Infantry in the fall of 1826. He spent at least some of that fall in Washington, D.C., visiting with his half-brother Stoddard, then in the Senate. Johnston made the social rounds in the capital as a brand new brevet second lieutenant, meeting such notables as Senator Johnston's close friend and political ally Henry Clay as well as the president, John Quincy Adams, another likeminded politician. It was here that the young officer ran into one of the first tests of his idealism and perhaps stubbornness when, doubtless because of who his brother was, he received an offer to assume duties on the staff of Major General Winfield Scott, perhaps the most dominant military figure in the United States in the first half of the nineteenth century. Both Senator Johnston and his wife pushed Sidney to accept the post, but he refused. His sister-in-law wrote that "although much gratified to have been mentioned by General Scott," the lieutenant "preferred to go off to the far West, and enter at once upon the duties of his profession." Johnston's son later remarked that he desired "to owe his advancement to meritorious service, not patronage." His already formed sense of honor and manhood was such that he desired to make his own way in life even at the cost of inflated status or peer affirmation; perhaps he was even a little bit ashamed of the help of his brother in getting into West Point in the first place. From here on in life, when he could, he would earn his own way.[22]

Johnston no doubt had second thoughts, however, when he first arrived at lonely and isolated Sackett's Harbor, New York, on Lake Ontario. His orders were dated December 22, but he arrived early, still in the dead of winter. Johnston had little to do except read, and his boredom almost got him into trouble when, during artillery practice over the frozen lake, he purposefully fired in the general vicinity of some recreationists on the ice. The shot landed far too close for comfort, and for a few seconds Johnston was afraid he had hurt or even killed some of the skaters. Fortunately, they were fine and beat a hasty retreat, though not without sending shouts and gestures his way. Johnston took this as a lesson not to be so foolish in the future.[23]

Johnston's next orders took him, in the summer of 1827, to a new regiment and garrison as second lieutenant in the 6th U.S. Infantry, stationed at Jefferson Barracks, Missouri, just south of St. Louis. He arrived there on June 1, 1827, to unfinished barracks amid a beautiful wilderness and described how he was "agreeably disappointed in its location." There, for the next seven years, the officer took part in his first active military campaigning, growing in his profession as well as in his manhood.[24]

Johnston utilized his time at Jefferson Barracks in many ways, among them learning to play the flute. He practiced religiously to the chagrin of his friends; "a wide difference of opinion existed between himself and his friends as to his musical aptitudes," his son later humorously acknowledged.

In fact, Johnston became "somewhat irritable" over the whole episode, especially about his inability to learn it quickly. His temper almost snapped one day when he found a comrade in an adjoining room upstairs tapping on his ceiling every time he practiced. Johnston stormed upstairs to confront the officer, whom he found cracking walnuts. He decided then and there, ashamed of his haste and temper, to give up the flute: "I did not think that a man so sensitive about his skill was fit for a flute player."[25]

More importantly, while stationed at Jefferson Barracks, Johnston realized his full manhood in two major ways. First, he gained a wife and family; as historian Stephen Berry writes in his study of Southern manhood, "the woman, once acquired, would sustain and bear witness to the male becoming." Lieutenant Johnston attended a ball in St. Louis in 1827 and there met Henrietta Preston, with whom he quickly fell in love. She was, like him, well educated in the classics and honorable society, and the two made a wonderful pair. She also hailed from a well-known family with many connections. Her father was a military man, a major who had served in the West during the Revolution. Her mother was the daughter of a Revolutionary War colonel who had also been a member of Congress in the early days of the republic. The family had later moved from their Virginia homeland to Louisville, Kentucky, where the familial relations continued to expand. For instance, Henrietta's sister married William Clark of Lewis and Clark fame, while another of their kin had married Thomas Hart Benton, then also in the U.S. Senate. The family also included kinship to future army general and president Zachary Taylor. The Prestons were certainly a well-known and connected family, perhaps even more so than the Johnstons. As the budding love relationship between Sidney and Henrietta blossomed, those larger bonds of kinship grew as well.[26]

Henrietta spoke French, was familiar with all the current and classic literature, and traveled widely to visit relations. She was thus visiting St. Louis when she met the young Lieutenant Johnston. Even better, Johnston spent much of the following year, 1828, on detached duty recruiting for the regiment, and probably not by happenstance he was detailed to Henrietta's home city, Louisville. There, he courted her, and they eventually married on January 20, 1829. The newlyweds moved into officer's housing at Jefferson Barracks, where life was happy but plain. "Some cut glass seems to have represented the splendor of their little establishment," one of their children later wrote.[27]

To this cheerful union soon came a child on January 5, 1831, born in Louisville and named William Preston Johnston, after Henrietta's father; she also had a brother by the same name. Mother and son remained in that city for a time but soon rejoined Lieutenant Johnston at Jefferson Barracks a few months later. There, the family remained together for the next year or so, until the rumblings of Indian trouble began to be heard.[28]

These rumblings provided Johnston with the second manhood attribute required in his life—legitimacy in his new profession, which could only come with active campaigning and combat. Historians such as James M. McPherson have described seeing combat as a "test of manhood." Johnston's first campaign came in 1827, when his regiment was involved in an operation into Wisconsin to dampen the enthusiasm of the Winnebago Indians. Later, Johnston participated in the Black Hawk War in 1832. The Sauk and Fox Indians under famed leader Black Hawk had been moved west of the Mississippi River as part of President Jackson's Indian Removal policy. They returned to their old sacred ground in 1832, however, after finding life across the river not to their liking. The small band refused further negotiations, at which time the army sent out its nearest force, units from Jefferson Barracks. Johnston and the other troops from St. Louis moved out under Colonel Henry Atkinson, the regiment's commander and, as a brevet brigadier general, the officer in charge of the expedition. The force followed the Native Americans northward through Illinois and into Wisconsin throughout the spring and summer of 1832. Ultimately, they cornered Black Hawk's Indians against the Mississippi River and defeated them at the Battle of Bad Axe in August.[29]

Johnston was not a frontline commander, but rather assumed several staff duties. He worked with the local militia, mainly from Illinois, which included a young Abraham Lincoln; also in the militia was future politician and general John A. McClernand. Among the regular force was Johnston's West Point friend Davis. Johnston's son later remarked on the irony of both Lincoln and Davis having fought together, men "who, forty [thirty] years later, measured arms on an arena whose contest shook the world." Another aspect of the lieutenant's work, which illustrates his standing among his superiors, was his duty first as adjutant of his regiment and then as assistant adjutant general on Atkinson's staff. Johnston's role, according to his son, was "necessarily keeper of his commander's conscience . . . [and] the historian of the campaign." Johnston kept a diary of the military events and wrote the report of the action later, although he was not present for the entire operation. At one point in early June, Johnston returned to St. Louis to oversee the equipping of new militia forces slated to join the expedition. It was during this short return home that Johnston first met his brand new daughter Henrietta Preston Johnston, who had been born in April while he was away.[30]

By the time Sidney Johnston reached his thirties in the early 1830s, he was well on the way to realizing the life of a Southern gentleman, albeit not yet through the ultimate role of a slaveholding elite. But he had firm kinship connections that were already built in his own family and only added to those substantial ties by marrying well into another prominent Kentucky family. Likewise, the connections made in his days at West Point added close friends, if not kin, to his network. These friends and relatives included governors and senators as well as future presidents, and although Johnston was adamant that he wanted to earn his own way, there is no doubt that some of these ties had already paid good dividends. But like most other young Southern men, he sought acceptance in the slaveholding elite for himself, not just through his family connections.[31]

In addition to his kinship network, Johnston also had a solid gentlemanly code already established for his moral bearing. He was by all accounts selective in his friends and sought to put his best face forward. And that played into his notions of manhood, including his relationship with females. He and his brothers had foregone another tenet of manhood, land ownership, by giving some inherited land to their sisters for their well-being. Likewise, his own care and respect for women was evident. One of his comrades during the Black Hawk War told of an episode in which Johnston confronted a fellow officer who was using "coarse and vulgar" language, saying he "did not believe in female virtue." Johnston simply reminded the offender, "you have a mother; and, I believe, you have a sister." He let it go at that, and the man "hung his head in shame." Certainly in this case, like many Southern men coming of age and seeking the status of a Southern gentleman, Johnston's code of honor in regard to women and even his own reputation led him to be at times aggressive and confrontational.[32]

Finally, Johnston's status was ensured by both his position as a U.S. military officer and his head-of-household status as a husband and father. While the Black Hawk War was comparatively benign (certainly with what was coming later in his career), Johnston was nevertheless growing in his profession, his status as adjutant an extremely important and honored position. In fact, some "revolutionary governments" in Latin America and even in Europe approached Johnston and others about coming to lead their forces. Likewise, his own family was growing, and more children would eventually be born. Johnston was thus master of his life and peers as much as almost any young man turning thirty could expect, particularly out on the frontier areas of the still-young United States.[33]

But as the 1830s continued, Johnston's entire world came crashing down around him. His comfortable faith in his achieved success and desire for more to come was severely shaken when almost every single defining factor of his life was swept out from under him, leaving him grasping for a new life and a new identity. The methodical chess player was about to be thrust into a high-stakes, fast-moving poker game.[34]

Not the least of his problems was the acute outbreak of cholera among the soldiers sent to fight Black Hawk's Indians in 1832. On the way home, the 6th Infantry faced a severe outbreak of the disease, and Johnston himself came down with a severe case. His son later wrote of the treatment his father received: "lying upon the floor, he was wrapped in heavy blankets, drenched with vinegar and salt, and then dosed with brandy and Cayenne pepper." He added that it would be up to others to "decide whether he recovered in consequence or in spite of the treatment."[35]

Johnston's other major disasters involved the loss of numerous members of his kinship community. Suddenly, he would no longer have these trusted people to advise him in the future. In 1832 came a tragedy in the form of the accidental death of his closest friend at West Point. Bennett Henderson had resigned from the army but was living near St. Louis when he was catapulted from a carriage as it overturned, killing him. Crisis after crisis also came among his family connections. Johnston's father passed away in 1832, his mother having been gone for decades now. The next year the man who was really more of a father figure to Johnston than even his own father, Senator Josiah Stoddard Johnston, also perished in a steamboat accident on the Red River in Louisiana.[36]

The senator was, in fact, elder brother and father figure all rolled into one, and he had continued to counsel Johnston throughout his early military years. Stoddard constantly urged on his younger half-brother the ideals of a gentlemen, writing that land ownership and plantation owning were the true marks of a man. The lieutenant already owned some land, particularly in Louisville that came from his wife's family, and he had a man in the city, Edward Hobbs, to see to it for him. Stoddard also pushed him toward politics as well as education. "Books are the source of the purest and most rational pleasures. . . . To a gentleman this taste is essential," he wrote Sidney in 1833. He also added that the young man's military pedigree was likewise profitable, especially if the nation ever blundered into civil war, which the senator predicted happening as early as that year: "military talents are held in high estimation all over the world, less perhaps than they deserve in this country; but no one knows how long we shall be peaceful neighbors." Stoddard possibly predicted a war with neighboring Mexico, but his next sentence amid the nullification crisis in South Carolina rings with haunting foreshadowing, even in 1833: "you may live to see not only war among the States, but civil and perhaps servile war."[37]

Yet Stoddard Johnston would not be there to help navigate his younger half-brother through those turbid waters. He and his family were traveling on the steamboat *Lioness* on the Red River in May 1833 when, early in the morning, an explosion occurred. Sidney's brother John wrote him of the bad news, stating that the senator and his only son, William, were in their stateroom and "in one instant, when all on board were unsuspecting, the boat was, by some unaccountable accident, blown to atoms by gunpowder." The total killed were fifteen or twenty people, with the senator perishing instantly and being blown into the water. His body was not found for several days. Young William survived but was terribly injured, taking refuge on a piece of debris in the river. A newspaper lamented the loss, writing that Stoddard was "an able statesman and one of the most useful members of the Senate. He was a gentleman of rare accomplishments—generous, faithful, and kind, of very courteous manners, and possessed of the most liberal feelings; a fast friend, and an honorable opponent."[38]

Yet the pain of loss hit closest to Johnston when members of his own immediate family started to pass away. He and Henrietta had a third child, daughter Maria Preston, in October 1833, but she died less than a year later, in August 1834. Losing a child provoked special suffering, especially when one of his three children did not live to be a year old and the other two were terribly sick during the same time. In fact, daughter Henrietta, born while Johnston was away serving in the Black Hawk War, became so sick and unresponsive that the family declared her dead; she was even laid in her coffin until one of the kin thought she heard a faint breath or felt a slight pulse and ordered her to be bathed in hot water. Other treatments brought the baby to respond, and Henrietta went on to live a long and productive life. But, of course, there was no way to know this future as both she and brother William Preston remained very sick for a long time.[39]

But no death compared, in terms of feelings or results, with Johnston's ultimate loss: that of his wife Henrietta in 1835. She had struggled under the strain of his being away during the Black Hawk War, caring at the time for two very sick children. She caught a cold that would not go away, and from there declined over the next couple of years. "I have so bad a cold that I can't be heard when I speak," she wrote her mother, "and I am often fatigued and sick." She had experienced some malarial exposure, but her slow failure occurred by such slight degrees that her son described her as being "lulled into a fatal security." Johnston's biographer has surmised it was tuberculosis.[40]

Henrietta admitted that the strain of motherhood with an absent husband was almost more than she could handle and begged Johnston to resign from the army so that he could be at home. Johnston immediately faced a crisis, his wife's wishes pitted against his desire for a military profession and the gentlemanly status that came with it, especially should war ever erupt. In addition, the federal government had spent a lot of money to educate him in the art of war, and he felt a degree of debt to continue to give it his services. But leaving the army would allow for a move back to Kentucky, where it was thought Henrietta's health might improve. Johnston was outnumbered in this fight, as Stoddard, before he died, had pushed him to exit the army and take up planting and politics. He wrote in his last letter, in fact, "if you should retire now, as you may do under the most favorable and flattering circumstances, you will carry with you your military character and services, which will always be a source of pride and pleasure, as well as of proper consideration, among your friends and countrymen. . . . If you should aspire to political life, your past career will be of the highest claim to public confidence and favor." Stoddard added that if war came, Sidney could always go back into the army "with much higher rank."[41]

Still, it was a grueling decision for the young officer to leave his chosen profession. He took a leave of absence in 1833 and the spring of 1834 to care for Henrietta. But she got no better, and Sidney Johnston finally resigned in an effort to please and try further to heal his wife. He definitely had second thoughts, however, telling the postmaster to send the resignation letter at noon only "if not recalled before that hour." He admitted to a friend, "I felt some little pain at seeing my letter glide into the letter-box." His resignation was dated April 24, 1834, to take effect May 31. In an effort to quickly morph into the status of a landed Southern gentleman, Johnston bought a small farm near St. Louis to work, but the couple first planned to travel to ease the terrible trouble with his wife's lungs.[42]

Johnston made one of the truly major decisions of his life when he resigned his commission in 1834 to care for his ailing wife. His half-brother Stoddard had long advised him to get involved in planting, yet another acceptable vocation for a Southern gentleman, but he had resisted as long as he could, preferring his military career. Yet as his wife grew more and more ill, Lieutenant Johnston spent less and less time at his post. After he ultimately resigned, the couple headed eastward to the best warm springs and baths in the hopes that she might regain her health. They traveled to New Orleans and Louisville, where doctors bled her and demanded she follow a strict diet that only served to neglect her crucial nutrients. Visits to the best springs in Virginia did not help much either, and travels along the East Coast did little to alleviate her suffering, despite visits to Baltimore, Philadelphia, and New York. Making the situation worse, the infant daughter they had left in Louisville, Maria, died in August while they were away; her parents only learned the sad news when they returned in October.[43]

Unfortunately, nothing could aid Henrietta's damaged lungs, and she spiraled to a slow death, passing away in August 1835. A friend wrote of Johnston's "tender devotion to his wife" and admitted that "he impressed me at first as an austere man, but I found him the kindest and gentlest of friends; a stoic, yet he had the tenderest nature, so mindful of others' feelings." But it was a significant blow. Once Henrietta died, Johnston was alone and grieving, and he became a recluse on the small farm near St. Louis where they had planned to lead a happy life together. His children remained in Louisville with her family, so he was alone to consider his future.[44]

Consequently, by 1836, Johnston was floundering. In a mere two or three years, he had lost the most important parts of his kinship network. He had more importantly lost many of the aspects that made his status of manhood secure, including his wife and one child, with the other two then remaining with his in-laws. And he had lost his chosen military profession, now being a simple farmer, which was not going very well as yet. Alone, Johnston soon developed a hatred for the small farm where his wife should have lived by his side. His son later wrote that his "plan of life was shattered."[45]

Johnston was consequently at a loss of what to do by 1836. None of the life he had carefully built over his first thirty years remained. He would have to begin to recast his future, but he was now behind, almost starting over from scratch, something hard for a grown man in his thirties to do. Unfortunately, Johnston would seemingly play catch up for the remainder of his life, trying hard to resecure his future. In doing so, he began almost to panic and gamble on decisions that were not always the best option. He first envisioned going west into Indian country to establish a colony in the Sioux territory, but the government logically turned down his request. Significantly, there was little of his close kinship network still alive to counsel him, in particular Stoddard, who had kept him from what all considered a rash decision to go into the navy as a younger man.[46]

Without any compass, Johnston returned to what family he had left, his children and in-laws in Louisville. There, he heard a speech by one Stephen F. Austin imploring Kentuckians to support the independence movement in Texas with their money and lives. This seemed perfect for Johnston. Significantly, there now was no one to talk him out of what would turn out to be a huge gamble, with even his life at stake.[47]

— 2 —

SIX FEET OF TEXAS SOIL

CRISIS AND RECOVERY

lbert Sidney Johnston once declared that all he wanted at the end of his life was "six feet of Texas soil." Such a statement spoke volumes about the man, acknowledging his own mortality as well as indicating the simpleness of his lifestyle. But most of all, it clearly spoke of his adopted land of Texas as his true love. Although having been raised in Kentucky, receiving his appointment to West Point from Louisiana, and owning a farm in Missouri, Texas would forever be his home.[1]

Despite all of the connections he had elsewhere, including large kinship networks in both Kentucky and Louisiana, Johnston was vulnerable to the lure of Texas, its wide-open spaces, and the freedom of the frontier. No less of a draw was the possibility for him to make a new life, one that would hopefully regain his place in the forefront of the social system of the time. It would even potentially allow entrance into the slaveholding elite. Texas had declared itself independent in March 1836 and won that status from Mexico in April at the Battle of San Jacinto, which made Sam Houston a hero. The first president of the new republic was David Burnet, although Houston won the presidency later that year in official elections. The excitement of the revolution was real to a military man, the possibility of upward mobility was real to a gentleman, and the attraction of cheap land and lots of it was very tempting to an ambitious man who desired to be among the slaveholding elite. Manifest Destiny called loudly to many young Southern men intent on making their fortunes in land and slaves; Johnston was no different. His life was currently in shambles, and he could not resist the call of Texas and all its possibilities in a move of desperation to regain all that he had lost. But he could not see all the dangers looming ahead.[2]

In his move to Texas, Johnston displayed numerous attributes of a desperate man gambling on the future to regain his self-worth and peer acceptance. He turned his back on what monetary wealth he had, leaving it all back east. Worse, he continually sold off land piece by piece to fund this continuing trek, which only dug an ever-deeper economic hole. He became increasingly desperate with each debt, which caused him to gamble more and more to try and right himself economically. Similarly, Johnston left his family behind, both those closest to him, such as his own and his wife's family members, and most notably his two small children, who he left in Louisville with his in-laws. Unfortunately, he also left behind what was left of any kinship members who might have talked some sense into him regarding his troubling new plan to go west. Had his brother Stoddard still been alive, he would no doubt have tried to talk Sidney out of such a gamble just as he had when his younger brother desired to join the navy. Unfortunately, there were no more father figures in Sidney Johnston's life to guide him in the right direction, so the lure of Texas became that much greater in the absence of any sound counsel. And unlike the methodical chess player he always envisioned himself as being, these frantic decisions were made in haste and perhaps without proper context and contemplation. In the end, they resulted in additional troubles that put Johnston further and further behind—and almost cost him his life.[3]

Johnston's 1836 move to Texas was not his family's first foray there, however. Two older brothers, Daruius and Orramel, had gone west in 1812 as part of a movement to support independence from Spain. The effort had not gone well, and they almost lost their lives as a result. Now, some twenty years later, Texas was not much more tamed, and Sidney faced many of the same hardships.[4]

Fortunately, Johnston had a calling card of sorts. Even if he did not use the letters of introduction he carried with him, once again in stubbornness to make his own way by merit, he did have a military pedigree from West Point and service time in the U.S. Army. Johnston arrived much too late to be involved in the famous actions of the Alamo or Goliad as well as San Jacinto, but his travels soon thereafter took him to New Orleans and Alexandria, Louisiana, where he visited with family for a time before heading west with a couple of partners.[5]

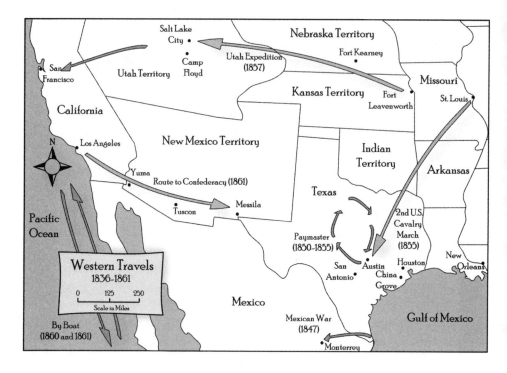

Once in Texas, Johnston met Burnet and Houston. He quickly rose in rank in the new republic's military, his West Point education and military experience being immediately noted and utilized. Johnston in fact joined the Texas army as a private but soon became a high-ranking officer. One general appointed him a colonel and adjutant general of the army, while President Burnet offered him the position of adjutant general of the entire nation. Houston also offered him a staff position with the rank of major. Soon, Johnston became a brigadier general, certainly a fulfillment of his desire for honor and reputation that had eluded him thus far.[6]

Johnston's quick rise brought troubles, however, which necessitated more gambles in order to stay afloat. Many of these problems came from his fast rise in power, which others took exception to. Other crises came when decisions made in lofty positions crossed those of other prominent Texans, some of whom had Johnston's future in their hands. And still other difficulties arose from Johnston's show of manhood, his bravery as well as honor often getting him into dangerous situations. One such episode occurred when two soldiers quarreled and drew weapons. Amid the dangerous confrontation, Johnston rode through at a gallop "and, with a tremendous grab," one of the participants confessed, "jerked his [opponent's] pistol out of his hand, which was all that saved my life." This episode demonstrated Johnston's willingness to make a difference, even at the possibility of endangering his own life.[7]

One event that combined his honor with willingness to face danger in a desperate situation indeed almost cost Johnston his life. By early 1837, he was the senior brigadier general in the Texas army, but there was an undercurrent of distaste over this, led by the junior brigadier general Felix Huston. A Kentuckian by way of Mississippi, the populist Huston had conspired to win the affection of most of the rough-and-tumble soldiers who ousted several leaders by vote. He made it plain that anyone who stood in the way of his assuming command of the army would do so at their own peril. Johnston, of course, was his senior and maintained his authority, whereupon Huston challenged him to a duel: "assuming the command under an appointment connected with the attempt to ruin my reputation and inflict a stigma on my character, . . . I therefore propose a meeting between us, in as short a period as you can make convenient."[8]

With his settled code of honor guiding him, especially concerning how his peers would view his response, Johnston could not let the challenge pass. He believed that his own honor as well as the state of the Texas nation was on the line. He firmly believed that Huston did not have the leadership qualities necessary to lead and would drive the republic into the ground if he became commander. For the sake of Texas, Johnston declared, he had to meet Huston on the dueling field. Furthermore, it would be seen as a personal sign of weakness and lack of manhood if Johnston declined, a tinge upon his honor. He thus wrote back: "After reciprocating the sentiments of respect and esteem which you have been pleased to express toward me, it only remains to accord to you the meeting proposed. I have designated 7 o'clock, A. M., to-morrow."[9]

It was indeed a gamble with his life, more so because Johnston was no duelist and Huston was known to be proficient with his aim of pistols. Johnston, as the challenged party, had the right to name the weapons, but for honor's sake he chose common pistols despite this placing himself at a disadvantage. Selecting something less deadly would have been better for him, but he knew that if he did he would never have won the allegiance of the Texas army, which after all was what this whole matter was mostly over. After some negotiating to fire from the hip to equalize the odds, Johnston confided, "I am not sure I could hit the side of a house in firing from the hip." He rather sought to take a mental advantage, knowing the pistols had hair triggers. Johnston planned to wait until the moment he saw Huston begin to squeeze his own trigger and then fire, hoping the noise and concussion would pull him off slightly. It was about the only real chance he had in this life-or-death gamble.[10]

The two men met across the Lavaca River from their encampment at Camp Independence, moving with a number of spectators to "an open, grassy spot, on the edge of the prairie." There, the seconds did their jobs and Johnston and Huston began their duel, going through five different shots; neither hit the other. Johnston believed the timing of his firing caused Huston to react and miss. On the other hand, one of Johnston's shots went "through his hair and grazing his ear." Huston would not call the duel off, however, and his sixth shot was nearly fatal. That bullet drove into Johnston's hip and the general, presumed to be mortally wounded, was taken away.[11]

One observer noted the feeling of despair as "the surgeon declared the wound so dangerous as to leave little hope of recovery, and the injured man was removed to the little hamlet of Texana, where he lay for weeks at the point of death." For what it was worth, Huston declared his honor satisfied and agreed peacefully to be second in command of the army. In fact, the two men showed a remarkable comradery thereafter, Huston giving up his post shortly afterward. For his part, Johnston even declared that, if he died, he wanted no ill-feeling toward Huston and for the army to obey him as their new commander.[12]

Fortunately, Johnston recovered, although slowly and painfully. He wrote, "my attempts to take exercise on horseback have proved exceedingly injurious, and I am compelled to refrain; and, of course, am greatly discouraged, as my suffering is without intermission." Amazingly, the bullet had gone through the hole in the pelvis and inflicted no structural damage. It did do nerve damage, however, particularly to the sciatic nerve. Still, the greatest effect was the lengthy recovery needed even after the life-threatening danger was gone. Doctors advised that his wound could only be healed with ample rest.[13]

Although Johnston tried to fulfill his duties as commander of the Texas army, he just could not do so; he could not even mount his horse. As a result, he had to resign on April 22 and leave the command to someone else. Returning to recover in Kentucky did not help his status in Texas. In fact,

Johnston would never again regain command of the Texas army. He had been too stubborn in defending his honor and what he perceived as the military viability of Texas in the face of Mexican aggression to regain the lost province. It was a gamble to be sure, one that cost Johnston his command and nearly his life.[14]

The duel aside, Johnston's most troublesome personal conflict, however, was with the unmistaken leader of Texas, Sam Houston. As Johnston rose in prominence in the republic, he began to be drawn into political actions, which he abhorred. That brought him even more into Houston's realm, and Houston was not a man to cross. Like Andrew Jackson, the former Tennessean (and former governor of that state) now put his mark on Texas, his victory at San Jacinto solidifying his place in the new country. Yet Johnston and Houston rarely saw eye to eye, and their relationship continually soured, to the detriment of Johnston's career. Certainly, his two top generals dueling did not make Houston happy: he (as well as the Texas secretary of war) scolded Johnston, "let harmony in camp be inculcated and by all means prevent *Duelling* in future!"[15]

In fact, Johnston (while still in command) and Houston struggled over the best ways to defend Texas, particularly with Mexico continually threatening another invasion throughout the latter part of the 1830s. Captured at San Jacinto, Mexican president Antonio Lopez de Santa Anna had not fulfilled his promises of assurance of independence given in exchange for his freedom. Texas continually faced being swallowed up again. Much of the fear was because of the paltry Texas army at the time and Johnston's serious dueling wound. Houston provided little support to the military and sought only to outwait the Mexicans. At the same time, he wanted to make treaties with the Native Americans on the frontier to stabilize at least one section of the area that needed defense. On the other hand, Johnston proposed an offensive into Mexico with his limited numbers. He argued that invasion would require fewer men than an all-out defense and would set the enemy back on their heels. Houston did not see it that way and forbid any invasion of Mexico, causing Johnston and others to slowly lose faith in him, not only as a military man but also as their leader. "Our Government wants energy and prudent foresight," Johnston wrote a friend. He accordingly spent more time recuperating in Kentucky in a couple of different stints, mostly because of his doctors but because of Houston as well.[16]

Matters for Johnston, despite his dueling fiasco, took a temporary turn for the better with the change of administration in Texas in 1839. With Houston leaving office because of term limits, Texans elected Mirabeau B. Lamar as president, and he brought in a new military policy. In particular, Lamar accepted the Johnston idea of defending Texas with more troops and little conciliation with the Indians. To put this new policy in place, Lamar appointed Johnston as his secretary of war, yet another lofty position that brought with it the desired honor and status of a Southern gentleman. Thus, with the changing of administrations, Johnston once again had a steady job, but not one that he enjoyed or had envisioned. Stuffy politics in the newly built frontier capital of Austin, encircled by a palisade wall for protection, was not what he desired. The constant bureaucracy, including anybody and everybody seeking positions, grated on him.[17]

Johnston nevertheless advised two major changes to Texas military policy. The first was to mount a major invasion of Mexico to stop the continual threats from that nation as well as to solidify the republic's independence. Without the means necessary, however, nothing came of this effort. The second policy change was taking the fight to the Indians, one that reversed Houston's strategy and angered the former president. Their conflict had begun brewing when Johnston was the army's commander, and Houston chafed at the general's insolence in bucking him. Now with the policy reversal officially put into effect, particularly against a band of Cherokees, Houston's wrath came in full. "Whoever else made their peace with him," Johnston's son later noted of Houston, "he never forgave General Johnston."[18]

Yet the mundane bureaucratic work continually grated on Johnston. Although in the field occasionally as secretary, he spent most of his time in Austin. There, he realized what he had fallen to, pushing papers within a high-level administration. Johnston quickly tired of such work, much preferring to be out with the army on the wild frontier. At the same time, his meager salary meant that Johnston, whose finances were already in shambles, was unable to provide the social finery expected of a cabinet official. And he was still seemingly public enemy number one to Houston, and their relationship continually deteriorated as Houston plotted a return and probably revenge in the next presidential election. In fact, the situation became so bad that when Johnston heard of Houston making disparaging remarks about him, he actually challenged the ex-president to a duel. Johnston wrote him, "you will not be surprised that I inform you that immediately after the termination of the present session of Congress I will hold you accountable."

Wiser in the ways of politics and life in general, Houston disavowed making any insult toward him, which in the manhood code of the day ended the situation. Johnston replied, "I will consider [it] satisfactory." But he should have known better than to issue the challenge in the first place; his earlier duel had not exactly gone very well for him.[19]

Johnston became increasingly unhappy in his position. He admitted to a friend: "I feel like an exile. . . . I sometimes fancy myself most miserable. I stand alone. But here I have cast my lot; and here, come weal or woe, I shall, unless Fate has otherwise decreed, spin out the thread of life." It certainly seemed that Johnston was wondering about his gamble of moving to Texas. Matters became so bad, in fact, that he resigned as secretary of war in February 1840, which relieved him not only of the tediousness of office but also of any income. It was yet another gamble made when matters of life boiled up to the point that he had to make long-odds decisions just to catch up. Johnston "during this period . . . was adrift."[20]

The 1841 reelection of Houston only brought more trouble. Johnston had broken with him publicly, and Houston's return to power meant that he had no future in Texas. During the canvas for president, Johnston's name was often mentioned in opposition to Houston. While he did not promote this notion, not even being in Texas, and certainly did not campaign, the mere mention of Johnston as an opponent solidified Houston's hatred for him. As Johnston's son put it, the development "was to imbitter the animosity of the new President toward him."[21]

Johnston's resignation as secretary of war thus initiated a period of utter flailing, during which he seemed a nomad not knowing where to go or what to do. He had no job, no roots, no advisors, and plenty of baggage—from enemies in high places to health concerns. Not surprisingly, Johnston spent the next few years wandering around aimlessly. He returned east for part of the time, being away from Texas for an entire year at one point. He traveled to Kentucky and dealt with the land he still owned elsewhere, even spending time on the East Coast, in Rhode Island, visiting family.[22]

Yet Texas was never far from his thoughts, and in fact Johnston returned there in 1844. Many had tried to get him to return and enter the political fray against his old nemesis Houston, but he declined each time, mainly because of a lack of funds. He assured his friends that he would be back but needed to remain in Kentucky for a while, "unless the men of Texas are needed for her defense. In that event I will not, if alive, fail to be with you." But the lure of Texas and its potential remained very real and very strong. Without anything else promising, Johnston again set out for the frontier to rebuild his fortunes, including replacing those parts of his life that had vanished in the terrible years of 1833–35. While he could not replace the relationship he had enjoyed with his late brother Stoddard, he had developed new friends in Texas. He also sought to replace his livelihood and Southern gentlemanly honor as well as to reestablish a love life.[23]

By 1844, Johnston would make much progress in this reinvention of himself, mainly by acquiring both a new wife and a plantation. While back in Kentucky, he had met Eliza Griffin, a cousin of his first wife Henrietta. She was from a Virginia family of military men, her brothers serving in the army and navy. Her parents had died when she was a child, and her grandmother and other family raised her. By the 1840s, Eliza was living in Kentucky. Born in 1821, she was barely over twenty years old when she met Johnston, then over forty. Johnston's son and biographer simply noted that "there was some disparity of years," he himself being only a few years younger than she was. Nevertheless, Johnston married Eliza in October 1843 in Kentucky. Their union would eventually produce five more children, ranging from a son named Albert Sidney Johnston Jr. to a daughter born in 1861, when Johnston was nearly sixty years old.[24]

Johnston's second marriage provided the companionship, stability, and honorable manhood attributes that he desired, although perhaps not the guiding mentors that he so desperately needed. His new wife also provided more responsibility, especially with additional children coming along. Johnston's duties to his wife and growing family required that he settle down and earn a living, and so he launched into another gamble that, like many beforehand, came up lacking and nearly ruined him financially. He had earlier speculated in land, buying a large tract of several thousand acres in North Texas when he arrived in 1836, but the title was not clear and became an albatross about his neck for years. Desiring to try his hand at planting and become that elite slaveholding master of his domain that almost all Southern men aspired to, Johnston and a friend bought a plantation in Brazoria County, just south of Houston, called China Grove. It consisted of around six thousand acres, mostly prairie but containing some good cotton land as well. Johnston first intended to rent it out for profit (unsuccessfully) but then dreamed of growing cotton on the fertile portion and sugar on the prairie, easing his financial burdens and providing his family a comfortable living all while propelling him into Southern gentlemanly status. Despite having attained high rank and high political office and having benefited from the kinship ties of two prominent families, that ultimate goal of becoming a slaveholding elite had thus far eluded Johnston. This seemed his chance to make that leap forward. Unfortunately, China Grove cost a whopping sum of sixteen thousand dollars. And financially, it only got worse; his friend soon faced bankruptcy amid other projects and requested that Johnston take the full ownership of the plantation, which he did. This action helped his friend, but it saddled Johnston with the whole debt, which he was never able to pay. His son admitted that the "purchase proved to be injudicious and disastrous." Johnston had to sell much of his land back east to keep his land in the west.[25]

Johnston never made a success of China Grove and, as a result, never entered the upper tier of society as a Southern slaveholding elite. In fact, he was not even able to pay the full interest on the mortgage and went further into debt. It was a vicious cycle, the assumption of the entire debt causing such a lack of capital that he was not able to hire or buy workers or slaves to work the plantation sufficiently to make money to invest back in it.[26]

But the failure of China Grove was not because of a lack of effort. Johnston only had one family of slaves to work his plantation: a man, wife, and three children—two girls and a boy. He could never generate enough profit to expand on this basic tenet of Southern manhood. Thus, much of the work was done with his own hands as well as those of his children and friends who visited, such as young William during his visits from Louisville. Johnston wrote a friend in 1849, "my own personal labor (it don't mean headwork) was necessary in conducting my small farming operations; and I have yielded it with cheerfulness, and have thus, after three years' toil, become a rugged farmer, with good habits."[27]

Money was the chief enemy. Johnston had sold most of his land back east but made sure his first wife's land inheritance in Kentucky was kept in trust for his children's education. As a result, he lived humbly in Texas, a "double-log cabin" with a porch and rude wood furniture as his home. He and his slaves worked hard to produce a small crop of cotton, sugar, corn, and vegetables, most of which went for his and the slaves' sustenance; only a little was left to sell for supplies. "We manage to raise almost everything we want," he wrote. But it had potential for more. "I possess a great treasure," he explained to his son, "but I fear I shall not be able to make it manifest to any capitalist." Thus, already in massive debt, he was unable to gain the necessary capital to make more money. While the niceties of life were not forthcoming—Eliza understood that—Johnston very much enjoyed the natural beauty of China Grove and its flora and fauna. He also spent a lot of time playing chess.[28]

Yet after a few years of struggling to make the plantation profitable without any success, Johnston came to the conclusion that he had to get out from under the debt. He had sold off his St. Louis property as well as much of that in Kentucky in a vain effort to keep financially afloat. The proceeds from the plantation and the sale of his landholdings back east were "gradually swallowed up by the expenses of living and the interest on his debt, without diminishing its principal." Eliza confided, "he is almost in despair, and often says he feels like a drowning man with his hands tied; but he tries to keep up his spirits." It was a no-win situation, made so because of Johnston's unwise decisions and gambles that did not pay off.[29]

The increasing economic problems also began to affect Johnston physically and mentally, especially when another son was born in 1847. "A heavy, increasing, and seemingly hopeless burden of debt taxed his energies, his pride, and his patience," his son and biographer wrote, and he described Johnston after years of toil as "sallow, gaunt, and ague-stricken in appearance." He added that "it was a campaign in which he might die struggling, but in which he did not intend to surrender manhood, cheerfulness, or hope." Johnston himself wrote of being "entirely secluded from the world and from all society whatever," that "a man in my situation is not likely to be overburdened by his friends." Perhaps at the lowest point, one neighbor even fed the Johnston family dog strychnine, and it died at home in convulsions in front of the entire family, including the children. They and Eliza wept bitterly, and while Johnston was terribly upset, he resisted retaliation; if he shot the neighbor, "it would make the man no better, and it would do himself and family no good. . . . The dog was dead, and nothing could restore him to life." In the depths of desperation, Johnston did not always react according to the honor code of Southern masculinity, especially in terms of retribution, but rather according to his own code of leniency and latitude.[30]

Then, even more problems came, likewise the result of Johnston's hasty move to Texas. The United States annexed the republic in 1845, becoming a new state immediately. Politically, this action cooled off Johnston's affection toward the Whig Party and especially for his deceased brother's friend

Henry Clay, who opposed annexation. But Mexico began again rattling its saber in relation to Texas. There were definite possibilities that could come of it for Johnston, including reentry into the American military now that he and Texas were a part of the United States. He could conceivably go back to the U.S. Army or even serve in the state forces, although Eliza was firmly against such a move, preferring he remain at China Grove even if that meant a paltry lifestyle. But should Johnston want to return to the military, there were old issues from his earlier decisions that continually affected him even in the mid-1840s. Unfortunately, Houston was going nowhere, and with Texas now only a state in the larger American nation, he was still a major player, either as governor in Austin or at times a senator in Washington. In both offices Houston could be counted on to restrict Johnston whenever he could. Houston's friendship with the president, Democrat James K. Polk (another Jackson protégé), was yet another reason the long-time Whig Johnston could expect no welcoming arms to greet his potential reentry into the army. Johnston's options seemed to be continually dwindling, so he persisted in working his isolated and now almost barren plantation.[31]

A sliver of hope appeared in 1846, however, as Polk led the nation into war with Mexico. This was, after all, what Johnston had been preaching for years, an offensive into the enemy's territory to teach them once and for all that Texas was sovereign territory, albeit now American. He also realized that in any buildup to war, there were always high command positions available. Johnston saw this opportunity and made every effort, over his wife's appeals, to get in on the action. He and Eliza came to a compromise that he would volunteer for six months and then come home for good. Yet Johnston found Houston continually at work against him—even his friend Zachary Taylor, now a major general in the U.S. Army, ran into problems getting him a command. Taylor nevertheless called on Johnston, and he went to camp immediately, leaving behind Eliza and the children at Galveston. Once there, he was quickly elected as colonel of one of the Texas units, the First Regiment of Foot Riflemen of Texas. But this was only a six-month regiment, whose term of enlistment ran out before the major movements into Mexico even began. Johnston tried to get his troops to reenlist, but the majority voted to disband the regiment and go home. Despite lofty descriptions of Johnston being able to change men's minds and lead them by his charisma, in this instance he was unable to change anyone's minds and the regiment disbanded, leaving him a colonel without a regiment. Fortunately,

Taylor graciously appointed Johnston to a staff position with one of his subordinate generals. But the post was not considered an army position, so even while fighting in the war Johnston was not being paid, something he desperately needed.[32]

As a staff officer, Johnston moved with the army up the Rio Grande and participated in the battle at Monterrey in September 1846. Coming under heavy Mexican fire, his horse shot three times as he aided in reforming some broken troops in a cornfield, Johnston admitted, "I, finely mounted throughout, escaped with my huge frame without a scratch." He also renewed his acquaintance with Jefferson Davis, now colonel of the 1st Mississippi. Johnston also served alongside other future luminaries such as Joseph Hooker.[33]

Danger still lurked even after the battle, namely in the negotiations for surrender, in which Johnston soon found himself involved. Taylor sent Davis, his son-in-law, on a mission to communicate with the Mexican commander. As the colonel stopped at headquarters on the way, Johnston asked permission to accompany him, which Taylor thought was a good idea. Johnston and Davis rode to the Mexican pickets, who were less than friendly, especially with the former dressed in rough Texas attire. Some residents nearby threw gestures and insults, one calling Johnston "Tejano!" This group became troublesome to the pair, who were glad to see a Mexican army captain ride up. Johnston whispered to Davis, "had we not better keep him with us," and the two refused to leave his side (basically taking him prisoner) as they were taken to see the Mexican commander. The Americans got what they desired and returned to their lines, glad to be safe, although in the chaos Davis lost a pistol Johnston had ironically given him in 1832 during the Black Hawk War.[34]

By October 1847, Johnston's time was up, not so much with the army—Taylor would have loved to have him stay—but with his wife. He had promised her earlier that he would be home and his time had now run out, so he returned to Galveston to get Eliza and his youngest son before heading back to China Grove. There, Johnston sat out the rest of the war, although keeping a close watch on the happenings and commenting freely on them, wishing, of course, that he could participate in those events.[35]

Once more, Johnston seemed to be at the end of hope, nothing economically or militarily working to launch him into the elite manhood status he desired. But his fortune again changed with the new presidential administration elected in 1848. Polk decided to serve only one term, and his successor was none other than Johnston's old friend Taylor. Yet even as beset with problems as he was, Johnston still would not lobby for a position or have his friends do so for him. Logically, any position offered by the former warrior now turned commander in chief to the wholly army man would be military in nature, and Johnston had promised his wife that he had retired from that line of work forever. He even had seemingly developed a distaste of all things military, going so far as to talk William out of attending West Point; Johnston's first-born son instead went to Yale and became a lawyer.[36]

Still, Johnston's current situation forced a rethinking of his ideas on the military. Eliza soon gave her blessing to this, realizing the effect China Grove was having on all of them, particularly her husband. But he was adamant: "I do not, therefore, wish my friends to ask General Taylor for any office for me. He knows me well; and if it should not occur to him to offer me a place, I shall only think that he has selected others whom he believed better capable of promoting the public interest." One of Johnston's friends agreed that "a gentleman ought not to ask" but related that Taylor had actually inquired about him: "he asked kindly after you," the friend related, adding, "I told him you were struggling along in Texas." Taylor "remarked that it was no place for you, and observed, 'I had not been informed of my election long before I determined to do something for Johnston.'"[37]

Several positions were available, though mostly in civilian clerical work, which did not interest Johnston. The only open military position was as a paymaster in Texas. Although the post was as "a mere disbursing officer and nothing more, without authority or command," it carried the rank of major in the regular army and offered a foot in the door, an entry position to a possible field command in the future. Johnston thus took the job in December 1849, cognizant that after all his hard work, he had not been able to make his own way but had to depend on the help of friends. It must have been a severe check to the honor-bound and stubborn Johnston, who remarked, "now, do you think that if I had been a sharp fellow, General Taylor would have taken the trouble to hunt me up in the mud of the Brazos bottom to make a paymaster of me?" Yet his acceptance of such charity illustrated just how low he had fallen, even giving up for a time on the dream of becoming one of the Southern slaveholding elite.[38]

But even this gift came with its own problems. A paymaster was not exactly the cream of the officer corps and offered little chance for glory. In addition, it required a vast amount of travel. Despite having a bout of malaria,

Johnston, after taking Eliza and the children to Kentucky, returned to Texas to begin his duties, later fighting off yellow fever as well. He once again followed the pattern of leaving family at home while he went to his work. Eliza and the children returned to Texas later in the year, Johnston meeting them in New Orleans for the return trip. There, he learned that another daughter, Mary, only recently born, had died.[39]

The paymaster work was grueling. Johnston had to make a trip to New Orleans every four months, later increased to two, to pick up the payroll, often as much as fifty thousand dollars in gold and silver. Obviously, the return to Texas was dangerous as were his travels to the various forts and garrisons in his district. The circuit of the various forts normally covered as much as seven or eight hundred miles and took several weeks. He headquartered himself in Austin but made his lengthy tour several times a year, guarded only by a troop of cavalry and accompanied by a clerk and his slaves John and Randolph (also his cook). Unfortunately, the wagons and mules available to him were afterthoughts, the best going to line officers and their men, Johnston having to make do with shoddy equipment and worn-out animals. It was a lonely, solitary life, and he could only revel in the beauty of nature, watching the birds and animals and enjoying the flowers along the route. Only occasionally did he have personal company, such as when his young son Sid accompanied him, Johnston writing that "he swam and fished in almost every stream on the route." His oldest son, William, also accompanied him on one trip in 1854. Meanwhile, Eliza continued to bear more children.[40]

By far the worst problem to come out of the job was the possibility of losing some of the money, which happened to an alarming degree over time. Johnston had finally lost China Grove to auction in 1849, although he was still responsible for the eight thousand dollars of debt it encumbered. Ironically, William, now a Yale-educated lawyer residing in Louisville, bought the plantation in 1852 to relieve the debt of his father, although the elder Johnston insisted on paying his son back. Then, Johnston's finances took another hit when it was discovered on several trips that he was hemorrhaging money from the payroll, and he could not identify the culprit. Eventually, the amount totaled to as much as seventeen hundred dollars, a large sum for that day. Johnston was beside himself, aware that his honor and trustworthiness were at stake, William later remarking that the episodes so "seriously threatened him with loss of property and reputation that he almost sunk under it." Rather than report the losses, Johnston made up for the deficits from his own pocket each time. William got into the sleuthing business during his 1854 trip with his father, but he, too, could not solve the mystery. Finally, Johnston ultimately found out that one of his slaves, John, had gotten a set of keys that worked the lockbox and had helped himself to the funds over the course of a couple of years. John was sold, the proceeds going to repay Johnston for his losses. But the benevolent Johnston would allow no further punishment of the slave, even when many recommended a severe beating. "The whipping will not restore what is lost," he argued, "and it will not benefit the negro, whom a lifetime of kind treatment has failed to make honest. It would be a mere act of revenge, to which I cannot consent." He certainly had different notions of the Southern gentleman's mastery than the majority of his peers.[41]

Although providing an income, the five years spent as a paymaster grated on Johnston and his entire family. "He will not last long with this sort of life," Eliza confided to her stepson William. But while Johnston floundered, others were reaching heights of success politically. No loftier extended family or friend had been Zachary Taylor, who had surged all the way to the presidency before his unfortunate death midterm. But he had drawn Johnston out of the "mud" of Texas and gotten him back into the army. Others were also attaining high positions that would definitely aid Johnston, including William Preston, brother of his first wife, who was now a member of Congress from Kentucky. But there were no greater coattails than those of his friend from Mississippi, Jefferson Davis, who became secretary of war under President Franklin Pierce. There was no doubt that Davis would look out for his old friend, classmate, and wartime partner Albert Sidney Johnston, and there was no doubt that Johnston would accept and even ask for that benevolent aid that he had so often refused in the past. Times were tough, and Johnston was not above asking Davis for his help in attaining a command.[42]

Davis came through. The Franklin Pierce administration beefed up the size of the army, adding four new regiments, two infantry and two cavalry. It was ironically a surge in the very force that Davis himself would have to fight a mere four years from the day he left office. Clearly, the moderate Davis was not a supporter of secession at this point. Regardless, competition was keen for the officer billets in these regiments, but Johnston had many who supported him. As much as he hated leaning on others for his advancement, he needed to escape the grueling paymaster duty and get a position in one of the new units.[43]

Many lobbied for Johnston when the bill expanding the army became law in 1855. Among them were Representative Preston as well as old friend Thomas Jefferson Rusk, who was active in the earliest Texas efforts of independence and was a warm friend of Johnston's through his years there. Now he was one of the state's senators. The entire Texas legislature as well as the governor and lieutenant governor also argued for Johnston to receive one of the highest positions among these regiments. But it was Secretary Davis who was the most influential, he being the leader the president would most listen to in making military appointments. It was no surprise that Johnston soon had a command very much to his liking: "repair to Louisville, Kentucky, and assume the command of your regiment," his orders read.[44]

Up until now, the only question had been what position Johnston would have and in what branch. His association with Texas almost required him to be part of one of the cavalry regiments slated to go there; it would seem a waste of knowledge to appoint him and then send him somewhere else. The question was also debated about his rank. Johnston was a major already, so obviously he could not go down to one of the captaincies. He could, of course, transfer laterally to become one of the majors in a regiment, but the top two positions of colonel and lieutenant colonel were also available in each of the four units. In the end, Pierce and Davis appointed Johnston colonel of the new 2nd U.S. Cavalry, although there were others who ranked him and there was some debate and recommendation, even from Lieutenant General Winfield Scott, that the new regiment's lieutenant colonel, Robert E. Lee, should have been colonel and Johnston the second in command. Either position would have likely suited Johnston. The majors and captains were also filled with a veritable who's who of later luminaries, with William J. Hardee and George Thomas as majors and six future Civil War generals as captains, including Earl Van Dorn, Edmund Kirby Smith, and George Stoneman. Others such as John Bell Hood held lower-level officer positions. The regiment quickly became the pride of the U.S. military.[45]

At this time, however, the 2nd U.S. Cavalry was merely a paper regiment. The officers thus were mostly called eastward for interim duties; certainly Johnston was. He and Hardee sat on the Cavalry Equipment Board in Washington to determine new uniforms and equipment. Meanwhile, the recruits were to assemble at Johnston's old home at Jefferson Barracks near St. Louis, which no doubt brought back some painful memories when he joined them of his time there during the lowest days of the early and mid-

1830s. Then both Johnston and Lee were detained sitting on a court-martial case at Fort Leavenworth in the fall, despite both wanting to get to their new command; "I am much annoyed at my absence from the regiment at a time when the presence of every officer is peculiarly needed," Johnston admitted. Meanwhile, Major Hardee assembled the troops and prepared them for their movement overland to Texas. But the regiment needed its commander, Hardee writing that the colonel's "presence is indispensable." Eventually, Johnston arrived and instituted pride among the companies, including color coordinating the horses in each. "The officers & men are making most encouraging progress in the drill and acquiring a good knowledge of their duties generally," he reported to Washington in late 1855.[46]

Johnston soon led the regiment, with numerous officer's families including Eliza and their children, southwestward through Missouri, the Indian Territory, and into Texas. Eliza kept a diary, noting at the beginning, "well, here I am . . . soldiering, my gude man appointed Colonel of Second Regiment of Cavalry, a new Regiment just enlisted." Leaving in late October, the regiment faced a cruel winter storm before it arrived at its post. The trip was hard on all, especially the accompanying family members, Eliza telling of one encounter she had with a civilian from whom she tried to buy milk for her sick baby: "That milk has butter in it," he exclaimed and refused to sell it to her. Fortunately, the regiment arrived at Fort Mason in Texas by mid-January 1856 and settled into a routine. Unfortunately, Johnston came down sick and almost died from a "violent remittent bilious fever." He recovered but relapsed on a trip to San Antonio that spring, which "brought him to the verge of the grave." It was not his first near-death experience, but Johnston recovered just as he had in the past.[47]

Despite his frequent illnesses, no doubt the result of years of hardship and toil as a struggling plantation owner and paymaster, Johnston finally had a position he was proud of and that brought him the pay and status he desired. In fact, he assumed even more responsibility quickly when, despite the heavy sickness, he also performed duties after only a couple of months as the temporary commander of the Department of Texas (he being the ranking officer in the Texas region), with headquarters in San Antonio. Next door to him was recruiting officer Dabney H. Maury, who wrote that Johnston was his neighbor "and a very good one he was." Major Don Carlos Buell was his assistant adjutant general. While no longer in direct command of his regiment, Johnston now commanded the entire area and many other troops as well. It was not bad for someone who was a mere paymaster in this same department just a few short months ago. In this expanded role, Johnston backed offensive tactics against the Indians, particularly the Comanches, an idea he had pushed for decades. Now, at last, he had the authority to make it happen.[48]

In the meantime, the colonel was becoming more and more mindful of the happenings around him as well, his views on current events showing up often in his correspondence. Johnston had always been an ardent Whig, probably because of the influence of his older brother Stoddard. But he had more recently begun to gravitate toward the Democratic Party. His views on slavery certainly ran more along Democratic lines than that of the old Whigs or certainly of the new Republicans. When an abolitionist later courted his daughter, Johnston made it plain that "being an abolitionist [should] make him despised by her as a viler traitor than Cataline; he had the redeeming trait of courage, these latter day Saints have no instincts above an assassin or incendiary." Still, Johnston cautioned calm: "let us make war against the world rather than against each other." But he made it clear that if a choice had to be made, he would fall on the Southern proslavery side despite never attaining the status of slaveholding elite himself. He wrote his son William, "I notice with sorrow the progress of fanaticism in the North," adding, "we want the rights and independence of the States and the security to individuals guaranteed by the Constitution. . . . With whatever sorrow, however heart-felt and agonizing, we will not hesitate to encounter separation with all its attendant horrors rather than bear the evils and degradation relentlessly heaped upon us by the heartless folly of fanaticism." These were words that could have just as well come from the lips of John C. Calhoun. Later, in remarking that he was "contented with the result of the [1856] election," Johnston desired only that "our Northern brethren will give up their fanatical, idolatrous negro-worship." Similarly, Eliza wrote, "where the darky is in any numbers it should be as slaves."[49]

Yet while the nation itself was dividing more and more, a more immediate threat appeared that required Johnston's attention and took him away from duties in Texas. A permanent departmental commander had arrived, Brigadier General David Twiggs, and Johnston returned to the command of the 2nd Cavalry. Then another duty arose. By 1857, the Mormons had become a problem to the territorial government in Utah, after having first been driven out of Illinois. Their leader, Joseph Smith, had died in 1844, leaving power to Brigham Young, who took the people to Utah to make their new life and following their new faith. There, around the Great Salt Lake, Young set up his own nation, not accepting U.S. control and hampering trade and emigration westward. Federal policy tried to placate Young by making him governor of the territory, but he was adamant that he was in charge and refused attempts to curtail his authority with the people. Ultimately, the federal government sent a new governor and other officials, including judges, to take over the territory, accompanied by a large military force to protect them. The commander of that force was Colonel Johnston.[50]

Unfortunately, like many of the other episodes in Johnston's recent life, this one was complicated, tiring, and fraught with danger. Nothing in life seemed to come easy for him, as evidenced by the fact that the originally named commander of the expedition, Brigadier General William S. Harney, declined to accept it. The colonel felt no such freedom and made his way to Fort Leavenworth, where he soon led two regiments of infantry, a regiment of cavalry, and two artillery batteries westward toward the Great Salt Lake, where "the community and, in part, the civil government of Utah Territory are in a state of substantial rebellion against the laws and authority of the United States." His mission was to convey the new set of civilian leaders to the territory and keep the communication routes open. Other than that, Johnston was to stay out of all political affairs.[51]

The danger came due to such a late departure from Fort Leavenworth. Johnston received his orders on August 28, 1857, and left the fort on September 17. It would be a miracle if the command made it through the Rocky Mountains before winter; indeed, they did not. In twenty-seven grueling days, the command moved nearly a thousand miles through South Pass, pausing only briefly at Forts Kearny and Laramie on the way. One captain wrote of the cold "racking the bones of our men and starving our oxen, and mules, and horses, already half starved." Fitz John Porter related that Johnston was right among the suffering, writing that "Colonel Johnston footed along at the head of the command, setting an example of endurance that checked complaint, and turned these trials into matter for jest and good-humor." The winter was harsh but mostly harmless, although the Mormons did everything they could to derail the government force, including building earthworks to defend their city and making threatening gestures; they even tried conciliation and trickery. Johnston would not go along with this, knowing that if he took their good will, the Mormons would claim to have saved the military force from starvation. "I can accept of nothing from him so long as he and his people maintain a hostile position to my government. . . . Peace or war is in their hands, and if they have war it will be of their own making."[52]

More trouble came from Johnston's own side. Some pro-Mormon civilians arrived to negotiate a peace between the two almost immovable forces, putting Johnston into a quandary even as Sam Houston, now in the Senate, publicly questioned the colonel's policies. A rumble even occurred between Johnston and the new territorial governor, Alfred Cumming, over what the military's role would be. Most concerning was Johnston's desire, like always, to take the fight to the enemy. The administration of President James Buchanan had a change of heart, however, and basically ignored the situation in Utah, resulting in a military occupation of the territory lasting several years.[53]

Ultimately, official negotiators arrived from Washington, and Brigham Young, perhaps realizing he had no other alternative, yielded to the new territorial government. That satisfied Johnston, who was only there to keep the peace and defend the new administration. He thus marched his troops through Salt Lake City in a show of force and went into camp just to the south. He chose a site between the city and Provo in Cedar Valley, naming it Camp Floyd after the sitting secretary of war, John B. Floyd. Johnston issued a circular assuring the people of the territory that "no person whatever will be in any wise interfered with or molested in his person or rights, or in the peaceful pursuit of his avocation." Unfortunately, as matters settled down, Johnston remained stuck in Utah for three years. Two general officers were assigned to the command above him when it looked like fighting might break out, but when peace was brokered each time the War Department considered the need for a general less important than elsewhere. Colonel Johnston, despite requests to be relieved, stayed on in the territory.[54]

Johnston remained in Utah until February 1860, braving summers and hard winters. Many times the temperature fell far below freezing, and he wrote home how, when he went outside, his "mustache soon becomes an icicle." He spent his time keeping the peace and keeping his troops ready if called upon, although no major altercations developed between the army and the Mormons. The same could not be said about Johnston and Cumming, who again did not see eye to eye on the military's role. The colonel at one point wrote the governor, "I am under no obligation whatever to conform to your suggestions with regard to the military disposition of the troops of this department." All the while, Johnston worked with neighboring Indian tribes, chiefs often coming to his headquarters for visits. He likewise scouted the country for potential routes for the proposed transcontinental railroad. He also oversaw numerous officers who came and went, including another stint commanding his old staff officer Major Buell. Still, it was a long period away from Eliza and the children, another of which was born in 1857. "I bear my exile here badly," he admitted, "my philosophy sometimes gives way. I try to be content, and hope for better times." Fortunately, in the meantime, in 1858 Johnston received the rank of brevet brigadier general, an unofficial promotion that carried higher authority but no higher pay.[55]

Better times came when Johnston was finally able to turn over command to Colonel Charles F. Smith and make his way home. He was so far out west that he found it easier to travel to California and return to the East Coast by boat and across Central America; trudging across the Great Plains alone, especially in winter, was not a practical option. It was a moving goodbye ceremony when he left, riding along the line of troops he had commanded for years now; most were sad to see him go.[56]

Johnston spent much of the remainder of 1860 in Louisville with his family, watching the nation fall apart. He knew another task awaited him, because General Scott and others were loud in their praises of how he had conducted his Utah campaign. Departmental command was again in his future, but he decided not to go back to command in the Texas department. With the sectional turmoil boiling over, especially after Republican Abraham Lincoln won the presidential election in November, Johnston knew that Texas would probably secede, and he would have to follow his adopted state: "my citizenship in Texas was obtained at the cost of the bloom of health and the prime of life spent in the service of the State." He did not want to be confronted with a situation where he would have to choose between his duty as an army officer and his loyalty to Texas. In fact, he decided he would resign from the U.S. Army rather than take the Texas command. Fortunately, orders came for him to assume control of the Department of the Pacific in California instead.[57]

Leaving for the West Coast the day after South Carolina seceded, Johnston did not know what his future would hold. But he had Eliza and the children with him this time, hopefully for what would turn into a long, prosperous, and peaceful command in California. Joining him, too, was his slave Randolph, whom he freed before leaving Kentucky (he also gave another slave to his son William). But having been with him in Texas and Utah, Randolph wanted to stay with Johnston, who agreed to take him along and pay him wages. The Johnston party moved by boat from New York to Panama, crossing the isthmus, and thence by another ship on to San Francisco, arriving on January 14, 1861, despite harsh weather. "The last four or five days . . . was quite rough from head winds," he wrote, so much so that Eliza had to lie down most of the way. Johnston took formal command the next day, the War Department having combined the Departments of California and Oregon into one Department of the Pacific.[58]

Johnston spent most of his time in this command dealing with budgets, replying to requests for protection from Indian raids, working on construction projects such as forts and roads, and guarding mail and stagecoach shipments. He worked mainly through his assistant adjutant general, Major William W. Mackall, as well as other staff officers such as his engineer, Captain Jeremy F. Gilmer, who loudly proclaimed his "strong Southern talk." Although agreeing with his sentiments, Johnston later told him that he "did not at that time feel authorized to say so." Yet after only a few weeks in California came the event that Johnston knew was imminent. On February 2, Texas formally seceded from the Union, which effectively brought Johnston's career in the U.S. Army to an end. "To continue to hold my commission after being apprised of the final action of my State, to whose partiality in a great measure I owe my position, could find no justification in my own conscience," he wrote. Johnston would never fight against Texas; additionally, the new Confederacy's views on everything from the Constitution to slavery fit his own almost perfectly. "I felt as soon as I learned the course adopted by my State (Texas), that it was my duty to conform to her will," he explained. Johnston had made the gradual switch from a Union-loving Whig to a diehard Democrat by this time and welcomed the change, although his heart hurt from the idea of warfare against the nation for which he had served so many years. His son later described his father's situation as a "choice of evils." Still, he was a Texan, so Johnston mailed his resignation on April 9. "I adopted Texas," he explained, "and its people have been my fast friends and are entitled to my best services."[59]

Johnston's resignation and request for a replacement was done in secret because he did not wish that his command or anyone else know of his actions until his successor arrived, at which time he would turn over the department. But Washington authorities, including General Scott, had anticipated his action and sent, just as secretly, his replacement. Brigadier General Edwin V. Sumner rushed to California to relieve Johnston even before his resignation—not actually accepted until May 6—arrived. Sumner showed up on April 24 unannounced and took command the next day. Such a lack of trust hurt Johnston, as did rumors that he was conspiring to turn over California to the Confederacy. He made it plain, and events and sources later bore it out without any doubt (including his replacement Sumner, who wrote the War Department, "it gives me pleasure to state that the command was turned over to me in good order"), that he remained loyal to the Union so long as he remained in the army, even after submitting his resignation but before his relief. Johnston had earlier written, "as I will do no one thing which my conscience does not approve as beneficial to my country, I shall always be without fear, and, I hope, without reproach." Even amid the crisis as rumors of his disloyalty emerged, he firmly told the governor of California: "I have spent the greater part of my life in the service of my country, and while I hold her commission I shall serve her honorably and faithfully. I shall protect her public property, and not a cartridge or a percussion-cap shall pass to any enemy while I am here as her representative." He added, "there is . . . no man in the Union more sorely afflicted than I am at the occurrences now taking place." But he was relieved to be out from under the stress of conflicting loyalties; when Sumner arrived he quipped, "then am I doubly relieved." Still, he was chagrined at the duplicity involved "without the customary notice."[60]

So now yet another crisis faced Johnston in his crisis-ridden life. His first thirty or so years had been almost perfect in every way, with a firm footing of kinship ties, an honorable position in life with the U.S. Army, and with a happy and growing family. But all that came crashing down in the heartbreaking mid-1830s, sending him into a tailspin from which it took him decades to recover. He later admitted, "a series of adverse circumstances have, with me, disappointed expectations most justly founded; and, although I am still confident of a final extrication, the effect has been to throw me beyond the sphere of motion of friends and acquaintances to a distance, I fear, at which sympathy languishes." The last twenty or so years had seemingly involved one crisis after another, whether political, economic, or social. But many of them were self-inflicted from poor choices Johnston had made in taking gambles trying to recover his equilibrium in life. Yet he took it all in stride, trying to remain upbeat and positive, once writing that "it ought to be held [just] as honorable to battle with adversity with unquailing front as to lead the way to the deadly breach amid the roar of cannon and the din of mortal combat."[61]

But the crisis Johnston now faced, that of momentous civil war against his former nation, was perhaps the biggest calamity of his life to date. It would prove to spur another set of supreme crises, even threatening his life, which had already hung so delicately in the balance on several previous occasions.[62]

— 3 —

THAT IS SIDNEY JOHNSTON'S STEP

TAKING COMMAND OF THE WEST

F anaticism will soon bring on a sectional collision between the States of the Union," Albert Sidney Johnston declared, "in which every man will have to choose his side. When it comes there will be no lack of blows." Then he added, "and may God help the right!" Johnston proved to be a prophet insomuch as his declaration came true in short order, although it was not a great leap of faith to declare such future events amid the hectic and toilsome chaos of the late 1850s. For good reason, William Seward proclaimed there was coming an "irrepressible conflict," and Johnston's sister-in-law, widow of the dead senator, wrote that the politicians of the day "seem to take pride in fanning the fire brand of discord between the north & south."[1]

For all of Johnston's clarity of thought, yet another major life gamble became necessary as the nation fell apart in 1861. When Texas seceded, there was no doubt what he would do: resign his commission and become a civilian again. Since Texas was a slave state, Johnston's resignation can be taken no other way than as a commitment to the elite slaveholders that he had always striven to become but had not quite reached. He refused to give up his Texas citizenship to remain in the U.S. Army after having struggled so long to reach the social position he had. But resigning and potentially taking up arms against the army he had served and so loved was potentially treasonous, although most Confederates argued that personal resignation and the secession of their individual states freed them from U.S. citizenship and thus removed the stigma of treason if they went to war.[2]

Sadly, this second resignation from the army did not start off any better than his first, as Johnston now had no place to go, no income, and no surrounding set of friends or kinsman in San Francisco. Worse, he was isolated in California, far away from most of his family and from the scene of major national events. "I must now look out for a livelihood for my poor family; how or where to find it is not apparent," he wrote his son William in Kentucky. Tangential family problems also emerged in the disruption of Albert Jr.'s life, his son having just been appointed a cadet to West Point. Perhaps this was an attempt at bribery, but Fitz Porter warned the War Department that General Johnston "cannot be bribed." Worst of all was the questioning of Johnston's character and honesty. He assured everyone he could that "the whole charge [of treason] is false in every particular, and that there is not the slightest ground for it." He further argued, "if I had proved faithless here, how could my own people ever trust me."[3]

Many people tried to convince Johnston to remain loyal to the Union, his sister-in-law (Senator Johnston's widow) one of the foremost: "your elder brother, my beloved husband, having felt for you as a father, gives me a right to speak as a mother; and I do affectionately request you not to act hastily and resign your commission." She told him she had just received a letter from Washington stating that General Scott himself "designs, when General Johnston arrived here, to place him in a position at once which will relieve him from the slightest imputation." She counseled, "therefore, my dear Albert, do not think of resigning. Remember your dear brother's love for the Union, his exalted patriotism, and his many virtues. You are his representative now."[4]

The idea of Johnston gaining high rank in the Union army was not an isolated hope of his sister-in-law. Many others contemporaneously described him as the best soldier in the army at the time. Porter wrote him in April that the secretary of war "has the utmost confidence in you, and will give you the most important command and trust, on your arrival here." Even General Sumner, upon relieving Johnston, told him: "General, I wish you would reconsider and recall your resignation. General Scott bade me say to you that he wished you for active service, and that you should be only second to himself." Montgomery Blair, Lincoln's postmaster general, likewise later explained to William Johnston: "I immediately told Mr. Lincoln the facts, and recommended him to send your father a major-general's commission, and he at once executed the commission. I had it forwarded to your father at

San Francisco." Johnston was gone by the time the document arrived, and there is some debate as to whether such offers were genuine or mere ploys to keep him loyal long enough to get someone not under suspicion in his place.[5]

But given Texas secession, there was never any real chance Johnston would remain loyal to the United States. He would go with his adopted state, which had become special to him even to the point of not renouncing his citizenship there even for monetary gain in court cases regarding his disputed land in its northern counties: "my citizenship in Texas . . . I will not give it up now, tho' I should lose in consequence every foot of land I have in the state, this I would regard as a mere mess of pottage in comparison with my citizenship." And Texas, it seemed, was about to enter another war. "I suppose the difficulties will now only be adjusted by the sword," Johnston wrote his sister-in-law in response to her call for remaining in the U.S. Army. But his actions brought other opportunities, namely with the newly organizing Confederate forces. His old friend Jefferson Davis had been appointed provisional Confederate president and would certainly offer Johnston a high command in the war all knew was coming. In fact, Davis later asserted, "I hoped and expected that I had others who would prove generals, but I knew I had one, and that was Sidney Johnston." He also told a friend, "there is one man above all others—he is now in California—I have written to him—I believe he is with us." William Johnston also sent word in April that he had been in Montgomery to meet with President Davis and came away with assurances that his father "would be second only to President Davis in rebel considerations and position." Johnston was well pleased. "It looks like fate; twice Texas makes me a rebel," he quipped to his wife. "We are all well," he wrote his son from California, "and almost as comfortable as we could desire, were it not for the unhappy condition of our country. I confess I can only expect a general disruption, for passion seems to rule."[6]

The major problem, of course, was that Johnston was in California, far away from the scenes of action. He would return east, but by summer, Union forces were looking for him. "The Secretary of War directs that you arrest General A. S. Johnston if he returns from California by overland route," Scott himself ordered on June 3. Soon learning of a group of "bold and enthusiastic Southerners" who planned to cross the continent and join the Confederate military, Johnston did just that. On June 16, he left and met up with the others, setting out eastward across the deserts of California and Arizona, heading for Texas.[7]

The desert trail ran for some eight hundred miles before reaching Mesilla on July 28. From there, Johnston moved on to El Paso and took a more formal stage to San Antonio, thence to New Orleans and on to Richmond. Time was of the essence. Johnston remarked that Southerners' highest passions would be at the start of the war, for "we are a proud people." He went on to argue: "If we are to be successful, what we have to do must be done quickly. The longer we have them to fight, the more difficult they will be to defeat." Johnston finally made it to Richmond by September 3 and went to see President Davis, whom Leonidas Polk described as very desirous of Johnston's arrival: "we want and he [Davis] wants Genl A. S. Johnston badly." The president, ailing and on his sick bed, heard footsteps on the floor below. His mood brightened and he exclaimed, "that is Sidney Johnston's step. Bring him up." Davis had the general he wanted.[8]

Johnston met with Davis in the ensuing days as the two hashed out his command. The first matter of business was Johnston's appointment as full general, to date from May 30. Davis initially made five such appointments, causing some argument from Joseph E. Johnston, who maintained that his rank as brigadier general in the old army was higher than the others had held and thus entitled him to be senior to them. The president responded that the rank was in a staff position, not a line post, and used other criteria as well in determining seniority of the full generals. He thus appointed Samuel Cooper as the Confederacy's adjutant general, a position he had held in the old army; he was destined to remain behind a desk in Richmond. Albert Sidney Johnston became the ranking field commander, followed in order by Robert E. Lee, the other Johnston, and P. G. T. Beauregard. A lot of the motivation for Davis's action stemmed from his semi-worship of Johnston. Biographer William C. Davis has termed it "filial love" and argued that the president thought of Johnston as his idol: "he worshiped Sidney Johnston as he did no other man in his life." Davis himself admitted as much: "I knew Sidney Johnston, I believe, better than I know any other man." Regardless, Johnston quickly replied, "I hereby signify my acceptance of that appointment and herewith enclose the oath duly executed."[9]

With his rank determined, the next issue was where Johnston would command. His assignment would be west of the Appalachian Mountains, from which the president had received numerous requests for Johnston to take charge. Davis later confided to Johnston's son that it was a difficult decision to send him out west, as he preferred to have him as secretary of war.

But he rationalized that "the West was a field vast and distant, where the chief must act without advice or aid, and he seemed the only man equal to it." Davis already had both Joe Johnston and Beauregard in the East, they having won the battle at Manassas in July 1861. Also, Sidney Johnston was from the West. Perhaps tipping the scales, those commanders Davis had in that vast region currently were only mediocre at best.[10]

Many Southerners asked for Johnston's appointment in the West as well, including his former major in the 2nd U.S. Cavalry, William Hardee, who commented to an acquaintance, "I am desirous . . . that Gen'l Sydney Johnston should be sent to command in the valley of the Mississippi, he has more experience than [Major] Gen'l [Leonidas] Polk & will inspire greater confidence." Even Polk, the current Confederate theater commander at this point as well as Episcopal bishop of Louisiana, wished for Johnston to supersede him, they having been roommates at West Point. He wrote President Davis bluntly: "I know of no one so well equal to that task as our friend General Albert S. Johnston."[11]

Accordingly, Adjutant General Cooper issued orders on September 10 that Johnston would command Department No. 2, which encompassed the heartland of the Confederacy: Tennessee, Arkansas, and the western portion of Mississippi along the Mississippi River. Also part of the department were the nonseceded states of Kentucky, Missouri, Kansas, and the Indian Territory. In effect, the command was for the defense of the Mississippi Valley. Johnston's orders explicitly stated that he go to Memphis first, one of the river's queen cities, although he also had leeway to make his headquarters wherever he saw fit. He also had authority to call on the various states in his department for troops.[12]

Discussions in Richmond varied about what to do out west, and certainly Johnston would not have a clear idea on how to proceed until he arrived on site. But the prevailing opinion was that Johnston would gather his forces in Arkansas and invade Missouri because of the importance of that area. Secretary of War Judah P. Benjamin later wrote, "when we sent General A. S. Johnston to take command of the Western Department it was believed that he would proceed at once to the west of the Mississippi and conduct the campaign in Arkansas and Missouri."[13]

Johnston did not tarry long in Richmond, of course, and was in Nashville just four days later, having traveled the main rail line from east to west via Knoxville (where he met with his new subordinate in East Tennessee,

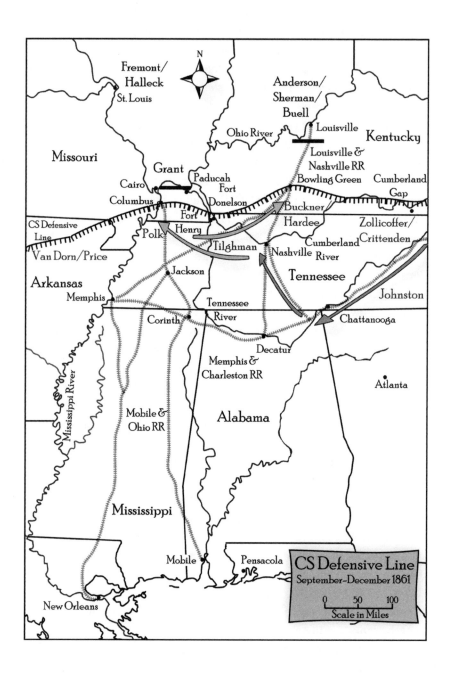

Fremont/
Halleck
St. Louis

Anderson/
Sherman/
Buell

N

Ohio River

Louisville

Kentucky

Missouri

Grant

Paducah

Fort

Louisville &
Nashville RR
Bowling Green

Cumberland
Gap

Cairo

Columbus

Donelson

Buckner

CS Defensive
Line

Fort
Henry

Polk

Hardee

Zollicoffer/
Crittenden

Van Dorn/Price

Tilghman

Cumberland
River

Nashville

Arkansas

Memphis

Jackson

Tennessee

Johnston

Corinth

Tennessee
River

Decatur

Chattanooga

Memphis &
Charleston RR

Atlanta

Mobile &
Ohio RR

Alabama

Mississippi

Mississippi River

Mississippi

Mobile

Pensacola

New Orleans

CS Defensive Line
September–December 1861

0   50   100
Scale in Miles

Brigadier General Felix Zollicoffer) and Chattanooga. He took formal command the next day, September 15, 1861, appearing before the people of Nashville at the capitol building and addressing them as "fellow-soldiers—I call you soldiers, because you all belong to the reserve corps." With the general was the beginnings of his staff, including his assistant adjutant general from California, William W. Mackall, as well as eventually his chief engineer, Jeremy Gilmer, who had also been with him in California. Randolph (or "Ran"), his former slave, was also his constant companion.[14]

Johnston's arrival in Nashville portended a new era in the command of the West, both for him personally as well as the troops already defending this vast stretch of the Confederacy. Personally, Johnston had a brief reunion with his son William, who was in Nashville and would eventually become an aide to President Davis in Richmond. There was some talk and advice for Johnston to place his son on his own staff, but both shied away from that despite many generals doing so throughout the war. The younger Johnston stated that his father "thought, and I agreed with him at the time, that, for my own sake, and to avoid even the semblance of partiality, it was better for me to forego the pleasure of this association." But he sadly added, "this was the last day that I ever saw my father."[15]

Despite the family interests, it did not take long for Johnston to survey the military situation and come to some hard decisions. He essentially stepped into a drama that was already unfolding and would not slow down to allow him time to catch up. Johnston had to get up to speed quickly and thus met with various officials and generals in his new department such as Zollicoffer and Tennessee governor Isham G. Harris. From them he learned that the situation was even worse than he had suspected in Richmond. His friend the president had given him a plumb assignment, but it was no favor. Davis actually expected Johnston to work miracles.[16]

Distance and size were major problems, the department stretching, in what historian Charles P. Roland has described as "a trace of a defensive line," more than six hundred miles from the Cumberland Gap to the Indian Territory. The most critical portion was the more than three hundred miles from the mountains westward to the Mississippi River, with three major rivers and one railroad piercing that vital defensive region. Worse, the rivers brought the two sides' navies to the table, the Federals far ahead on that score than the Confederacy. Davis had given Johnston authority to call on the Confederate naval forces in his department, but they were minor and weak. Johnston's land forces would likely be on their own.[17]

The major problem was, of course, the enemy confronting Johnston, threatening him at multiple points. At least three major clusters of Federal forces were along his defensive front from the mountains of eastern Kentucky and Tennessee to the Indian Territory. One was in Missouri, although it had been defeated at Wilson's Creek in August 1861 and its leader, Brigadier General Nathaniel Lyon, killed. This force was probably not a serious threat at the moment. Not so was a larger army astride the Mississippi River, first under Major General John C. Frémont and then Major General Henry W. Halleck. The departmental commanders and their subordinates such as Brigadier Generals Ulysses S. Grant and John A. McClernand, as well as Johnston's old friend Charles F. Smith, were already pushing southward and making noise even in September. And then a large force under a series of commanders such as Johnston's West Point comrade Robert Anderson as well as Brigadier General William T. Sherman and finally Johnston's former assistant adjutant general in Texas and Utah, Don Carlos Buell (now a brigadier general), threatened eastern Kentucky and Tennessee. All were well aware of Johnston's arrival, Frémont writing in some panic on September 17, "information of the most grave character reaches me that General Johnston has arrived at Columbus, Ky., and taken command." He called for immediate reinforcements. William Johnston later declared that he had personal knowledge that General Johnston also used what he thought were Buell's opinions of him to his advantage.[18]

In addition to his military woes, Johnston stepped into another major problem when he arrived, this one political: the touchy issue of Kentucky and its declared neutrality. This status had offered a tenuous defense of the western Confederacy all along, and Tennessee governor Harris put a lot of stock in Kentucky's neutrality for protecting his northern border. But then an ill-advised movement by Major General Polk, while still in theater command before Johnston arrived, saw Confederate forces invade Kentucky to acquire and occupy the very defensible location at Columbus on the Mississippi River. This action having occurred just days earlier, Johnston stepped into an ongoing and developing strategic headache as he reached Nashville. President Davis tried to clean up the mess, his secretary of war telling a frantic Governor Harris that the "movement was wholly unauthorized," but even Davis soon came to the conclusion that what was done was done and there was no going back. As such, he now wanted Johnston to take the best defensive positions in Kentucky if warranted, particularly moving up to the Barren River at Bowling Green. In fact, a message reached Johnston while still en route to Nashville that he should confer with the western leaders and then "decide in relation to Bowling Green." But there was little time to think, as the Federals responded to Polk's actions by moving forces southward from Louisville as well as to the mouths of the Tennessee and Cumberland Rivers at Paducah and Smithland; Grant and Smith garnered for the Federals those extremely strategic positions. As a result, Davis could not get Johnston to the West quickly enough, wiring Polk at Columbus on September 13, "General A. S. Johnston is *en route* to join you." He also assured Harris the same day that "General A. S. Johnston has been directed to confer with you at Nashville." Everyone seemingly looked to Johnston to arrive and be the adult in the room, but historian Larry Daniel has surmised that he faced "a largely unsolvable strategic/political dilemma."[19]

So, Johnston had a mess across much of his extended line of defense, facing Federals who were moving forward to gobble up as much of Kentucky as they could until they met Confederate forces doing the same thing in a wild episode similar to a land rush. Obviously, there were political as well as military issues involved too, but the Confederate civilian leadership basically left it up to Johnston to decide how to proceed and whether to take positions in Kentucky. By the time he arrived in Nashville, of course, the political questions had been answered for him, thus "the occupation of Bowling Green became necessary as an act of self-defense," as Johnston informed President Davis. But staking claim to as much of Kentucky as possible was also problematic for Johnston for many reasons. One was a severe lack of soldiers at his disposal as well as sufficient arms for those men. Likewise, there was a severe shortage of generals to command those troops. Johnston would have a hard enough time defending the western Confederacy with plenty of troops, much less with the paltry numbers he now had. To Governor Harris, for instance, he wrote that "the defenseless condition of this department was patent from the moment I arrived and had a hasty view of the field."[20]

Military concerns now prevailed, and Johnston set forth his many reasons for taking Bowling Green and other areas in Kentucky. In fact, he put his thoughts down on paper on September 16, only a day after taking command of Department No. 2. On the big question of Confederate troops remaining in Kentucky, particularly at Columbus, he asserted that the decision had already been made prior to his arrival, and his forces would have to do the best they could with what they now had. Specifically, the legislature and governor now called for the Confederates to withdraw all forces from Kentucky, but Johnston forcefully responded, "the troops *will not* be withdrawn." He argued that a withdrawal, particularly from Columbus and near Cumberland Gap, was not possible "without opening the frontiers of Tennessee and the Mississippi River to the enemy, and this is regarded as essential to our present line of defense as well as to any future operations. So far from yielding to the demand for the withdrawal of our troops, I have determined to occupy Bowling Green at once." Essentially, with no thought of giving up Columbus and removing those troops from Kentucky now that the irrevocable political damage had been done, occupying Bowling Green would not create any more transgression against Kentucky itself. Johnston might as well take advantage of having Bowing Green and southern Kentucky if troops were going to remain elsewhere in the state anyway. Likewise, Polk's taking of Columbus extended the Confederate left flank in a salient far above the rest of the defensive line, inviting attack if Johnston did not take possession of Bowling Green.[21]

Johnston implemented his Kentucky strategy immediately, and that meant holding the critical position at Columbus as well as the Barren River line at Bowling Green. On September 15, he ordered Brigadier General Simon Bolivar Buckner, a native Kentuckian who held almost as much sway as anyone in that state perhaps apart from ex–vice president John C. Breckinridge, to move northward and occupy the town along the Louisville and Nashville Railroad. Johnston reminded him of the need for stealth because of the slanted numbers: "secrecy in preparation and promptness in execution give the best if not the only promise of success, and the general is confident you will be wanting in neither." Buckner occupied Bowling Green with fewer than five thousand men on September 18 and sent an advance farther forward to the Green River at Munfordville. Johnston considered Bowling Green to be easily defended because of the Barren River, a good depot for supplies along the railroad, and easily accessible from Tennessee, but he ordered Buckner not to go beyond Munfordville, certainly not to Muldraugh's Hill. Because the Green River would be in their rear, Buckner's forces could easily be cut off if they advanced all the way to Muldraugh's.[22]

Yet even at the same time as occupying portions of Kentucky, Johnston was trying to patch over the breeches in protocol and neutrality. Although sensitive to the political implications of his military actions, Buckner issued a scathing proclamation to the people of Kentucky when he took Bowling Green. Johnston issued a countering proclamation on September 22, written in Richmond and only tweaked by him and his staff to make it fit the immediate situation. It basically gave the "motives" for the Confederate incursion and promised "no hostile intention towards its [Kentucky's] people." Johnston also promised that his "army shall be withdrawn from Kentucky so soon as there be satisfactory evidence of the existence and execution of a like intention on the part of the United States." Nothing seemed to work, however, and he later reported that "no enthusiasm, as we imagined and hoped, but hostility, was manifested in Kentucky." Johnston badly overestimated his fellow Kentuckians, most of whom sided with neither belligerent.[23]

But what really overshadowed the Kentucky policy were the paltry number of troops and arms Johnston had to work with. He explicitly told Davis, "we have not over half the armed forces that are now likely to be required for our security against disaster." It was indeed a dismal situation, as those troops were spread far and wide along Johnston's lengthy defensive line, from the Indian Territory all the way to the Cumberland Gap. He had only four small concentrations of forces, mainly covering transportation routes leading directly into the Confederate heartland. Out west was Major General Sterling Price's command that had just defeated the Federals at Wilson's Creek and then again at Lexington, for which Johnston congratulated the Missourian while approving his operations. Price occupied northwestern Arkansas and southwestern Missouri with a force of about ten or twelve thousand men. There was also a small force in northeastern Arkansas under Brigadier General Hardee, along with nearby independent commands such as one under Brigadier General M. Jeff Thompson. In the more important area from the Mississippi River to the Cumberland Gap, Polk and his eleven thousand troops occupied Columbus on the Mississippi River. Zollicoffer, a politician and newspaperman but importantly a Whig to help offset all the Democrats who had been appointed generals in the Confederate army, operated on the extreme other flank in front of the Cumberland Gap with around four thousand men. In between them, along the line of the Louisville and

Nashville Railroad, was another force of around ten thousand at Nashville and now extending to Bowling Green. In between each of these concentrations were long stretches without any significant numbers of troops or, at places, only a motley assortment of sick and unarmed recruits; one Confederate described his camp "being merely one large hospital."[24]

The most critical of these uncovered areas was where the Tennessee and Cumberland Rivers pierced the defensive line a mere ten or twelve miles apart. Two small forts had been started to guard these approaches, Fort Henry on the Tennessee and Fort Donelson on the Cumberland, but neither was strong enough or had much more than a regiment garrisoning it. Fortunately, Johnston had the gift of interior lines, whereby he could shuffle troops if needed. The Memphis, Clarksville, and Louisville Railroad ran generally parallel with the defensive line for much of the way, intersecting the various north–south railroads that led to the major garrisons. The problem spot was where the rail line crossed the Tennessee River at Danville, just south of Fort Henry. If the railroad was broken there, Johnston's position would be cleaved in two, with the wide and impassable (except by boat) river splitting his wings. The track also crossed the Cumberland River at Clarksville, but the bridge there was of lesser importance, as the Cumberland did not affect troop movements farther south nearly as much as the Tennessee, which dove in a much deeper bowl even into the cotton states of Alabama and Mississippi.[25]

After issuing such a dismal warning, Johnston set to work doing something about each problem. Manpower was a definite issue, and Johnston took advantage of the authority he had received to call on the various states in his department for more troops. To the governors of Tennessee, Mississippi, and Arkansas he wrote a basic form letter telling each the same thing: he needed armed troops for the duration of the war but would take twelve-month regiments whose members brought their own shotguns and squirrel rifles. He designated points in each state for their rendezvous, with the idea that they would be sent northward to his defensive positions as soon as possible. Johnston thus called for thirty thousand troops from Tennessee and ten thousand each from Mississippi and Arkansas. The governors did what they could, often issuing proclamations to their people, but were not able to provide much help. A grateful Johnston nevertheless asked that all armed companies be immediately lumped together and sent forward while the others waited for weapons. He also tried to requisition any troops moving through his department destined for other areas as well. Overall, the response was lackluster at best, Johnston admitting at one point to his aide Major Edward W. Munford: "I am disappointed in the state of public sentiment in the South. Our people seem to have suffered from a violent political fever, which has left them exhausted. They are not up to the revolutionary point." Munford asked if the general doubted final success: "he looked at me gravely for a moment, and said, 'If the South wishes to be free, she can be free.'"[26]

Equally concerning were arms and equipment for those troops, Johnston informing President Davis that "thirty thousand stand is a necessity to my command." He once ordered a staff member to pick up two shiny new horseshoes that had been dropped by a quartermaster, telling him, "that's something saved to the Confederacy, and our duty is to save everything we can." But arms were the major need. The first wave of patriotism and volunteerism was still having its effect, with more troops than weapons available. In fact, during the fall of 1861, Johnston had two whole brigades, one under Brigadier General Leroy P. Walker in northern Alabama and the other under Brigadier General William H. Carroll in East Tennessee, completely ready for service but unarmed. He wrote Governor A. B. Moore of Alabama that "the condition of the defenses of our northern frontier requires every possible assistance from the South. We have men in large numbers. We are deficient in arms." He made the "strongest appeal to your excellency's patriotism to aid me in this respect." To Mississippi's governor, John J. Pettus, Johnston stipulated, "all the troops you can send armed are needed at once." He even sent Colonel St. John R. Liddell to Richmond to lobby for arms, to which a despondent Davis responded with uncharacteristic frustration toward Johnston: "why did General Johnston send you to me for arms and reinforcements, when he must know that I have neither?" Later, after calming down, the president simply told Liddell as he ushered him out the door, "tell my friend, General Johnston, that I can do nothing for him; that he must rely upon his own resources. . . . May God bless you."[27]

There were few arms to be had anywhere. Governor Joseph E. Brown of Georgia wrote: "It is utterly impossible for me to comply with your request. There are no arms belonging to the State at my disposal." Alabama's governor replied that he had no weapons either, with four full regiments in camp but unarmed. Johnston also tasked the Confederate government with supplying his men, making a case directly to President Davis for a shipment of rifles that he heard had landed at Savannah, Georgia. Other forms of munitions and supplies were also lacking, including powder and commissary goods. Johnston started a department-wide collection of supplies at various points such as Nashville, Memphis, and Grand Junction, Tennessee, and opened smaller depots elsewhere, normally at railroad junctions.[28]

Also of concern was a lack of generals to command whatever troops came forward. Johnston wanted Buckner as a general, appointing him a brigadier commanding several new Kentucky regiments and tasked with moving the troops to Bowling Green. Other officers fortunately arrived in the department, including John P. McCown. Other colonels already within the department were also elevated, men such as Lloyd Tilghman, who was unfortunately sick some of the time; Johnston even requested that Major Alexander P. Stewart receive promotion. Major John C. Breckinridge, former vice president and senator from Kentucky, was also tapped as a general officer, Johnston quipping that "he has gone to Richmond to get his musket." Engineers, while not general officers, were also at a premium, and Johnston complained about how much he needed them. He received "the only engineer officer we have to spare," Captain Gilmer, who had been with him in California. Otherwise, Johnston had to find engineers among his line officers who were West Point trained or in private business.[29]

Any number of other military administrative issues faced Johnston during these months, including the disposition of prisoners of war prior to the famous Dix-Hill Cartel, which formalized a process to exchange them. The exchange system at this point was individual to each commander and often required a local back and forth. At one point, for example, Napoleon Buford visited Polk under a flag of truce. The bishop informed Johnston of their negotiations and reminded him, "the flag was borne by Buford (N. B.), whom you recollect as my classmate at West Point from Kentucky." Later, Johnston and Buell also developed a system on their front near Bowling Green to exchange prisoners "grade for grade." In addition, Johnston set up a military board to try civilians under military arrest.[30]

Getting acclimated to his new surroundings as well as to the civilians and officers of the region also took time. With his genial nature, Johnston misjudged some of his subordinates, at one point having a high opinion of a certain colonel until he saw him one day berating his regiment with vitriol and cursing. "That man has not as much sense as I had believed," he told a staff officer as they passed, "he does not know how to command men. It is an error to suppose it can be done by fear. The true secret of command lies in the exercise of moderation, united with superior sense and justice. No man can command others with permanent success unless he has learned to command himself." On the other hand, Johnston judged some others correctly, as one found out when he angrily burst into the general's tent and blurted out: "I would like to know, General Johnston, why all my suggestions and recommendations are overslaughed or treated with silent contempt?" Johnston, the only other person in the tent, simply turned slowly and mumbled, "was your remark addressed to me, sir?" The man wilted. Civilians could also cause trouble. One came to him with a plan to arm the troops with spears fitted with pruning hooks to cut cavalry reins, and he would not take no for an answer. When Johnston finally had enough, he quietly asked, "what do you think the Federal horsemen would be doing with their revolvers, while our spearmen were trying to cut their bridle-reins?" At another point, he harangued a civilian who came to headquarters with a plan to assassinate Andrew Johnson, a Tennessee Unionists still serving in the U.S. Senate, "at a trifling cost of money." Johnston told him firmly, "sir, the Government which I serve meets its enemies in open and honorable warfare. It scorns alike the assassin's knife and the debased scoundrel who would suggest its use!" An indignant Johnston turned to a staff officer after the man hurriedly left: "that scoundrel wanted me to bribe him to assassinate Andrew Johnson."[31]

More personal issues needed to be attended to as well, including the proper dress of a full general. In late September, Johnston ordered over fifty dollars' worth of clothing from a Memphis store, including a coat, pants, two pairs of "drawers," undershirts, and handkerchiefs. Also included was an officer's coat, a cravat, and a kepi. At the same time, Johnston worried about Eliza and "our dear children," another of whom was born recently. He counseled, "you must name the baby for yourself." Unfortunately, Johnston had no idea where his wife and children were, hearing only rumors that they had arrived in New York and made it to Louisville. The rumor was that his old friend Buell was giving them every consideration he could. Ultimately, the rumors proved incorrect, but Johnston did have some family nearby. His son William was a Confederate officer in Virginia, but his daughter-in-law Rosa and grandchild were close to Nashville. In all the chaos of not knowing exactly where anyone was, Johnston nevertheless told his wife, "be courageous

& hopeful. I think of you always. God Bless you dear wife & our children."
On a less worrisome note, the U.S. War Department in Washington actually
wrote him requesting information on expenses and receipts from 1857![32]

Even something as mundane as assembling his staff was important, as
those men would be the arm of Johnston's decisions and the support for the
army. He had as his assistant adjutant general Lieutenant Colonel Mackall,
gruff and often described as "about as amicable as ever" and "generally . . .
cheerful for him." The general also had two members who would be with him
for the duration of his time in command, Captain Henry P. Brewster and
Captain Nathaniel Wickliffe. Major Albert J. Smith took charge of the quartermaster department, while Captain Thomas K. Jackson oversaw the commissary. Lieutenant Joseph Dixon was his engineer, pending the arrival of
Captain Gilmer, who arrived just as Johnston traveled to other parts of his
department, necessitating a chase to find the department's headquarters. As
a personal staff, Johnston had a lone aide, Lieutenant R. P. Hunt, although
he had volunteer aides such as Arkansas senator Colonel Robert W. Johnson, Missouri's Confederate governor in exile Colonel Thomas C. Reynolds,
and Colonel Samuel Tate, a West Tennessee businessman and railroad official. Major Dudley M. Hayden and Major Munford were also military aides
who would be with Johnston for the duration of his command. Surgeon
David W. Yandell became departmental surgeon. And Johnston needed a
surgeon. He wrote Eliza later, "I suffered all October with inflammation of
the lungs, which the Doctors said was the effect of Malaria." Not all were enthused with his staff, however, one person writing Johnston that he hoped
"you have stopped the orgie, which those young & frivolous officers Capt
Wickliffe, Capt Brewster & Maj Mumford indulged in."[33]

Other personal issues also developed, including the almost immediate
and steady correspondence arriving from those unknown to Johnston but
who knew someone who knew him, all requesting high-ranking staff positions. Some even came from governors and the secretary of war. Gifts also
arrived for the new general, perhaps to curry favor with him. Most notably,
Johnston was offered several horses when he arrived in Tennessee. One
named Umpire, given by James H. Meriweather of Memphis, was described
as "the finest thoroughbred stallion in the Mississippi Valley." Umpire was,
it was noted in sending him, "also a Kentuckian." Johnston also received another horse from W. B. Smith of Tippah County, Mississippi, through the
efforts of Mississippi statesman Alexander M. Clayton. He wrote that the

horse would be presented "as a present, and as some evidence of the estimate which he [Smith] in common with our whole community places upon your service & character." Clayton assured Johnston the animal, "a large gray horse, young, strong—of good action and will be able to bear a soldier thro the labors of a campaign," would be sent to him "without parade, and without any flourish of trumpets."[34]

Most notably, an Arkansan, Captain J. D. Adams of Little Rock, "was & is still anxious to have you suited with a very fine horse." Adams and his agents spent six weeks seeking out the perfect animal but could not find one, eventually settling on another gray one that the agent nevertheless declared was "one of the finest military horses I have ever seen." Adams and the others were not as enthused ("[it] did not suit me but was the best that could be done at the present") but finally had to agree to it. In the letter accompanying the animal, Dr. L. Blackburn wrote, "he is five years old last spring without a fault kind both under the saddle and in harness." The horse had actually been owned by Arkansas officer (referred to as general but never appointed as such) Thompson B. Flournoy before his death in August, after which it was then tuned out to pasture, where the "heavy dews of night" softened its hooves, which then wore down "nearly to the quick." But a week's rest in normal surroundings would have the horse ready for work, although Captain Adams made plain, "if you do not think him equal in every respect to any horse you have ever seen upon the military field, then notify me of the fact and I will replace him." In a postscript to his letter, he added, "This horse is a thoroughbred, name Fire Eater."[35]

Amid the whirlwind preparations to remedy all these problems and get settled in his new command, Johnston nevertheless faced pushback and bureaucracy. He quickly complained to Adjutant General Cooper in Richmond that "of the funds promised by the Quartermaster General to Colonel Stevenson, quartermaster at this place, not one dollar has been received. Their immediate transmission is absolutely necessary." That brought a curt reply from Quartermaster General A. C. Myers that "the Quartermaster-General does not promise funds to any person whatever." Secretary of War Judah Benjamin often corrected Johnston as well. For instance, writing in reference to the rifles landed at Savannah, he told him that there were a mere thirty-five hundred that became available and many were already promised out; nevertheless, he sent him a thousand of them. Benjamin also corrected Johnston's use of supplies gathered at Nashville, saying those were intended to supply the army in Virginia; he informed Johnston that he should "draw your supplies by purchasing from the country around you." More problematic, he censured Johnston (even calling his request for troops issued to the governors an "unlucky proclamation") on many of the decisions he was making early on, including calling on the states for large numbers of twelve-month volunteers. The war secretary described such troops as "immensely expensive and utterly useless," raised only to sit in garrison for the winter. Benjamin also disliked Johnston's willingness to accept the troops already brigaded, which removed from the president's hands the ability to organize them as he saw fit and thus to dictate the brigade commanders. He even faulted Johnston for not preparing returns quickly enough. Even Davis had to check Johnston at times, replying in reference to the request for the arms arrived at Savannah that the government received "less than a sixth of your requisition. . . . You shall have what can be sent you. Rely not on rumors." Johnston stayed mute on most issues but balked at the lack of authority to use the stores at Nashville for his army.[36]

Worse than the pushback, which Johnston apparently took "as a rebuke," was the potential for enemy movements as September moved on into October. While little actual major Union activity resulted, there were plenty of rumors that had to be treated like the real thing until disproven. Thus, it was a tense time as numerous threats popped up here and there, causing Johnston to warn his local commanders of such possibilities. To Buckner, for instance, he cautioned as early as September 25, "four thousand Federals have landed at Henderson [Kentucky] to co-operate with the Union men. Look to your left and rear."[37]

At the time of Johnston's arrival in the West, the most likely avenue of Union invasion seemed to be on the Mississippi River at Columbus. As a result, he traveled from Nashville via Humboldt, Tennessee—where future Tennessee senator Gustavus A. Henry met and accompanied him—to Columbus to oversee the defenses there. One of the Confederates there wrote of the well-known commander's impending arrival: "we are expecting and anxiously awaiting the arrival of Gen Johnston tonight." Johnston was on site by September 19 and went immediately to work. "I am about completing the works here," he wrote Cooper in Richmond, "to meet the probable flotilla from the North, supposed to carry 200 heavy guns." He asked for anything extra that could be shipped to him, acknowledging that the government had to make tough decisions about where resources should go. "At the same time," he continued, "it is my duty to represent my own wants, and I may be pardoned if, entrusted as I am with the defense of this department, I should find the upper part of this river as important as its mouth."[38]

Johnston kept his headquarters at Columbus for several weeks, watching closely the Federal moves as well as reports in the papers. At one point reading of the massive staff his opponent Major General Frémont had gathered, Johnston quipped, "there is too much tail to that kite." He also taught his young staff the lessons of life. When they asked his opinions on where the final line would be when the South won the war, Johnston replied simply, "in the beginning of a great war like this, I never try to prognosticate final results. I do the duty which, for the time being, lies before me, and I leave the rest to providence." He also showed his bravery to both his staff and his troops, especially when Union gunboats came down the river and tested Columbus's guns on occasion. At one point in early October, when enemy shells began to fall too close to him, some cautioned Johnston to take cover but he replied, "we must all take our risks."[39]

Columbus seemed to be the area most in danger during the latter weeks of September and into early October, but other positions on his line faced the same problems of too few troops and resources to meet potential Federal activity. "I need re-enforcements at this place very much," Buckner wrote from Bowling Green, but all Johnston could advise was to "call in your detachments, and make your stand there." He promised, however, to send Buckner as many of the troops even then being raised because of his call as he could. Buckner ultimately held out because no major Union advance came. He continually built up his defenses along the Barren River and hoped for a delay in the enemy's movement southward. Fortunately, he received re-inforcements by early October, when Hardee brought the equivalent of two brigades from Arkansas and took command, he being the senior brigadier. At the same time, Zollicoffer farther to the east was also loudly calling for aid; Johnston planned to send him troops as well when he could.[40]

Contrary to popular opinion today, Johnston also gave some attention to what was undoubtedly his weakest link, the fortifications on the Tennessee and Cumberland Rivers east of Columbus. Several Union forays on the rivers came closer and closer to the Confederate works, easing along to find out what they could of the defenses. Johnston received word of these scouting activities from various concerned officials, including Gustavus Henry, who wrote, "it seems to me there is no part of the whole West so exposed as the valley of the Cumberland." The Tennessee River and Fort Henry also presented a major problem. Henry insisted, "if the enemy's gunboats should succeed in passing Fort Henry, two hours' run will take them to Danville, and there is nothing to prevent the destruction of the railroad bridge." Johnston is often perceived as having completely ignored the twin rivers, which indeed became the case later on, but at this point he was acutely aware of the possibilities of disaster there. As early as September 17, just three days after arriving in Nashville, Johnston began to show concern, ordering an engineer (Dixon) to Fort Donelson. In early October, he sent another engineer to mount the guns that had been sent there, a week later prodding Polk to "hasten the armament of the works at Fort Donelson and the obstructions below the place." Yet Johnston never went there himself to check on the progress. The two forts remained extremely weak defenses at this point, their garrisons consisting of only one regiment, the 10th Tennessee under Colonel Adolph Heiman at Fort Henry with a detachment under Lieutenant Colonel Randal W. McGavock at Fort Donelson. McGavock reported as late as October 17, "we are in a defenseless condition here, having only three companies of raw recruits, poorly armed, and not one artillerist to manage what heavy guns we have."[41]

By the second week in October, however, action also seemed to pick up at Bowling Green, forcing Johnston to move there. Hardee, having arrived and taken command, immediately panicked, in part because of reports of an enemy movement southward as well as Buckner having begun a withdrawal of his advance forces from Munfordville. Hardee wanted to maintain the Green River line at Munfordville but saw that a higher authority was needed. He wrote Johnston on October 12, "your presence here much needed." Johnston made immediate preparations to move eastward the next night, informing Richmond, "to-night [I] will repair there myself and take command in person." Despite the sickness he was enduring with his lungs, Johnston left on time during a cold snap. After utilizing the Confederate rail network via Humboldt and the critical Tennessee River bridge at Danville, he arrived on October 14, conducting a review of his troops as one of his first actions. Of course, the Federals kept up with him closely, following his movement eastward. Johnston also pushed up troops manning rear areas, such as Tilghman's force at Nashville, to Bowling Green for a potential confrontation. Ultimately, the Confederate contingent at Bowling Green totaled as many as twelve thousand troops. Among those meeting Johnston there was his brother-in-law, Kentuckian William Preston, a colonel who joined his staff.[42]

In such a critical situation, with too few men, too little resources, too long a line to defend, and too much bureaucracy, Johnston was seemingly in the same old desperate straits he had found himself in since the mid-1830s. Events threatened to overwhelm him, and he had to react to the situation rather than mold it. In a moment of despair, he warned Richmond, "I will use all means to increase my force, and spare no exertion to render it effective at every point, but I cannot assure you that this will be sufficient, and if re-enforcements from less endangered or less important points can be spared, I would be glad to receive them." The irony was that the circumstances were not necessarily of Johnston's own making; he had literally inherited them when he took command in mid-September. Regardless, this was his problem now, but fortunately events were moving so slowly that he had time to think carefully through all aspects of the situation, as he so often did. This allowed his methodical, chess-like mind to strategize and maintain his defensive line.[43]

In giving his problems long thought, Johnston nevertheless responded with patterns from his past that had become his way of doing things when confronting overwhelming difficulties. One pattern was to gamble, although many of Johnston's bets had not paid off in the way he had hoped. In Texas, the foolish duel had nearly taken his life, and other episodes such as buying China Grove, taking his paymaster position, and his trek across the desert had nearly done him in. Faced with overwhelming odds and desperation, Johnston had continually resorted to bold if sometimes necessary gambles to keep afloat. But here in the western Confederacy, perhaps, was the biggest set of odds he had yet faced in life, and he had no other recourse than to risk his command to keep it intact. As such, another pattern was to seemingly go on the offensive to show force while actually defending, something he had proposed often with the Mexican threat to Texas and then actually done with the Indians on the frontier. Now, Johnston ordered Hardee to "make a rapid movement upon Greensburg, with a battery, 900 infantry and 300 cavalry, to disperse the insurgent force and return without delay to your present position." He essentially had to gamble what little resources he had to maintain his line against a possibly substantial threat. Johnston knew he had to bluff his way through this critical time until more help could arrive, even developing a plan to utilize wooden mock cannon to bolster his lines in place of actual artillery pieces. To President Davis he admitted, "I magnified my forces to the enemy." It was a bluff worthy of a good poker player.[44]

Johnston accordingly began his bold gambit by showing offensive force but, like many outnumbered belligerents in the past (George Washington included), determined to hazard no battle until he could build up his forces. On the far right, Zollicoffer advanced from the Cumberland River to the London area. In Bowling Green, Johnston canceled the withdrawal of the forward forces at Munfordville, arguing that "the backward movement from Green River might, and probably would, be interpreted by the enemy into a retreat." One staff officer wrote that Johnston wanted Hardee to continue to show force to "impress the enemy with an expectation of an advance by us." Johnston later followed that up with orders "to suggest to the enemy by his movements our intention to cross that river." The bold bluff worked for the time being. The Federals, if they ever really intended to move forward, did not. Hardee, in fact, quipped that "the Yankees had a vague idea that we were their superiors in courage and skill," and the reactions of Sherman and Buell, the departmental commanders facing Johnston, bore this out.[45]

Problems still abounded, even though matters settled somewhat at Bowling Green as Johnston bluffed his way through October and November. While showing force to the enemy, he plainly told Richmond of his problems but otherwise kept them to himself; engineer Gilmer wrote that the general was "not very communicative." In actuality, Johnston viewed an attack at either Bowling Green or Columbus as a given and warned Richmond that, "as my forces at neither this nor either of the other points threatened are more than sufficient to meet the force in front, I cannot weaken either until the object of the enemy is fully pronounced." Worse, Kentucky was not warming to the Confederacy as hoped; Johnston wrote that there was "no such enthusiastic demonstration" as expected and that the people there "appear to me passive, if not apathetic." And then there were actual moves taking place during early November at Columbus. Polk was loudly calling for more troops, guns, and gunboats to defend his highly defensible area, much more so than anywhere else along Johnston's line. He was obsessed with his lair at Columbus, writing that once it was completely fortified, "I shall be at liberty to look around me, if need be." Thus, Forts Henry and Donelson, now in Polk's area of command, suffered growing neglect, with only a smattering of troops on site and only trifling attention paid to them by the bishop, despite Johnston's insistence that he do so.[46]

By late October, the theater commander divined three major potential Union areas of advance: on Zollicoffer near the Cumberland Gap, on Hardee at Bowling Green, and on Polk at Columbus. He only added a nod to the twin rivers, noting that the enemy might "endeavor to use the Tennessee River in aid of the movement [against Polk]." While Johnston continually warned the bishop "to keep a vigilant eye on the Tennessee River," Polk was more consumed with Columbus and gave it and the Cumberland River little attention. In fact, by the end of October, he amazingly wrote Colonel Heiman, "your report of dispositions for defense of Forts Donelson and Henry are satisfactory." Polk also recommended sending Brigadier General Tilghman to command that area, which eventually occurred in mid-November. Unfortunately, Tilghman's first impressions were not good: "I have completed a thorough examination of Henry and Donelson and do not admire the aspect of things," he informed Johnston. He similarly reported to Polk, "it is but too plain that instant and powerful steps must be taken to strengthen not only the two forts in the way of work, but the armament must be increased materially in number of pieces of artillery as well as in weight of metal." In order to add some protection for the low-lying Fort Henry, Tilghman immediately began work on defenses on the higher ground on the west side of the Tennessee River, to be known as Fort Heiman, but he continually reported his problems—"I am not secure at either Henry or Donelson," he wrote in mid-December—and constantly called for more troops.[47]

Polk's mind was firmly on the Columbus area itself, however, and perhaps with good reason. In early November, the Federals made a foray forward under a little-known brigadier general, Ulysses S. Grant. Johnston did not know Grant, having left the army well prior to the Illinoisan's cadetship at West Point and did not return to line service until after Grant had resigned from the army in 1854. Grant nevertheless was a factor in Johnston's defenses starting in late 1861, when he moved southward on the west side of the Mississippi River and attacked a small Confederate camp across from Columbus at Belmont, Missouri. The fight on November 7 was sharp but small, and the Federals had to get out quickly once Polk sent reinforcements from Columbus. Johnston pronounced the result as a "glorious victory" and gave his thanks for "the work well done." Nevertheless, Grant's move, along with corresponding yet not as bold probes east of the river, even more firmly fixed the bishop's attention on his Kentucky bastion.[48]

The affair at Belmont was not Johnston's only reality check, however.

Reports of advances arrived from all along the defensive perimeter almost daily, including even the effects of saboteurs burning railroad bridges in the Confederate rear in East Tennessee. Johnston described the effort as "this insurrection," and Secretary of War Benjamin replied that he "hope[d] to hear they have hung every bridge-burner at the end of the burned bridge." Some indeed were executed, while others were taken to jail in Alabama.[49]

Easing some of the burden as the winter loomed, which in itself would hopefully provide even more of a grace period since most armies did not operate in the winter months, were continually arriving generals, troops, and arms. More generals appeared in Johnston's department throughout the fall, including Brigadier General Charles Clark. Former vice president Breckinridge, now a brigadier general, also arrived and took command of one of the Kentucky brigades at Bowling Green. Also arriving were Brigadier General George Crittenden as well as Johnston's requested A. P. Stewart, whom he had identified as "Stuart" and thus fouled up the bureaucracy, delaying the appointment. Most notably, the Kentuckian Crittenden went to the Cumberland Gap region and took command from Zollicoffer, who had no experience in the military per se and had been placed in a safe sector originally, when Kentucky neutrality still shielded East Tennessee.[50]

Manpower and arms remained an issue, but one that was getting better as well. Johnston ultimately told the governors in his department that he would accept nothing but three-year volunteers, but as matters continued gloomy in November he had to revoke the order and later wrote, "I will muster into service all you may be able to arm." He thus made another round of calls on the states of Tennessee, Alabama, and Mississippi. Fortunately, more resources flowed in, regiments and supplies from all over the Confederacy, including from Major General Mansfield Lovell in charge at New Orleans. Lovell at first refused a request from Brigadier General Gideon J. Pillow but then acquiesced to Johnston, explaining, "I thought your danger more imminent than mine." Lovell also later admitted that in refusing Pillow's request, "I should have attached more weight to the call if it had come from General Johnston." Another shipment of European rifles in November also netted the western commander forty-five hundred desperately needed Enfields for his troops. Finally, the War Department authorized Johnston to begin work on riverine ironclads to combat the Federal navy's presence. Johnston put Polk in charge, and the bishop began converting vessels on the Tennessee and Cumberland Rivers to support the forts. But a lack of resources and knowhow led Chief Engineer Gilmer to rely mainly on "batteries ashore, in combination with such obstructions as may be devised in the channel under the guns of the works." Of course, the Achilles' heel for fixed fortifications was the turning movement, a constant concern for Johnston.[51]

The theater commander's major problem, however, was his subordinate leadership, namely his old roommate Polk at Columbus. The bishop seemed unable to let go of his need to control, even at one time in November writing Johnston, "could you not, in a private way, let me know of the strength of your force, and as far as it is safe let me hear some idea of your plans." Polk could also be, in historian Thomas Connelly's words, "insubordinate"; for example, it took three orders to get him to let loose of one of the few engineers in the western Confederacy. Then, with the increase in Union activity on the twin rivers and the lack of defenses there, Johnston ordered him to send Pillow and five thousand men to the Clarksville area to bolster that section. Polk refused, offering his "views in regard to the proposed movement" first to his commander directly and then to his old friend President Davis; he even sent Pillow, who was probably behind the stubbornness anyway, to confer with Johnston in Bowling Green about the move in early November. Johnston refused the bishop's arguments and noted somewhat curtly, "that order, then, will be executed." Polk then found a convenient excuse to keep Pillow around with the Union advance that resulted in the battle at Belmont. Still, Johnston took that victory as a sign: the Federals "were routed with great loss, and I now consider his [Polk's] situation better than before the conflict [at Belmont]." He repeated the orders the next day for Pillow to move eastward, arguing that "the necessity for General Pillow's force at Clarksville is greater now than when ordered." He urged haste over the next few days as well. Polk continued to delay and gripe, however, again refusing to send the troops even while requesting reinforcements for Columbus.[52]

Polk was obviously not in a good state of mind, and an explosion of a cannon as he stood watching it fire made his mentality even worse: "General Polk is still very unwell from the effects of his injury from the explosion." Even Pillow wrote Johnston that "General [Polk] is not so well" and reported how the bishop had ordered Pillow back. Johnston then moved the troops anyway, perhaps because loud calls regarding Pillow's lack of ability came in as well: "if General Polk is not well enough to take command, I pray General Johnston will put some man of more prudence there," one advisor wrote. In the midst of it all, Polk took offense and offered to resign, telling Davis, "within the last few weeks you have been able to avail yourself of a distinguished military commander, our mutual friend, who was not in the country at the date of my appointment, upon whom you have devolved, partly at my insistence, the duties of the office I consented to fill." He wanted to return to his ministry in the Episcopal Church, but in one of the many mistakes Davis made throughout the war, the president refused the resignation.[53]

Even later in December, when it seemed Bowling Green would come under a major attack, Johnston again ordered Polk to "send to this place 5,000 of your best infantry by rail direct." But Polk again demurred, arguing that he had too few troops himself, and "I was on the eve of calling upon you to send me 3,000 men immediately to enable [me] to hold my position." Polk ended with a warning, stating firmly that "to send the force ordered would be to sacrifice this command and throw open the valley of the Mississippi." Oddly enough, the supposedly decisive Johnston backed down and countermanded the order. He was a firm commander, but his old West Point roommate seemed to know just how to get him to concede. In fact, at one point when Polk complained of his treatment in the press, Johnston quickly came to his defense, telling him, "never mind, old friend; I understand and appreciate what you have done, and will see that you are supported."[54]

Polk's second in command, Pillow, also made trouble, as he and the bishop continually interfered with the fortification work at the twin rivers. He as well as Tilghman gave orders to the local engineers on site, which were directly the opposite of what Johnston's departmental engineer demanded. A staff-line controversy soon erupted, leaving the engineers on site to wonder whose orders to obey—the generals there or the departmental engineer. Lieutenant Dixon understandably wrote Captain Gilmer, "I would like to know whose orders I am to obey."[55]

Even as the meek and genial Johnston had trouble forcing his will on his peers, he faced continual reports of Union advances all along his line. Polk and Pillow repeatedly sent panicked messages from Columbus, where the bulk of Johnston's troops—now some twenty thousand—were situated. "He [the enemy] is now making preparations upon a gigantic scale to invest this place," Pillow wrote in mid-November. But the Federals were doing the exact same thing to Johnston that he hoped to do to them—bluff in an aggressive way to make the opponent think an attack was coming in a bid to defend territory currently occupied. Report after report said as much, although at times local commanders admitted the falsity of the information, such as when Zollicoffer remarked that he "beg[a]n to suspect the movement was a feint, and that their forces may be withdrawing to support concentration on General Buckner's front." Warnings also came from west of the Mississippi to "call to your [Johnston's] attention the war on the borders of Arkansas, in Missouri, Kansas, and the Indian Territory"; the correspondent labeled Confederate forces there as "the disorderly and illy-united army of General Price." Fearing that the main confrontation would be at either Columbus, which stabilized after Belmont, or Bowling Green, Johnston nevertheless remained at the latter position in personal command most of November, apart from a quick trip to Nashville on the eighteenth to determine with Governor Harris the protocol for calling up more troops. All the while, Johnston ordered that bodies of troops go forward often to "create the impression in the country that this force is only an advance guard." Faced with what he described as "the choice of difficulties" in moving men to where they needed to be, Johnston could only bluff his way through his defense. But his scheme worked, scaring the Union commander in Kentucky during this time, Brigadier General Sherman. He wrote Brigadier General George H. Thomas on November 12, "I am convinced from many facts that A. Sidney Johnston is making herculean efforts to strike a great blow in Kentucky; that he designs to move from Bowling Green on Lexington, Louisville, and Cincinnati."[56]

By the time the calendar reached December, Johnston thus began to feel better about his situation and even that of the Confederacy. He reported "intense excitement" in the West over the contemporary Trent Affair and the possibility of foreign intervention, although Johnston calmed his excited staff officers with the prediction that "Mr. Lincoln will eat dirt—will eat dirt." Closer to home, despite continued panicking by subordinates, particularly Zollicoffer and Polk (Pillow deceitfully, according to Connelly, pushing the latter to alarms at Columbus), Johnston on occasion reported little activity to Secretary Benjamin. On December 8, for example, he explained that "the enemy, from the best information I am able to obtain, have made no material change in the disposition of their forces in front or on either flank." He similarly reported on the thirtieth that "the enemy have made no forward movement since my last communication, nor have I any information of any change in the position of their troops since then." Continual thrusts northward, or at least the appearance of them, kept the opposing Federals off balance, although occasional alarm still developed when an attack seemed eminent. One such panic occurred in late December, Johnston reporting that "the enemy in overwhelming numbers are crossing Green River." This was again a false alarm, but it nevertheless contributed to the call for support from Polk and his refusal to provide it.[57]

Much of the ease in worry came from the slow but continual beefing up of Johnston's forces. Many of the regiments that he had called for from the states were arriving by December, and now he had some arms to give them. Others came already armed. In addition, regiments and brigades already in service were transferred to Johnston from the interior as well, such as, in the largest movement, an entire brigade of Virginians and one tagalong Mississippi regiment from western Virginia under former U.S. secretary of war John B. Floyd. By early December, Johnston counted some twenty thousand troops at Bowling Green and a like number at Columbus. There were also several thousand to the east under Zollicoffer and Crittenden, who by mid-December had unwisely moved to the Cumberland River at Mill Springs and then, without orders and with "more spirit than wisdom," as historian Charles Roland described it, moved on across to Beech Grove. Price had another twelve thousand troops west of the Mississippi River in Arkansas and Missouri, where he was pushing his own pet project of capturing St. Louis— "of this I have more than once advised General Johnston," he wrote Davis. There were also smaller garrisons interspersed between these larger posts along the line.[58]

As a result, Johnston thought that he had turned the critical corner in his defense for the winter. The weather had been surprisingly dry for much of the recent months, causing considerable concern. But by December 21, he felt that conditions were about to deteriorate, probably shutting down activity for several months. "The weather has been very fine for some weeks and the roads of every kind are excellent," he informed Richmond. But "I think a change is about to take place. It is now cold and cloudy, and snow and rain we hope will soon make the country roads very difficult to travel over, which would be greatly to our advantage." He added significantly, "I have made every effort to gain time to strengthen our defenses here and increase my force."[59]

The only major area of concern continued to be the twin rivers, which were much less weather-dependent for travel. The condition of the defenses at Forts Henry and Donelson still concerned Johnston as well as those in Nashville and northern Alabama and Mississippi, knowing that if Fort

Henry fell there was nothing else to stop the Federals from getting to those regions. By early November, Fort Henry was in better shape, but Fort Donelson still lagged far behind in development, although a series of barges had been sunk north of the fort near Ingram's Bar to stop Union movement further down the Cumberland. Johnston dispatched engineer Gilmer to Fort Donelson to prod the work along, and he began to get the fortifications there completed. Additional reinforcements followed, including a Tennessee cavalry regiment under Lieutenant Colonel Nathan Bedford Forrest and several more large guns. Yet Johnston did not supervise Gilmer any more than he did other major officers in his department, believing they were acting faithfully. In fact, the captain was not because he was homesick from missing his wife and enduring the death of his mother. He thus took little interest in the work. Thomas Connelly has argued that it was a major "command failure at the departmental level." It also indicated a slow but sure lessening of concern for the twin rivers that developed during the late fall and would become critical after the turn of the year.[60]

For now, however, Johnston had gambled on his defensive line, bluffing like a poker player to stay in the game. But the lack of enemy movement had allowed him time to think through his options and defensive schemes. By the end of 1861, he had done so long enough to enjoy some winter cover, which he could also use to further strengthen his defenses. It seemed he had survived the seemingly unsurvivable autumn. It had been a necessary gamble—a calculated risk—but he, and this time his nation, had somehow lived through it.

But troubling issues were developing under the surface even in this seasonal calm. Johnston had a plethora of terribly incapable subordinates to whom he gave too much trust, allowing them to command their own districts mostly as they saw fit. Generals such as Pillow, Polk, Zollicoffer, and Crittenden were troubling to a high degree, yet Johnston instead placed himself with probably his most dependable generals, Hardee and Buckner. Likewise, he fell into the trap of believing his own area, Bowling Green, was the center of enemy plans and thus became fixated on defending that locale to the detriment of others, particularly the Tennessee and Cumberland Rivers, which seemed to be falling through the cracks already. He even failed to respond to many of Governor Harris's many calls for support.[61]

But he was not alone in this. The Confederate government in Richmond was closeminded to significantly aiding Johnston's command in Kentucky despite numerous calls for concentration. Perhaps President Davis and others believed, too much, in their miracle worker and savior of a commanding general. Historian Thomas Connelly certainly argues that faith in Johnston's record and image led to apathy on the part of Tennesseans, thinking he had everything under control. But many in addition to Johnston were sounding the alarm: Major General Braxton Bragg in September wrote, "Mobile and New Orleans are being fortified at great expense, when they should be defended in Kentucky and Missouri." General Beauregard similarly wrote, "we must give up some minor points and concentrate our forces to save the most important ones, or we will lose all of them in succession." Johnston himself argued, "New Orleans is to be defended from above by defeating the enemy at Columbus." But few would listen to any of them.[62]

Unfortunately for the Confederacy, Johnston soon faced an oncoming advance in several areas that proved just how thin the western defenses were. And it would come sooner rather than later, the winter months that normally, and logically, provided temporary cover having little bearing in the late winter of 1862. The Federals were about to call Johnston's bluff.

In sum, Johnston's first four months at the helm of the Confederate western department were not without problems, but he somehow managed to survive, mostly because of a lack of opposing grit and resolve in the Union high command facing him. The lack of enemy effort, sometimes a result of Johnston's calculated and necessary bluffs, allowed him time to think through and respond methodically without having to resort to massive gambles. But his emerging command style had already shown major problems that against more spirited opposition would bloom into disaster in the new year. According to his personality as more of a methodical, gentlemanly chess player than a rough-and-tumble poker player, Johnston had shown more leniency than needed with his subordinates while he had proven unable to convince his superiors of a brewing crisis. And he was falling into the dreaded tunnel vision of deeming wherever he was as the predominant location, the focus of the enemy's attention. All his old personal attributes of leniency, meekness, and methodical thinking were combining to create a perfect storm of trouble that would soon see him fall from his acclaimed status as the savior of the South.

And thus has Johnston been portrayed largely in history, only a few historians questioning that idea. Connelly, for instance, has rightly doubted the general's status as the savior, writing that "Johnston's past record did not merit such acclaim." Although Connelly seemingly looked at everything associated with Johnston from a negative starting point, his claim does seem logical. Johnston had spent only small periods of his life in the army, whether serving Texas or the United States, and most of these years were at lower ranks. His big chance came with his appointment as colonel of the 2nd U.S. Cavalry, but he soon left that position for the Utah command that neither he nor anyone else wanted. Then he spent a mere few weeks commanding the Department of the Pacific. Johnston was high ranking, but his had been a bumpy and perhaps benevolent rise; what would the army do with a sixty-year-old major? And now, what would the Confederacy do with a full general who on the surface seemed to have his department well situated but was rumbling underneath and ready to fall apart upon the first sustained pressure the enemy put against it?[63]

— 4 —

IF BLAME THERE BE

FORTS HENRY AND DONELSON

O n assuming command of this department," Albert Sidney Johnston wrote Mississippi governor Pettus around the beginning of 1862, "it was my chief object to collect a sufficient force to shield the valley of the Mississippi from the enemy and assure its safety." Unfortunately, he added, "there is not now a force at my disposition equal to the exigency of my situation." Yet that situation would soon grow more and more troubling, causing the first major crisis of Johnston's tenure in the West. And it would be one to which he would not respond well, vacillating between weak leadership commensurate with his own chess-playing personality and taking major gambles in more of a poker-playing style that would risk entire wings of his army.[1]

Certainly, Johnston's forces were growing ever so slightly as the crisis in the West became better known, but the enemy's strength was likewise growing in the meantime. Comparatively, Sidney Johnston had about the same number of troops that General Joe Johnston had in northern Virginia at the turn of the year, but he had a defensive line some thirteen times longer. Historian Richard McMurry has revealed the large disparity in resources sent to the eastern and western Confederacy, and this obvious slant in manpower in early 1862 toward the East undergirds his argument perfectly. A fight of mammoth proportions was obviously coming; the question was simply when. "A conflict is to be expected here," Johnston announced on New Year's Day, 1862, to the people of Bowling Green, and he recommended they leave the area. He noted that this was particularly necessary for those around the newly erected fortifications, "as their houses will be used as a part of the defense or removed to make the defense more perfect."[2]

But there was no clear idea of exactly when or where the blow would fall. "The positions of the enemy's forces and those of the Confederacy stand relatively as reported in my last letter," Johnston informed Richmond on January 5. There were hopeful signs, such as the recent turn in the weather that he still gambled would give him at least a few more months to prepare, as armies normally did not campaign during the worst winter months of January and February: "the fine weather which prevailed till within two or three days past has been succeeded by rain, which usually falls here in sufficient quantities when the winter sets in to make the unpaved roads difficult and for large trains impassable." Likewise, new troops were supposed to be coming in as new arms now arrived on the Southern coasts in more rapid fashion. Any weapons he could get would aid Johnston in arming the new troops. He reported that his numbers at Bowling Green had in fact swelled to around twenty-three thousand in early January. Additional generals likewise aided the growing command, including Brigadier General Bushrod Johnson to command a brigade and Major General Earl Van Dorn to command "the Trans-Mississippi District, . . . with orders to report to you [Johnston] in person on his way to the West." Van Dorn was well known to Johnston, having been one of his captains in the 2nd U.S. Cavalry in Texas. He was also a prewar personal friend to him and Eliza; a dabbling artist as was Eliza, Van Dorn even painted a portrait of the Johnstons' daughter. But there was still a sense that the preparation was a slow and methodical plodding forward rather than a burst of energy to prepare for the inevitable. It certainly was a slow-enough buildup that could be matched by the enemy. In reality, only the shaky Federal command structures throughout the fall in all three departments facing Johnston's extensive command area had allowed him a grace period, allowing his forces to survive unscathed into the new year.[3]

This lull in operations allowed Johnston time to see to other facets of his command as well as his personal life. He still did not know for sure where Eliza and the children were: "I have been deluded for the last six weeks with the belief that you were in Louisville." But they had actually moved to her cousin's house in California. "If you are comfortable, although our separation is most painful to me, I think it will be best for you to remain . . . for the present," cautioning her to continue with the children's education. "You &

the children occupy every thought not devoted to business. You are always present to my mind." He assured her that he had recovered from his autumn sickness: "I am well & in better health than I have been for years." Johnston also worked with Colonel Preston as well as his son William on the family's financial issues.[4]

Johnston spent a good deal of time working on that official business he mentioned, including supply issues such as where and how to obtain them and how to distribute them to the troops. Despite his earlier problems with his own personal financial affairs, Johnston looked scrupulously at prices, trying to find the best deals on everything from beef to pork to corn. He had agents all over the western Confederacy finding the best bargains and purchasing what was needed to keep the armies fed. Johnston also worked to get the railroad systems in efficient shape, at times even ordering engines and cars from as far away as the Western and Atlantic Railroad in Georgia to operate in the Mississippi Valley.[5]

Unfortunately, despite his relative ease in December and early January, a couple of troubling patterns began to develop. Johnston still found himself severely outnumbered everywhere, and squabbling continued with the government about the need for more arms and men, with even some twelve-month troops being turned away. There was even some deletion of troops from his command, including regiments loaned from Lovell at New Orleans. Polk continually complained of having an inadequate force at Columbus, and Johnston was never quite able to stand up to his old roommate. He even brought some of the trans-Mississippi force eastward to remedy Polk's declared lack of troops. And then there were the continual rumors and indications of an enemy advance, Johnston writing in the second week of January that a force estimated at eighty thousand planned "to invade the Confederacy through Central Kentucky towards Tennessee." In his growing fixation with Bowling Green's defense, much like Polk's at Columbus, he assured Secretary Benjamin that "no doubt the strongest attack the enemy is capable of making will be made against this place." In late December 1861 and early January 1862, this became so acute, in fact, that Johnston had practically made himself a district commander, which has attracted the deserved ire of historians ever since. Benjamin F. Cooling has noted that "it took only ninety days for Albert Sidney Johnston to descend from theater to district commander." The larger significance, of course, was the effect this had on the entire western department, especially the defense of the Cumberland

and Tennessee Rivers. Richard McMurry has asserted that, with Johnston's fixation on Bowling Green, "there was no one exercising effective command in the West during the crucial winter of 1861–1862." Both Cooling and McMurry have extremely valid points.[6]

This tunnel vision on Bowling Green led to escalating problems outside that narrow front. One was Zollicoffer's forward move to Beech Grove, Kentucky, north of the Cumberland River. A defeat there would trap that entire wing north of the formidable river and bring about the destruction of Johnston's right flank, offering the enemy clear and unfettered access to the Cumberland Gap and East Tennessee. Johnston did not authorize the movement but could do little now in the face of the enemy. Still, he was not comfortable with the situation to the east, telling one colonel who requested transfer to Bowling Green that "the position of General Zollicoffer is too important and too exposed to permit any reduction of force, so great as the removal of your regiment would be." Nevertheless, Johnston did little to remedy the situation, fixated as he was on the defense of central Kentucky.[7]

Even worse was Johnston's sudden forgetfulness about the importance of the twin rivers and his lack of strength in place to guard them. As 1861 closed and certainly as the new year emerged, Johnston's former major concern for this region, as seen in his repeated messages to Polk, was apparently forgotten in January. Despite continual warnings from Tilghman at the forts, Johnston focused entirely on Bowling Green and even Columbus, with occasional attention going to the eastern flank. He even recalled his chief engineer away from the work on the twin river defenses to build fortifications at Nashville in case he had to fall back there from central Kentucky. But Captain Gilmer was scoffed at as "Johnston's dirt-digger," no one around Nashville thinking the war would come to their doorstep.[8]

As defending the twin rivers fell into a void of inattention, Johnston was not served well by his subordinates either. He had sent Brigadier General Tilghman to take command there, and this probably caused him to assume that the situation was under control, elevated as it was to be one of the primary defensive spots under a general officer. But Tilghman, who was very cognizant of the difficulties along the Tennessee and Cumberland Rivers, was not the problem. He continuously railed against the dearth of men, supplies, guns, and attention in his weekly reports and even wrote President Davis that "no one point in the Southern Confederacy needs more the aid of the Government than [these] points." But most of Tilghman's communications logically went directly to his district commander—Major General Polk in Columbus; he had little direct communication with Johnston, the department head. Polk, himself fixated on his own defense of Columbus and figuratively convinced the entire Union army from Virginia to the frontier was concentrating solely on his position, almost never sent Tilghman's concerns on up the chain to Johnston. When his concern was mentioned, it was in combination with problems in other areas, such as on January 11 when the bishop informed Johnston that "the unarmed regiments are stationed at Forts Pillow, Donelson, and Henry, at Trenton, Union City, and Henderson Station." The combination of the twin-river forts with many other areas diluted the concern expressed for them, and it almost goes without saying that it is obvious why there were no unarmed regiments at Columbus itself. As a result, there was a critical lapse in information making its way to Johnston from the twin rivers. What did come out got no further than Polk, who ignored it in deference to his own Columbus defenses. In fact, when Johnston learned in late January that the bishop had done little to facilitate construction of Fort Heiman on the west side of the Tennessee River, he uncharacteristically lashed out at one of Hardee's staff officers: "it is most extraordinary— I ordered General Polk four months ago to at once construct those works; and now, with the enemy on us, nothing of importance has been done. It is most extraordinary, most extraordinary."[9]

Despite all the problems, Johnston still prepared as best as he could, hoping his bluffs and the weather would forestall any enemy activity. But that did not happen, as events began to transpire in mid-January that would not stop until disaster struck. Operations began to move swiftly, and with them came a lack of time for Johnston to methodically respond; essentially, he had to shift from being a chess-like thinker to a quick-moving poker player in response to quickened enemy movements. Unfortunately, he did not respond well.

The chaos started with more calls from Polk, two in fact on January 12, that told of dire circumstances and an overwhelming force bearing down on him: "The time for the enemy's attack on this post, for which he has been making such formidable preparations, is at hand. I have reason to believe he will attack by land and water in a few days." Later, Polk gave specifics: "I am advised of his purpose to make that attack in the next three or four days." This was obviously not the first time Polk had cried wolf, and it would not be the last, but this time there was some truth to it. Johnston braced for a

Union advance once more, calling again for all the troops he could get and for Richmond to allow any and all who would volunteer to come to his aid. "A decisive battle will probably be fought on this line, and a company on that day will be more than a regiment next year," he wrote.[10]

Polk certainly sounded the alarm, but the same warning was being raised elsewhere as well. Rumors reported a Federal force moving toward Zollicoffer's position north of the Cumberland River near Mill Springs, Kentucky. Indications also went out from Fort Henry that a large force would "move up [the] Cumberland and Tennessee Rivers on next Thursday." That intelligence, of course, went first to Polk in Columbus, who was in full-prepare mode for resisting his own attack. Still in his Bowling Green and Columbus tunnel vision, Johnston even sent word to the bishop that "great preparations are making to attack Columbus." A frightened Polk fumed, blaming any resulting defeat on Johnston, who "felt himself so pressed as to make it necessary to draw on me for re-enforcements (about 5,000)." With all the concern for Columbus and the Mississippi River, however, little thought was given to the frantic messages from the Cumberland and Tennessee Rivers. In fact, in responding to one of the few direct messages from Tilghman, Mackall simply replied: "We now require vigilance and energy, and he [Johnston] is satisfied that in these you will not fail. He hopes to stop the movement for some time on this line, and that Generals Polk and Tilghman will delay them on the others." It did not sound as if Johnston was overly concerned about Tilghman's exposure.[11]

But then the Federals made an actual move that got everyone's full attention—and quick. Ironically, it was in response to a Confederate movement, namely the shifting of troops eastward to within supporting distance of Bowling Green. The Union high command, even Lincoln and General in Chief George B. McClellan in Washington, construed this as the beginning of an attempt to advance on Buell's forces in central Kentucky. In that regard, Johnston's probing and offensive feints were indeed working. In order to keep the Confederates pinned down and not moving into central Kentucky, however, Washington ordered Halleck to make a demonstration along the Mississippi River. "As our success in Kentucky depends in great measure on our preventing re-enforcements from joining Buckner and Johnston," McClellan wrote Halleck on January 3, "not a moment's time should be lost in preparing these expeditions."[12]

The job fell to Grant, despite terrible weather in January. In fact, the movement was delayed significantly due to the elements, but it eventually lurched forward on the fourteenth. Grant sent out two columns, aided by naval forces from Cairo, Illinois, and Paducah, Kentucky. The westernmost foray under McClernand, accompanied by Grant himself, ranged southward all the way to Milburn, near Columbus, and thoroughly frightened Polk. Ironclads showing up on the Mississippi north of the Confederate stronghold were concerning enough, but then ground troops appeared outside Columbus's fortifications. Polk had been warning that an attack was coming, and this was his proof. Obviously, Grant intended no such thing, only to scare Polk and force him to keep troops at Columbus rather than sending them toward Bowling Green.[13]

The easternmost Union force proved more important in the long run. Under Brigadier General Charles F. Smith, this column moved from Paducah down muddy roads to Murray but then marched eastward when supplies began to run low. They made it to the Tennessee River and supply vessels, but this inadvertently seemed to the Confederates like an advance on Fort Henry. The navy was also active, with the timberclad *Lexington* even taking Fort Henry under fire for a short time. Smith was also under orders not to fight but merely to show himself as often as he could wherever he could, which he did before heading back to Paducah while McClernand moved back to Cairo.[14]

The effects were significant throughout the Confederate defensive line. At Columbus, Polk nervously advised Johnston, "the enemy is in motion to attack this place, as I have already advised." Consumed with his own position, he declared Columbus "the key to the whole Mississippi valley" and that, significantly, "the attention of my army is now being fixed in this direction." As a result, the bishop dramatically wrote, "I have resolved, therefore, to stand a siege, and look to the general for such aid as the War Department and the country may afford him for relief." Consequently, Polk showed little concern for Forts Henry and Donelson. But worry was understandable on site with actual gunboats taking Henry under fire, one officer reporting, perhaps thinking it would be his last message, that "everything will be done that can be accomplished by energy and industry." Johnston himself reacted with great alarm as well, informing Richmond that Polk was under an attack "of immense magnitude."[15]

Once the Federal movements were completed, few knew what to make of them. "What the particular object of it was has not clearly transpired,"

Polk admitted on January 24, although he had determined that Grant and Smith had been involved. Nevertheless, the major result, and one that would actually come back to haunt them, was that Johnston suddenly awoke from his lethargy concerning the twin rivers. Even during the crisis on January 17, he pushed Polk to look to Forts Henry and Donelson and to reinforce them. Johnston also ordered his Ordnance Department at Nashville to fulfill requests for ammunition from Tilghman. He also ordered forward other regiments in the rear to Fort Henry, some all the way from Alabama. "Fort Henry, on the Tennessee River, is attacked," Mackall wrote on January 18. "General Johnston directs you to move all the efficient men of your regiment by railway to the crossing of the Tennessee and thence to Fort Henry."[16]

While Polk was still fixated on his own situation at Columbus in the days after the chaos, it fell to Johnston to see to the defense of the Cumberland and Tennessee Rivers. Details still slowly filtered in, but Johnston responded firmly to events in western Kentucky over the next few days. On January 20, he ordered a major portion of his force at Bowling Green to move westward to Russellville to stabilize the situation there. Participating in the move were eight thousand troops, including Floyd's recently arrived brigade and much of Buckner's division. Other guns and troops were also forwarded to the twin-river forts and Clarksville. News soon grew better from the region as the Federals withdrew, but calls for more defensive capability there were growing louder. Gustavus Henry declared that the forts "[are] unfinished, and in the present condition do no earthly good, and are no more effective for defense than if they were in their original condition before a spade of dirt was removed." Such news continued to impress upon Johnston the importance of Forts Henry and Donelson. Polk, on the other hand, never did understand their significance and continued his fixation on Columbus even after the mid-January Union reconnaissances. The result was a continued massive imbalance of defense at the twin forts. While Columbus and Bowling Green reported having well over 20,000 troops each in their end-of-the-month returns, Tilghman reported a measly 4,640 men defending perhaps the weakest link in the Confederate chain of defense.[17]

Even as the demonstration against Columbus went on, however, another crisis emerged on Johnston's right flank. Word first came into Bowling Green on January 18: "I am satisfied that the enemy are concentrating a large force to attack General Zollicoffer." Union commander George H. Thomas was indeed moving southward to the area immediately north of

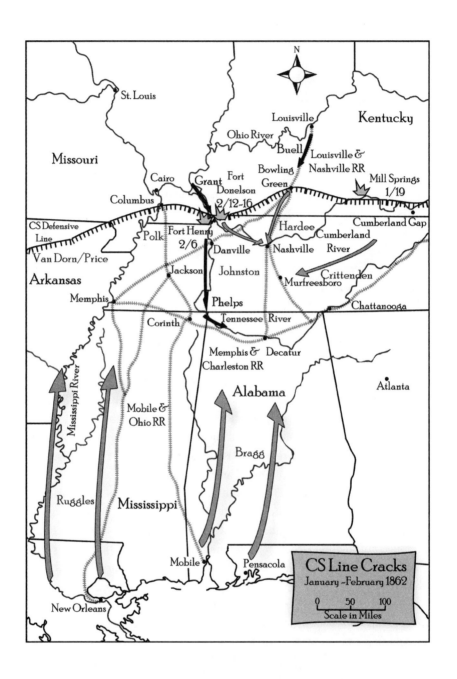

N

St. Louis

Kentucky

Missouri

Louisville

Ohio River

Buell

Louisville &
Nashville RR

Cairo

Grant

Fort

Bowling
Green

Mill Springs
1/19

Columbus

Donelson
2/12-16

CS Defensive
Line

Polk

Fort Henry
2/6

Hardee

Cumberland Gap

Van Dorn/Price

Danville

Nashville

Cumberland
River

Arkansas

Jackson

Johnston

Crittenden

Memphis

Phelps

Murfreesboro

Chattanooga

Corinth

Tennessee River

Memphis & Decatur
Charleston RR

Alabama

Atlanta

Mississippi River

Mobile &
Ohio RR

Bragg

Ruggles

Mississippi

Mobile

Pensacola

New Orleans

CS Line Cracks
January–February 1862

0   50   100
Scale in Miles

the Confederate position. Crittenden wired Johnston that same day: "I am threatened by a superior force of the enemy in front, and finding it impossible to cross the river, I will have to make the fight on the ground I now occupy." He called for a diversion even while advancing from his river campground to the battlefield variously known as Logan's Crossroads, Mill Springs, and Somerset.[18]

The battle itself was small but very important. Lincoln had long pushed for an offensive into East Tennessee, which at this point and long into the future would remain only a possibility. Conversely, Zollicoffer and Crittenden were the entire right flank of the Confederate defensive line, and a fight there would threaten the rest of Johnston's defenses if it ended in defeat. The theater commander certainly was aware of that possibility but had no more armed troops to assign to the area, especially when he had so many other even more seemingly threatened points along the line. Some of these had even fewer soldiers than the right, the critical twin rivers being among them. All Johnston could do was gamble that his shows of force and offensive threats would bluff the Federals into doing nothing in this critical area as well.[19]

Then Johnston's subordinate commanders failed him again on January 19. Zollicoffer and Crittenden, whom historian Steve Woodworth has described as "irresponsible, lazy, [and] alcoholic"—"Davis's main mistake in the handling of the eastern Kentucky front"—advanced to the attack, which resulted in a major defeat among the high hills of the battlefield. It was a slugfest involving small numbers of troops, but the net result could not have been worse for Johnston. The Confederates were defeated and retreated southward to their encampment on the northern side of the Cumberland River, where the Federals followed and shelled them. Crittenden managed to slip across the river during the night, saving a portion of the army that otherwise would have been captured or destroyed (as the rest were). The news was still bad, however. The Confederates suffered "the loss of our artillery, ammunition, cavalry horses, teams, and camp equiptments," one of Crittenden's staff officers reported. The loss also included the nearsighted Zollicoffer, who had ridden toward Union lines by mistake and was killed. Federals tampered with the body, but a Union surgeon later assured Johnston personally that it was done in the heat of battle and before it was identified as Zollicoffer; his body as well as that of a lieutenant were embalmed and sent back to Confederate lines. Conversely, rumors of Crittenden being drunk began circulating immediately. The worst part, of course, was that

Johnston's careful bluff of threatening an advance to mask his actual paltry numbers was now revealed for all to see. His gamble had failed because his commanders laid down their cards too soon.[20]

With advances on both his right and left, not to mention whatever was happening west of the Mississippi River, it seemed that Johnston's gambit was coming to an end; the Federals were calling his bluff. Johnston nevertheless took time as part of his official business to put his thoughts on paper in a letter to Adjutant General Cooper in Richmond on January 22. Obviously, he wrote, "that they [the Federals] will suspend them [operations] in Tennessee and Kentucky during the winter months is a delusion." While he reported having "hear[d] of no movement of the enemy on my front here," Johnston did comprehend the desperate situation he was in. The Federals under his old comrade Smith were wandering around western Kentucky and planning on, "it is presumed, . . . investing Forts Henry and Donelson." Fortunately, Johnston had already sent the eight thousand troops out toward Russellville, where they would be able to respond to threats at the twin forts or Clarksville: "they will be in a position to act effectively in either direction." He also sent more men directly to Tilghman, even though they were badly armed and equipped, carrying powder horns. But the news of Zollicoffer's defeat was a real blow, not just a potential one. He continued his report: "I have just received a telegram from [Brigadier] General [Thomas C.] Hindman, commanding the advance from this position, announcing the defeat and death of General Zollicoffer." Johnston immediately perceived the problems there, adding, "if my right is thus broken as stated, East Tennessee is open to invasion." But having strongly reinforced Tilghman, he had no more available troops to send eastward, fearing it would "leave this place untenable." Plus, he had to protect Nashville, describing the Tennessee capital as "the special object to defend." Taking everything together, Johnston explained the critical nature of his situation: "if force cannot be spared from other army corps the country must now be roused to make the greatest effort that they will be called upon to make during the contest. No matter what the sacrifice may be, it must be made, and without loss of time. Our people do not comprehend the magnitude of the danger that threatens. Let it be impressed upon them. . . . All the resources of the Confederacy are now needed for the defense of Tennessee."[21]

There were resources to be had, but the Davis administration refused to release them. In their politically motivated strategy of defending every nook and cranny of the South, Richmond authorities at the time had some twenty-five thousand troops along the Gulf Coast from Florida to New Orleans, even though facing little looming threat. Johnston had repeatedly called for support, often to the chagrin and exasperation even of his friend Davis, but there was only a trickle of help coming to Kentucky. Evidently, it would take some sort of crisis to get the president to budge on these reinforcements, but by the time the crisis came, it would surely be too late.[22]

Without much support, then, Johnston shuffled what troops he could in the West, protecting Nashville at all costs. He also tried to keep his supplies maximized, even amid a lead shortage beginning in late January. And Johnston had to contend with the lack of command ability to his east. Zollicoffer, never really a major commander, was now dead and Crittenden, despite being from a luminary family in Kentucky, was a poor replacement. In fact, calls for his removal were numerous amid the rumors of drunkenness, some demands even made directly to Davis. "Can not you, Mr. President, right the wrong by the immediate presence of a new and able man," one wrote in late January. Governor Harris went so far as to tell a member of the Confederate Congress that "Crittenden can never rally troops [in] East Tennessee. Some other general must be sent there." Secretary Benjamin wrote Johnston of "some pain[ful] rumors . . . [of] the intemperance of General Crittenden" and told him to investigate and remove him if necessary. Crittenden himself called for a court of inquiry, which Richmond granted, but the forgiving Johnston delayed the proceedings.[23]

As bad as matters seemed in late January, the next blow was much worse. Tilghman sent a note to Polk on February 4, followed by direct messages to Johnston himself, stating that "the enemy is landing troops in large forces on this side of the river within 3 miles of the fort." Tilghman was writing from Fort Henry. This was obviously the critical point for Johnston, whose line was still somewhat intact though turned to the east. A blow at the weakly defended twin-river forts in the center, however, would be devastating.[24]

Since Columbus and Bowling Green were heavily defended, the Federals not surprisingly decided to attack along the much-less-defended Cumberland and Tennessee Rivers in between them, where the Union's obvious advantage in naval resources could be well used. All that blocked these rivers, now that they were high enough for navigation, were three small earthen fortifications, only two of which had cannon large enough to stop armored gunboats. It would be in essence a large turning movement outflanking primarily Columbus to the west, since it came in Halleck's department, but also essentially turning Bowling Green to the east as well. Accordingly, a confident Grant and Flag Officer Andrew H. Foote soon landed troops and prepared to attack Fort Henry on February 6. The advance came in Halleck's domain, but the quickness of the offensive-minded Grant and Foote frightened the more methodical Union department commander. Likewise, Buell in front of Bowling Green somehow construed the rapid action as possibly turning into a threat to his forces as well.[25]

Word of this new Union advance rocked the Confederate high command even more. Polk still thought the ultimate goal was Columbus. Johnston, who had been awakened to the twin-river threat by the January Union reconnaissance, had started to build his strength there but had not made the situation as sure as it was at Columbus and Bowling Green. Only a mere few thousand troops manned the forts, although Johnston had sent forces to be in the vicinity if needed, including Buckner at Russellville and Pillow at Clarksville. Closest to the scene, Tilghman continually called for more men, keeping his commanders alert to the developments throughout February 5 and on the morning of the sixth. He reported to Polk that the Federals were reinforcing their initial landing force, which was indeed a second wave of soldiers brought down from Paducah because of a lack of vessels to carry them all at once. Tilghman fairly demanded of him: "Don't trust to Johnston's re-enforcing me; we need all. I don't want raw troops who are just organized; they are in my way. Act promptly, and don't trust to anyone." Of course, with his attention firmly fixed on Columbus's defenses, the bishop sent no troops whatsoever.[26]

Johnston, on the other hand, had indeed sent all those troops to the vicinity, but made the mistake of not getting them to the actual point of crisis. Thus, when the flotilla under Foote attacked around 11:00 A.M. on February 6, they immediately overpowered the fort despite a hard fight put up by Tilghman. Knowing the disparity in numbers that would only grow as Grant's forces moved southward on both sides of the river, Tilghman consolidated what he had, first at Fort Henry on the east side of the river, giving up Fort Heiman willingly, then sending that force off to man Fort Donelson while he fought as long as he could before surrendering. His infantry and field artillery made it out as Tilghman indeed fought with about eighty gunners in the lopsided fight at Fort Henry. Ultimately, with the Federal gunboats bearing down on him and the river rising even into the fort, Tilghman surrendered. Despite other Confederate forces in the vicinity, none were within the close distance needed to support the vulnerable fort. Pillow at Clarksville, in fact, reported on the sixth, "we hear firing to this place constantly."[27]

It was the major blow of the war thus far. "Fort Henry fell yesterday," a distraught Governor Harris informed Richmond the next day. He added: "A large increase of force to defend this [State] from Cumberland Gap to Columbus is an absolute and imperative necessity. If not successfully defended the injury is irreparable." Others knew the consequences as well. At Clarksville, Pillow, who actually thought the firing he heard on February 6 was at Fort Donelson, nevertheless knew what the loss of that post would entail: "If Donelson should be overcome, we can make no successful stand without larger force."[28]

General Johnston knew best of all what the fall of the Tennessee River fort, and Tilghman's surrender, meant. With Tilghman captured, his immediate need was for a general officer to take command at Fort Donelson. Fortunately, he had Bushrod Johnson in Nashville, having sent him westward on the sixth, arriving the next night; "take instant command of Fort Donelson," Johnston ordered him. Thinking more broadly, the department commander also ordered riverboats along the Tennessee to move southward away from danger. But in actuality, it was not so much Fort Henry itself that was important or even strategic. Nothing regarding that post was of primary importance except that it blocked access to the river upstream. But that area farther south contained numerous important points, not the least of which symbolically was the newly gained Federal access to the Deep South cotton states. In fact, as soon as Fort Henry fell, Foote and Grant sent the three timberclads (*Lexington, Tyler,* and *Conestoga*) under Ledyard Phelps southward, traveling all the way into Alabama and Mississippi and terrifying the population and Confederate authorities alike. Nothing, of course, was on the river in terms of fortifications or gunboats to stop the Federal navy, which by extension meant that transports could likewise funnel Union armies deep into the South by the same route.[29]

This naval penetration also brought up a new concern—enemy attacks on the Confederate railroad network in the cotton states, which was vital. Two of the most important trunk lines of the South ran in this general area, including the north–south Mobile and Ohio, at points just a mere twenty or so miles east of the river, and the east–west Memphis and Charleston Railroad, which ran almost adjacent to the river once it made its big turn in north Alabama, even crossing the river at Decatur. Former Confederate secretary of war Walker, now a brigadier general in Alabama, lectured that these two railroads were "the vertebrae of the Confederacy." The Memphis and Charleston, in fact, came so close to the Tennessee River at Bear Creek in Alabama that there was major concern Phelps's raid would steam up the creek and destroy the vital bridge there, breaking the line. Obviously, where these two major trunk lines intersected was highly important as well— Corinth, Mississippi, itself a mere twenty or so miles from the river.[30]

The possibilities for disaster were endless if the Federals spilled southward along the Tennessee River in large numbers. But for Johnston, the immediate concern now was for his original defensive line and the garrisons still stationed along it. Thus, the most prized possession along the river for the Confederates was not necessarily Fort Henry but what it initially defended farther south, the bridge at Danville, where the Memphis, Clarksville, and Louisville Railroad crossed the Tennessee on a revolving span. This was not only the lone railroad bridge across the river below (north of) Florence, Alabama, but also the only bridge of any kind spanning the Tennessee between Florence and the Ohio River. Part of Johnston's plan of defense utilized interior lines of communication to shift units quickly to a threatened sector, which the railroad allowed as it ran essentially just south of and basically parallel to his line from the Columbus area to Bowling Green. The track had already been used heavily to shuffle troops back and forth from one side of the uncrossable Tennessee River to the other, among them Johnston himself in October 1861.[31]

But now that the bridge was damaged and unusable, that link was gone and the next place to connect the two wings of Johnston's defense by rail across the Tennessee River was at Florence, Alabama. As historian Larry Daniel has described it, the Confederate line "had length but not depth." Depending on Alabama as a connection point was not feasible, as Florence was over 160 miles south of Bowling Green and nearly that far from Columbus. Thus, Johnston's line was split with the fall of Fort Henry, his eastern forces under Hardee and Crittenden, along with those sent to the twin rivers region, being separated from Polk's forces at Columbus. Worse, the Federal navy was already in between and far in rear of both; logically, Union armies would soon follow. Both of the bastions Johnston was so worried about (Columbus and Bowling Green) were now turned, outflanked, and with the enemy far to their rear. The Confederacy's remaining line was untenable.[32]

Although Johnston had been begging for arms and men for months now, only after the major blow at Fort Henry did the Confederate government understand the pending crisis and act. Richmond had provided a trickle of guns and troops in the months previous, but nothing large enough to turn the tide of war. President Davis had even sent westward another full general, P. G. T. Beauregard, to act as a support for Johnston in his defense of the long, expansive western theater. Beauregard had, of course, run afoul of the president earlier as a result of the fighting at Manassas. Davis sent him west on January 26 to confer with Johnston and then move on to take command at Columbus. Obviously, the president realized the Polk influence was not a good thing.[33]

Beauregard arrived on the evening of February 4 at Bowling Green, where he met with Johnston over the next several days about the unfolding catastrophe. And events were indeed catastrophic, Johnston later confiding to Davis that Beauregard "expressed his surprise at the smallness of my force and was impressed with the danger." Ironically, the Creole's movement west was at least partially responsible for that mess. The Federals, unbeknown to Johnston and his commanders, had picked up on reports of Beauregard coming from Virginia, and the rumor was that he was bringing with him numerous regiments to solidify Johnston's line. In actuality, Beauregard brought no more than a few staff officers, but the perception was that the Confederates in the West were about to be reinforced heavily. Consequently, Halleck allowed the hastily conceived Fort Henry attack as a chance to land a blow before those additional enemy forces arrived. Grant and Foote went on and took the fort, leaving Johnston and his new help to pick up the pieces.[34]

As Johnston, Beauregard, and Hardee huddled together at Bowling Green's Covington House on February 7 (Mackall attending part of their meeting), the stark reality set in on what had just happened. They drafted a memorandum that spelled out the effects plainly. An air of defeat came through the document, mentioning the fall of Fort Henry "yesterday" and labeling Fort Donelson as "not being long tenable." Thus, major moves were required because "the possession of the Tennessee River by the enemy, resulting from the fall of Fort Henry, separates this army at Bowling Green from the one at Columbus, Ky, which must henceforth act independently of each other until they can again be brought together." Rejoining the two wings was paramount, and the only way to do that was for each to fall back.[35]

The document plainly stated that "preparations should at once be made for the removal of this army [at Bowling Green] to Nashville, in rear of the Cumberland River." The problem was that if Fort Donelson fell, and they believed it would shortly, the Federal navy could range all the way up the Cumberland to the Tennessee capital and cut off Hardee's forces north of the river. These Confederates would thus be caught in the shallow bowl of the Cumberland's basin, with no place to cross except under the enemy's guns. And because the Federals were already operating along the Tennessee River all the way ultimately to Florence, Alabama, any movement across that river had to be made far to the east; fortunately, the bars at Muscle Shoals precluded any farther Union naval advance on the Tennessee. The plan thus stipulated that "should any further retrograde movement become necessary," it was to be done to the southeast for a crossing at Stevenson, Alabama, along the railroad to Chattanooga. That would get the army well eastward of any potential Union effect as well as cover East Tennessee. Of course, a howl went up from the Kentuckians around Johnston, including from the Confederate governor, George W. Johnson, at abandoning their state. Yet Johnston had no other choice.[36]

At the same time, the Columbus garrison was not safe either, although fewer geographical features such as the Tennessee and Cumberland Rivers stood in its way of retreat. Still, the officers realized it was time to abandon Columbus as well: "it becomes necessary, to prevent such a calamity, that the main body of that army should fall back to Humboldt, [Tennessee]." Afterward, tiers of defensive lines could be held, the generals even mentioning Grand Junction, Tennessee, as well as Grenada and even Jackson, Mississippi. Because of the lack of a clear threat to the rear, however, the western wing's retreat was not as time sensitive, and the memorandum recommended leaving a slight garrison at Columbus for now to slow the Federals as long as possible. Thereafter, successive defensive points along the Mississippi River were also to be held at Island No. 10, Fort Pillow, and even Memphis, "where another bold stand will be made." Beauregard even asked for the department's chief engineer to work on the Mississippi River fortifications, but Johnston could not spare Gilmer and sent someone else. In the meantime, fortifications and batteries continued to go up all the way southward to Vicksburg, Mississippi.[37]

The mood in Richmond was just as panicked. Secretary Benjamin wrote to Johnston that the fall of Fort Henry "has filled us with solicitude." But it finally woke them up to the dangers of such an extended defensive line that could easily be broken anywhere, which it now was at two different places. Responding with too little too late, however, the Confederate government nevertheless acted, first collecting a new force of some fifteen regiments to go to East Tennessee to cover that region. This allowed Crittenden's broken command, withdrawing first toward Nashville and then diverted to Murfreesboro, to join Johnston's forces retreating from Bowling Green. Secretary Benjamin wanted Buckner to lead the new East Tennessee force, but at this point the Kentuckian was getting more and more involved in the Fort Donelson defense and could not be spared. Eventually, in late February, Major General Edmund Kirby Smith took command at Knoxville.[38]

To stabilize Johnston's line itself, the Confederate government also acted more strategically, although once again too late to prevent or recover the losses already incurred. More weapons were somehow found and diverted to Johnston, which the general no doubt appreciated but likely wondered why they had not been sent earlier when he was predicting just such a catastrophe as had occurred. There was also yet another round of calls for the states to provide more troops, and soon the Confederate Congress would get involved and pass the famed Conscription Act in mid-April.[39]

Drafted soldiers, or even those joining the armies to keep from being drafted, were months out from actually taking their positions in the armies at this point, so immediate help was also needed. Davis provided this as well, although once again too late to make a difference when it mattered most. Calls went out in the immediate days after Fort Henry to the Gulf region commanders, Lovell and Bragg, to send aid for the broken Kentucky line. Benjamin wrote to Lovell on February 8, just two days after Fort Henry fell, "the President desires that as soon as possible on receipt of this letter you dispatch 5,000 men to Columbus to re-enforce that point, sorely threatened by largely superior forces." He went on to explain that "the menacing aspect of affairs in Kentucky has induced the withdrawal from points, not in immediate danger, of every man that can be spared to prevent the enemy from penetrating into Tennessee or passing Columbus." To Bragg went a similar call: "The President desires that you will as soon as possible send to Knoxville all the troops you can spare from your command without immediate danger." Benjamin added, "the condition of affairs in Kentucky and Tennessee demands from us the most vigorous effort for defense, and General A. S. Johnston is so heavily outnumbered, that it is scarcely possible for him to maintain his whole line without additional re-enforcements." A grudging Lovell sent "his best troops at New Orleans," while Bragg ultimately sent thousands of men from his positions defending Mobile and Pensacola. Bragg even sent a messenger to learn Johnston's plans; he returned with news of the "deplorable state of affairs." Troops from the Gulf defenses nevertheless moved northward in the ensuing days and weeks and ultimately began to collect around the critical railroad junction at Corinth. Once he met Bragg later on, Johnston warmly told him: "Your prompt and decisive move, Sir, has saved me, and saved the country. But for your arrival, the enemy would have been between us." Although one Mississippi regiment was described as being "in a state of mutiny" over pay, a spattering of other troops were also ordered to Johnston. All was the result of the fall of Fort Henry.[40]

Johnston was able to place his thoughts again on paper on February 8, when he addressed a detailed report to Secretary Benjamin. He admitted that "no reliable particulars of the loss of Fort Henry have yet reached me," although he was assured that most of the garrison had gotten out and retreated to Fort Donelson. Johnston explained how the loss gave the enemy control of the Tennessee River, "and their gunboats are now ascending the river to Florence." He noted the enemy's logical next step: "operations against Fort Donelson, on the Cumberland, are about to be commenced, and that work will soon be attacked." Therein lay the worry, that "the slight resistance at Fort Henry indicates that the best open earthworks are not reliable to meet successfully a vigorous attack of iron-clad gunboats." He dolefully added, "I think the gunboats of the enemy will probably take Fort Donelson without the necessity of employing their land force in co-operation, as seems to have been done at Fort Henry." Johnston continued that "should Fort Donelson be taken, it will open the route to the enemy to Nashville, giving them the means of breaking the bridges and destroying the ferry-boats on the river as far as navigable. The occurrence of the misfortune of losing the fort will [thus] cut off the communication of the force here under General Hardee from the south bank of the Cumberland. To avoid the disastrous consequences of such an event I ordered General Hardee yesterday to make, as promptly as it could be done, preparations to fall back to Nashville and cross the river." Left unsaid was the obvious solution: to hold Fort Donelson as long as possible until Johnston and Hardee could get south of the Cumberland.[41]

With the decisions made and Beauregard en route to Columbus after a delay due to a reoccurrence of his throat illness, the critical effort thus became holding Fort Donelson long enough to get Hardee's command from Bowling Green across the Cumberland River at Nashville. Johnston later explained, "I determined to fight for Nashville at Donelson, and gave the best part of my army to do it." Other forces north of the river were to likewise remove south of the Cumberland, particularly those troops near Clarksville, but the major threat was to Hardee's force perched some sixty miles north of Nashville. Depending on how quickly the Federals took Fort Donelson, it would be a race to get across the river in time. "The probability of having the ferriage of this army corps across the Cumberland intercepted by the gunboats of the enemy," Johnston wrote Secretary Benjamin, "admits of no delay in making the movement." Any and all efforts at slowing the enemy were thus appreciated, including a project to block the river. Mackall instructed on February 9, "the General is anxious that the experiment of Mr. Armstrong in blocking the Cumberland should be made promptly"; Nashville depots would provide anything necessary, including railroad spikes to finish a raft. With Gilmer gone once again to Fort Donelson, Mackall found another engineer, Victor Skeliha, and put him in charge of fortifying Nashville. Johnston particularly wanted the railroad bridge over the Cumberland River floored for vehicle traffic, anticipating the need to get Hardee's troops and wagon trains across quickly.[42]

Logically, Johnston thought the larger the force blocking the river at Fort Donelson, the better able they would be to delay the enemy. He accordingly began an ill-fated reinforcement of the fort, first from nearby garrisons but ultimately including those farther out at Clarksville and even Russellville, Kentucky. Slowly but surely, under Johnston's orders, these garrisons began to congregate at Fort Donelson, with Pillow's troops from Clarksville first arriving and that general taking command on February 9, calling in his grandiose way for his men to "drive back the ruthless invader from our soil and again raise the Confederate flag over Fort Henry." Soon thereafter, Buckner's command arrived as well, on the twelfth, adding another general officer (along with Pillow and Bushrod Johnson) to the command situation. But Pillow and Buckner did not get along at all, and as historian Nathaniel Cheairs Hughes has pointed out, "why Albert Sidney Johnston entrusted these two enemies with the fate of Fort Donelson, when it was common knowledge they could never be expected to cooperate, challenges one's imagination." Perhaps with that in mind, Johnston had yet another general soon on site who ranked both. By February 8, Brigadier General

Floyd was in Clarksville with his command and heading toward Fort Donelson as well. But the former secretary of war informed Johnston that day that the situation did not look good. Tensions were boiling over, as Floyd, now the senior commander in the area, had decided to evacuate Fort Donelson; Pillow refused and talked him into not only keeping the garrison there but also bringing his own command in as well. From what Floyd could gather on the ground, the enemy's ironclads "are nearly invulnerable, and therefore they can probably go wherever sufficient fuel and depth of water can be found, unless met by opposing gunboats." Left unsaid, of course, was the assumption that Fort Donelson itself would not stop the Union ironclads, nor would the meager defenses at Clarksville farther upriver. "The defenses here amount to about nothing," Floyd explained from Clarksville, "I think they have mistaken the location of the work upon the river hill about 200 yards, whilst the one in the bottom is nearly submerged."[43]

The bottom line was that little stood in the way of the Federals moving toward Nashville, and Floyd begged Johnston: "I wish, if possible, you would come down here, if it were only for a single day. I think in that time you might determine the policy and lines of defense." He nevertheless assured him, as the ranking commander of all generals in the vicinity, "I will, however, do the best I can and all I can with the means at hand." Despite the call, Johnston did not go to Donelson, perhaps his biggest mistake, but continued to affirm that Floyd was in command: "use your judgement," he ordered, although adding that it seemed from what Floyd reported about Fort Henry that "if at the long range we could do so much damage with the necessary short range on the Cumberland we should destroy their boats." Yet he still did not see the need to go take personal command, even as the days swirled into chaos as Floyd buckled. His almost begging for Johnston to come personally should have been enough to cause him to go there, as should the department commander's later scolding: "I do not know the wants of Gen. Pillow—nor yours, nor the position of Genl. Buckner. You do. You have this dispatch. Decide."[44]

Unfortunately for the Confederacy, there was developing at Fort Donelson, without Johnston's presence, a different mindset than the one employed at departmental headquarters. It is clear that Pillow certainly, and perhaps Floyd also once he was caught up in the chaos that engulfed the operations, saw the defense of Fort Donelson as the main objective. It became to them the line in the sand where the big battle was to be fought and victory or defeat determined. Certainly, Pillow took the post's defense personally, as he did superior officers arriving at his new lair. But Johnston saw the situation in a totally different light; Fort Donelson was not to be the site of the main battle—it was simply a delaying action to hold Union forces long enough for Johnston and Hardee to get their units out of central Kentucky and south of the Cumberland River. In fact, Johnston issued orders to Floyd on February 14 that, "if you lose the fort, bring your troops to Nashville if possible" and had even earlier made sure that he knew to keep his men on the west bank of the Cumberland "to have his route open to Nashville." Evidently, Johnston did not make his wishes known clearly enough, however, and letting Floyd remain in local command due to his own absence from the area brought huge problems. Nevertheless, reinforcing Donelson was not a catastrophic decision in and of itself; historian Steven Woodworth has argued that "what he [Johnston] did was a mistake, but it need not have been a disaster. The disaster was the work of the men he sent to command the reinforced garrison." But it is questionable whether even moving some troops to Donelson was a mistake; Johnston had only so much to work with, and he did with his limited means what President Davis would not do earlier—move troops to the crisis zone. Obviously, unless historian Thomas Connelly is to be believed that Johnston never thought that a Union land force would move eastward from Fort Henry, which seems highly improbable and not borne out by evidence, ground troops would be needed to temporarily defend the river batteries against the gunboats. Johnston effectively tried to cover the most threatened point with troops, which was reasonable as long as they did not get trapped there themselves.[45]

That said, it was certainly a major mistake for Johnston to leave the critical situation at Fort Donelson in Floyd's incapable hands. For all his work as governor of Virginia and U.S. secretary of war, Floyd had pitifully little actual military experience, which showed in the coming days. Yet Johnston left the entire defense at Fort Donelson to him, often reminding him that troop movements have "been left to your discretion" and providing him with "full authority to make all the dispositions of your troops for the defense of Fort Donelson, Clarksville, and the Cumberland you may think proper." Worse, Floyd was easily swayed by his subordinates Pillow and Buckner, who were themselves at odds politically and militarily, barely even speaking to one another. With such importance placed on delaying at Fort Donelson, it is intriguing why Johnston did not go there himself, sending only his brother-in-law Colonel Preston.[46]

As the days between Fort Henry's fall on February 6 and operations at Fort Donelson commenced on February 12 passed agonizingly slow, Johnston continued to gather information even as he traveled on February 13 to Edgefield, directly across the Cumberland River from Nashville. There he made his headquarters, outfitting it with newly bought furniture. He even had another conference with Beauregard the following day. But the news was still not good. Word from Alabama arrived that the Federal gunboats were at Florence on February 9. They even took control of the telegraph station there and "found out nearly everything that was passing over the line." Governor Harris was in an understandable panic and loudly calling for arms, saying he could put ten thousand men in service if he had weapons: "without them Nashville is in great danger." About all Richmond could tell Johnston was to "do your best and we will spare no effort." Chief Engineer Gilmer was at Fort Donelson and reporting that things did not look good there either: "the greatest danger, in my opinion, is from the gunboats"; he scarcely feared "a land attack." Pillow, before Floyd arrived on site to take command, also reported that matters were going to be close but warned that forces at Clarksville would not delay the enemy at all. But he added, "upon one thing you may rest assured, viz, that I will never surrender the position, and with God's help I mean to maintain it." That in and of itself should have been an indicator of the mistaken thought process of the Fort Donelson high command.[47]

Of course, the biggest problem was that, in addition to the arrival of a severe cold air mass that blanketed the area with snow and brought freezing temperatures, Grant's forces from Fort Henry were also arriving. The bickering Confederate generals on site let slip away the golden opportunity, in some historians' estimations, of an ambush in the barrens between the rivers. Grant began to surround the Confederate fortifications that day (February 12), and several attacks went forward the next, including a muted naval advance basically to show some force but that actually succeeded in heightening the morale of the Confederate garrison, who viewed it as a repulse of the gunboats. By the end of the day on the thirteenth, Floyd wired Johnston, "we have maintained ourselves fully by land and water." He expected the most significant fight the next day: "I presume [a major] battle will be fought to-morrow. We will endeavor to hold our position if we are capable of doing so." Although it was not a ringing endorsement, Johnston sent the message on to Richmond with little comment except that it was "the latest information from Fort Donelson."[48]

Better news came to Johnston the next day. The Federal flotilla had arrived during the night and made their attack on Valentine's Day, both sides assuming that this would be another Fort Henry type of fight. But Fort Donelson's guns were situated farther above the water than had been Fort Henry's, and Flag Officer Foote made the mistake of boring in too close. The result was a severe repulse for the Union ironclads (the timberclads remained mostly out of the fight), just as Johnston predicted, something that took everyone else on both sides by surprise. Floyd had wired Johnston amid the fight that "the fort cannot hold out twenty minutes" but then tempered his messages as the unthinkable happened. Pillow informed Polk and Johnston, "we have just had the fiercest fight on record between our guns and six gunboats," and Floyd confirmed that "the gun-boats have been driven back."[49]

Even with the good news, a nervous but relieved Johnston could still do little in Nashville besides wait and hurry his forces falling back across the Cumberland. To Crittenden he sent two messages that day to move southward quickly, watching the enemy in case they followed: "every exertion [should] be made, day and night." To Hardee he also sent two messages of haste, forwarding the reports he was receiving from Floyd. Hardee had left Bowling Green on February 11 but was then hit by the same massive winter storm that engulfed Fort Donelson two days later, delaying the withdrawal. Still, Johnston urged speed. "You will perceive," he wrote, "the necessity of hastening your march as much as possible. It must be continued day and night until the army crosses the Cumberland." In a separate message, he added that his units "should be concentrated here as rapidly as is consistent with an orderly march." Hardee himself left Bowling Green with the rear guard, the Federals following up and bombarding the town as the Confederates left. "I shall move on as rapidly as possible," Hardee assured his commander.[50]

By February 15, much of the needed delay Johnston had required had been provided, and the Confederate commanders inside Fort Donelson, with news of additional Union troops arriving to reinforce Grant, wisely decided it was time to get out. The plan had been slated even for the day before, when Floyd messaged Johnston, "I will fight them this evening." That attack was delayed until the next morning, February 15, when Pillow launched a surprise assault on the Union right, driving back McClernand's division far enough to open up the Forge Road, which allowed an escape. But then Pillow, imbued with the success and still thinking this was a fight to the death at the fort rather than a delaying action, amazingly ordered his troops back into his trenches, giving up the fiercely won battlefield as well as the escape route. Buckner argued vehemently against staying at the fort, but the weak Floyd sided with Pillow. It was the fatal mistake; the Confederates were trapped once more, this time for good. Throughout the night, the comedy of errors continued as the Confederate commanders deliberated on what to do. Only Buckner seemed to grasp the larger situation: "I understood the principal object of the defense of Donelson to be to cover the movement of General A. S. Johnston's army from Bowling Green to Nashville, and that if that movement was not completed it was my opinion that we should attempt a further defense, even at the risk of the destruction of our entire force as the delay even of a few hours might gain the safety of General Johnston's force." Floyd had evidently heard from Johnston that Hardee's troops were already to the Cumberland River, at which news Buckner urged an immediate surrender; Floyd and Pillow agreed. Then things became even more ludicrous as Floyd turned over command to Pillow and ran. Pillow then did the same thing. Buckner, now in command, immediately questioned Grant as to terms and received the famous reply, "no terms except unconditional and immediate surrender." Buckner did just that at daylight on February 16. Ironically, the Union land forces at Fort Donelson had been the real threat to the defenders, not the vaunted gunboats.[51]

Johnston knew little of these events and continually worked to get more men and arms for his scattered army, unaware that he would lose nearly fifteen thousand of both the next morning. Harris was almost beside himself and addressed the general: "Will you pardon me, my dear sir, for suggesting and respectfully urging the immediate re-enforcement of our gallant and glorious little army there [at Fort Donelson] to the extent of our ability. A few thousand men thrown to their aid immediately may turn the scale and make our victory complete and triumphant." The governor, too, was mistakenly thinking of a major fight that would decide things taking place at Fort Donelson, while Johnston saw the defense as only a temporary holding action. More good news arrived that afternoon, however, evidently sent at 1:00 P.M. from Fort Donelson, stating that the Confederates were driving the Federals (and opening up an escape route). Johnston sent the message on to Richmond, though reminding them, "there is no intelligence since 1 o'clock." Word arrived later that night that the day had been successful, Johnston duly reporting to Richmond: "We have had to-day at Fort Donelson one of the most sanguinary conflicts of the war. Our forces attacked the enemy with energy and won a brilliant victory."[52]

But then matters unraveled more than Johnston could have imagined. He and Major Munford, occupying the same room, had gone to sleep "jubilant over the result. All went to bed happy." But Johnston knew something was up when, during the night, he received a note from Floyd: "We are completely invested with an army many times our own numbers. I regret to say the unanimous opinion of the officers seems to be that we cannot maintain ourselves against these forces." Then early the next morning came a knock on the door by a courier with messages. Munford lit a candle and read the dispatch to Johnston. He remembered that "the general was lying on a little camp-bed in one corner; he was silent a moment, and then asked me to read the dispatch again, which I did. He then ordered the staff to be awakened, saying, 'I must save this army.'" The note was from Buckner and said he had sent Grant a flag of truce. Johnston surmised it was for surrender negotiations, although official word did not come until later. But this message only raised more questions. The last he had heard, the Confederates had won the victory; now there was talk of surrender. What had happened? And why was Buckner sending the messages and potentially surrendering? Where were Floyd and Pillow? What the message meant other than taking it at face value was not known. Johnston nevertheless alerted Hardee's forces, especially the commander in the column's lead, to hurry on, as "news from our flank makes this advisable." Fortunately, the head of the column under Colonel John Bowen reached Edgefield by late that day and was deployed as a shield by Johnston himself, while the last elements, having left Bowling Green on February 14, moved on southward. Johnston, in fact, explained that the decision to withdraw from Bowling Green was "ordered before and executed while the battle was being fought at Donelson." Hardee's command was now at the Cumberland River, however, with bridges available to pass over quickly, which Johnston set in motion even on the fifteenth. It seemed the race had been won.[53]

But news soon broke to the public that Fort Donelson had surrendered with most of the garrison, official confirmation coming with the arrival of Floyd and Pillow at Nashville the next day. Johnston was astonished at the quick reversal. "At midnight on the 15th I received news of a glorious victory; at dawn, of a defeat," he explained to President Davis. Fortunately, by that time Johnston had Hardee's troops mostly across the river, informing Richmond that "this army is across the Cumberland."[54]

Just getting his troops beyond the river was crucial, but it was not the only, and easiest, decision Johnston had to make. Next he had to determine what to do about Nashville. Should his forces defend it, and if so, how? There were pitifully few defenses prepared and not enough troops to man even those, much less big guns to stop the Union ironclads all knew would be arriving, probably in a matter of hours. Plus, Buell was bearing down from the north and Thomas still lurked to the east, with Grant's forces to the west. A fighting stand would only destroy the city and probably the army. Johnston informed Richmond that he had "no alternative but to evacuate Nashville or sacrifice the army." Unlike the commanders at Fort Donelson (and so many other Confederate commanders throughout the war), Johnston decided that saving the army was the priority. He thus marched his troops across the Cumberland River and through the capital city on February 17, much to the chagrin of an astonished populace. He left Floyd in command of the rear and tasked the cavalry under Lieutenant Colonel Forrest, who had himself escaped the doomed fort, to keep the calm and get out all the supplies possible; his orders stressed "do not fight a battle in the city." Neither task was done totally, the citizens and soldiers of Nashville panicking even while the army left tons of stores and supplies behind. Meanwhile, Johnston and his withdrawing army made their way southeastward toward Murfreesboro, where he hoped to meet up with Crittenden's similarly broken troops.[55]

Obviously, "the disaster of Donelson" and the twin rivers had been a major blow. The western defensive line, cracked at Mill Springs in January, was completely shattered in early February, and any future defense was severely hampered by losing a quarter or so of the entire western army at Fort Donelson. Making the loss even more insulting was that the capitulation did not have to happen. Hardee was to the Cumberland and there was an open avenue for most of the troops to escape from Fort Donelson on the afternoon of February 15. And the consequences were not lost on Richmond either; the terrified president simply wrote the theater commander on February 18, "inform me of your condition & plans."[56]

Johnston's subordinates, whom historian Steve Woodworth has described as his "foolish underlings," certainly had not served him well during this most critical of high-stakes games: "every blunder by an inept general would have disastrous effects on Johnston's thin-stretched line." Polk's intransigence at Columbus, Crittenden and Zollicoffer's ill-fated advance across the Cumberland River that led to death and disaster in the Appalachians, and Floyd, Pillow, and Buckner's comedy of errors at Fort Donelson, depriving Johnston of much-needed men and arms, were all examples of mediocre at best subordinates failing their commanding general in making even common-sense decisions. Certainly, the Fort Donelson generals, all three appointments made for political reasons, could have made a better attempt to extricate the garrison after attaining the main goal of buying time for Hardee's troops to escape. Perhaps if Tilghman had not given himself up so easily by remaining at Fort Henry, he would have made the case for evacuation successfully; he wrote in his report, significantly dated February 12—before Fort Donelson fell—that "the fate of our right wing at Bowling Green depended upon a concentration of my entire division on Fort Donelson and the holding of that place as long as possible." Perhaps Tilghman himself had let Johnston down as well by not remaining with the largest body of his troops that left Fort Henry and continuing the fight, although Floyd and Pillow would have ultimately outranked him. Still, he understood Johnston's desires better than those generals and would no doubt have made them known had he been there. Nevertheless, Johnston had plenty of time to make his desires to save the garrison crystal clear even after Tilghman's capture—if indeed that needed to be emphasized in the first place.[57]

Thus, Johnston was not without blame either, operating in what historian Stephen Engle has termed "the darkness of indecision." Although labeled as a strong and charismatic leader, Johnston had ample problems asserting his will on his subordinates. He never seemed able to stand up to and forcefully deal with his old roommate Polk or even Pillow, another luminary from the past who appeared to keep Johnston in awe. His tolerance of their obsession with Columbus—at the same time being obsessed himself with Bowling Green—was illustrative of this problem, even to the point of not securing the truly endangered points on the Cumberland and Tennessee Rivers; even Pillow's biographers have asserted that he mostly "sabotaged Sidney Johnston's attempts to strengthen the river forts." In addition to them, Floyd was a former governor and secretary of war. Johnston seemed unable to command these former luminaries, perhaps feeling they were equals if not superiors; they certainly had been superiors earlier in his life. Thus, the meek Johnston could never bring himself to command them efficiently or to lay blame on them, writing of calls for explanations that he had to "fix blame, if blame there be, on those who were delinquent in duty." Likewise, Zollicoffer and Crittenden seemed to be running wild in East Tennessee and Kentucky, with little restraint. Only where Johnston was actually present did he seem to have the charismatic effect over men as handed down so long in popular memory.[58]

Specifically, Johnston did not recognize until it was too late where the fatal blow would land on his western defense line. This was the problem, but all military commanders have that challenge of not being able to see into the future amid the fog of war. Still, when events began to play out much more swiftly, Johnston's response was inadequate, given that the only positive actions he took were those he seemingly saw to himself. Johnston could not be everywhere, but Beauregard (and even biographer Charles Roland) later faulted him for not concentrating his army at the twin rivers to combat Grant; Beauregard later said he recommended this, but no supporting evidence exists. Rather, William Preston wrote contemporaneously that the Creole "fully approved" the memorandum written on February 7 as well as Johnston's larger plans. Certainly, concentrating at the twin rivers on arguably the smallest Union force confronting him at the time opened up strong possibilities of defeat on other portions of the line. But Johnston sent a large portion of his command to that area anyway, something Larry Daniel has described as "a disastrous middle course." It seemed that matters were moving so fast in this high-stakes gambling game that Johnston simply did not have the needed time to think through his options or responses, as was the custom of the self-proclaimed methodical chess player.[59]

That Johnston never went to the twin rivers to take personal command over Forts Henry and Donelson and the troops there seems to rank highest on his list of errors. Even though he might have been captured himself, he most certainly would have tried to get the Donelson garrison out rather than surrender. At the least, his presence and direction would seemingly have ensured that everyone understood the plan during that fateful February 15 breakout attempt. Ironically, even though Johnston was not there, rumors of his capture were rife in the days after Fort Donelson, he being confused with Brigadier General Bushrod Johnson, who was indeed captured but then walked away days later while not under guard. Halleck clarified to McClellan after the stories circulated widely, "General A. S. Johnston was not there; it was General Bushrod R. Johnson." Diarist George Templeton Strong later corrected the error as well: "The captured General Johnston is not the genuine A. S. Johnston. He is a bogus Johnston, a 'Bushrod Johnston' [Johnson] that nobody ever heard of." Still, the bottom line is that Johnston never went himself to take command of the decisive point of his line, leaving the defense to an odd assortment of political appointees who served him terribly. If he saw the delaying action at Fort Donelson as so critical, indeed the key to Hardee's escape, perhaps Johnston should have made it his top personal priority. In Texas, he had once described Hardee as "a good friend of ours & one of the best officers in the service especially cavalry." Certainly, Johnston could have left the retreat to this capable officer he trusted.[60]

Likewise, because of his absence, the mix-up at Fort Donelson was ultimately Johnston's fault, as was his middle-of-the-road response. He had indeed realized the chaotic nature of the operations, writing Pillow on February 7: "Reports are so contradictory that you must do the best you can under orders you have recd., until Floyd arrives—when he will execute them. If your services or Buckner's or both are most important at Donelson, go there." He similarly wrote Floyd the next day: "In the absence of accurate information . . . I cannot give you specific instructions—I place under your command the entire force at Donelson & Clarksville. You will therefore ascertain the probable movements of the enemy and distribute your forces as you think proper." The mix-up engulfed a large portion of his forces as division after division, and their generals, swirled down the drain into Fort Donelson. Certainly, as Roland has argued, Johnston would have been better served either to leave only the minutest force to fight the fort as long as they could or to go in with all he had to make a sure thing of the defense. Johnston did neither and split the halves, which cost what Davis described as "the disaster at Fort Donelson." In fact, Roland argues that this was "the most grievous error of military judgment of his [Johnston's] career. . . . [T]his defense had to be all or nothing at all." But Johnston himself later explained, "had I wholly uncovered my front to defend Donelson, Buell would have known it and marched directly on Nashville." He also argued that he did not have the transportation needed to send his entire force to Donelson. It seems, then, that the best option would have been to hold the fort as long as he could with as small a force as possible to provide the necessary time the other troops needed before giving in. Still, the middle-sized force he sent there could have accomplished this, but with the priority to get the garrison out before it became too late to do so.[61]

In such a situation of quick-moving events, Johnston reverted to the patterns he had established over and over in his life, including his slowness in thinking, whether in chess or military movements, that many noted. Even biographer Roland has admitted, in comparing Johnston and Beauregard, that the latter was "quicker than Johnston in thought and word." Another pattern was that of taking huge gambles to make up the difference. Essentially, Johnston gambled on his subordinates acting in good faith for the greater cause, which they did not. Likewise, he gambled on the Federals attacking where he thought they would, which they did not. Most significantly, Johnston gambled on Fort Donelson holding long enough for Hardee to escape south of the Cumberland River, which it did, but at the cost of a large portion of his overall forces. "The blow was most disastrous and almost without remedy," he confessed. The chess player who preferred to methodically plot his every move was essentially out of place in a fast-moving poker-style game of war. This was a hand he lost, along with quite a large wager.[62]

He could only hope that the next deal would give him a better hand to play.

Early photo of Albert Sidney Johnston in dress uniform.
Courtesy of Library of Congress.

Albert Sidney Johnston in Confederate uniform.
Courtesy of Library of Congress.

Classmate, longtime friend, and president of the Confederacy
Jefferson Davis was a constant force in Johnston's life.
Courtesy of Library of Congress.

Robert E. Lee served as Johnston's lieutenant colonel in the 2nd U.S. Cavalry
and was a constant source of encouragement during the Civil War.
Courtesy of Library of Congress.

Governor of Tennessee Isham G. Harris worked with Johnston to defend the
state and was with the general at the time of his death at Shiloh.
Courtesy of Library of Congress.

Classmate and friend Leonidas Polk produced political woes
and generated near-constant concern from Johnston.
Courtesy of Library of Congress.

Former U.S. secretary of war John B. Floyd commanded Confederate forces at the disastrous fight for Fort Donelson, where Johnston himself should have taken personal command.
Courtesy of Library of Congress.

P. G. T. Beauregard, sent to serve as second in command in the western
theater, did not see strategy the same as Johnston and
was a continual counterweight to his plans.
Courtesy of Library of Congress.

Johnston fell at Shiloh near where his mortuary monument
stands today, dying in the ravine in the background.
Courtesy of Library of Congress.

Johnston's remains originally lay in a New Orleans cemetery before being moved to this elaborate tomb in the Texas State Cemetery in Austin. Courtesy of Library of Congress.

— 5 —

THE IRON DICE OF BATTLE

TOWARD THE SHILOH GAMBLE

T he citizens of Nashville were startled and confounded by the intelligence," one observer noted of the developments in mid-February 1862. They were especially panicked at word that enemy gunboats were on the way unopposed. Indeed, nowhere was the consequence of Fort Donelson's surrender felt more than at the Tennessee capital. Word of the disaster had slowly leaked out to the surrounding areas, and it was especially devastating after the morning newspapers in Nashville had just printed elevated stories of victory a day earlier. Johnston himself described how "the people were terrified and some of the troops were disheartened." A mob showed up at the general's headquarters, and a seemingly drunk man whipped them to a frenzy: "yes, fellow-citizens, we have a right to know whether our generals are going to fight for us or intend abandoning us and our wives and children to the enemy. We will force them to tell us." Governor Harris tried to keep calm and planned to fight for the city, calling anyone who could shoulder a weapon to report. "Impress upon your soldiers," he ordered the commander of the local militia, "that the Revolution of '76 was won by the Tennessee rifle, and that we fight in defense of our homes and all that we hold dear." But he knew there was no defense likely and informed President Davis that "no stand can be made. . . . I will rally all the Tennesseans possible and go with them myself to our army." He soon made plans for the legislature to convene in Memphis.[1]

Polk at Columbus was similarly left not knowing what was happening, even though Fort Donelson was in his military district. All he had heard

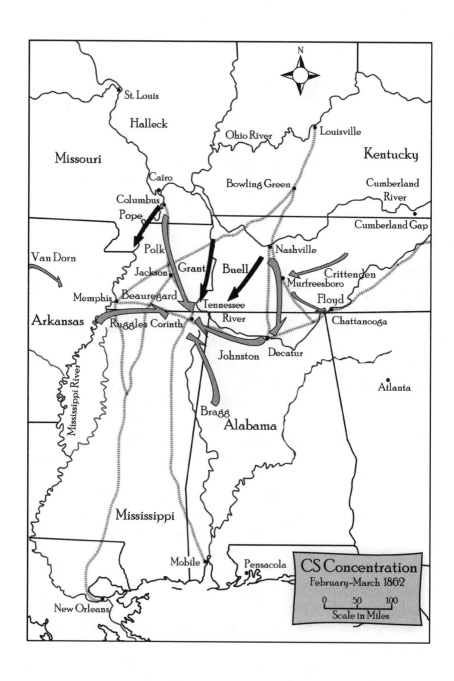

N

St. Louis

Halleck

Missouri

Ohio River   Louisville   Kentucky

Cairo   Bowling Green   Cumberland
River

Columbus   Cumberland Gap
Pope

Polk   Nashville

Jackson   Grant   Buell

Memphis   Beauregard   Murfreesboro   Crittenden

Arkansas   Ruggles Corinth   Tennessee   Floyd
River   Chattanooga

Johnston   Decatur

Atlanta

Bragg   Alabama

Van Dorn

Mississippi River

Mississippi

Mobile   Pensacola   **CS Concentration**
February–March 1862

0   50   100
Scale in Miles

New Orleans

were rumors that Johnston had abandoned Nashville, having no firm news and reporting that Beauregard had not arrived yet to take command. Beauregard himself was sick, having stopped his trek in Jackson, Tennessee, for the time being. But he was no more sanguine than anyone else regarding the situation, writing amid the Donelson fiasco: "I am taking the helm when the ship is already in the breakers and with but few sailors to man it. How it is to be extracted from its present perilous condition Providence alone can determine, and unless with its aid I can accomplish but little." He had predicted that the loss of Fort Donelson "would be followed by consequences too lamentable to now be alluded to" but saw little recourse: "General Johnston is doing his best, but what can he do against such tremendous odds?"[2]

In north Alabama, Leroy P. Walker reported the news to Richmond, writing that "the Kentucky line of defenses has been lost, with a large part of our army." In the Confederate capital, the authorities paced nervously despite preparing for the president's official inauguration just days away. In writing to Bragg on February 18, Secretary of War Benjamin even had few details: "I am still without any satisfactory information from General A. S. Johnston. I know not the nature nor extent of the disaster at Fort Donelson, nor the disposition of his troops, nor his plans, and am only aware of the very large loss we have suffered." And much of that information came from Northern papers. "Send such information of your present condition and intended movements," Benjamin politely intoned on February 18, knowing Johnston was probably swamped at the time.[3]

Johnston himself could not believe the developments. "Fort Donelson has fallen, and General Floyd's army is captured after a gallant defense," he reported. Yet there was nothing Johnston could do at this point besides simply continuing his withdrawal, needing now to get beyond the Tennessee River as well; officers went forward as early as February 22 to begin scouting the best places to cross. Nashville could not be defended, the ordered fortifications having never been built by an uninterested Gilmer or an uninterested populace and not overseen by Johnston himself. He assured the people that he was not giving up, however, telling one official, "go tell your people that, under the favor of Providence, I will return in less than ninety days and redeem their capital." But it would be hard until then, Johnston telling Harris: "Your first duty, Governor, is to the public trusts in your charge. I regard it as all-important that the public archives should be removed to some place of safety, and for this purpose have ordered transportation to be furnished you." He also recommended that the legislature adjourn and flee.[4]

Johnston nevertheless ordered Crittenden to join him at Murfreesboro, for which he left Nashville on February 18. With the addition of his forces from East Tennessee and "the fugitives from Fort Donelson," which one officer reported were "passing through here all going to their relative places . . . as though they were deserting" (he also had Union prisoners to deal with, later transferred to Memphis), Johnston's immediate command numbered a respectable seventeen thousand men, not counting a brigade sent to Chattanooga under Floyd. But he could not stay still long, having to escape south of the Tennessee River as soon as possible. Federal gunboats had been far south of his current position in the preceding weeks, and Johnston simply could not stay between the rivers, writing, "the complete command which their gunboats and transports give them on the Tennessee and Cumberland Rivers renders it necessary for me to retire my line between the rivers."[5]

The same problem existed for the troops at Columbus, although Beauregard had not made it all the way there yet because of his "nervous affection of throat." He summoned Polk and Governor Harris, then in Memphis securing the state's archives, to Jackson, Tennessee, for a conference, but the decision about the evacuation of Columbus was basically already made. Beauregard prophesied that the Kentucky stronghold "must meet the fate of Fort Donelson" and, after some consultation with the War Department in Richmond about options, received the confirmation: "evacuation decided on." The main hope of the War Department was "to save the cannon and munitions of war, which we cannot replace and cannot afford to lose." Ultimately, as preparations went forward, it was not until March 3 that an extremely reluctant Polk marched his troops out of Columbus for good.[6]

Bigger decisions loomed, however, including where Johnston would go once below the Tennessee River. "The force under my command cannot successfully cover the whole line against the advance of the enemy," he bluntly told Secretary Benjamin on February 25, adding that he recommended making East Tennessee its own department as "it would be almost impossible for me under present circumstances to superintend the operations at Knoxville and Chattanooga." As a result, he continued, "I am compelled to elect whether he [the enemy] shall be permitted to occupy Middle Tennessee, or turn Columbus, take Memphis, and open the valley of the Mississippi." Johnston did not have troops enough to cover both regions, as plainly seen in the preceding weeks, and he had to make a choice between defending Middle Tennessee or the Mississippi Valley. He revealed his decision by sending Floyd to Chattanooga to defend East Tennessee as best he could, then writing expectantly on February 25: "to me the defense of the [Mississippi] valley appears of paramount importance, and, consequently, I will move this corps of the army, of which I have assumed the immediate command, towards the left bank of the Tennessee, crossing the river near Decatur, in order to enable me to co-operate or unite with General Beauregard for the defense of Memphis and the Mississippi." A linkup in West Tennessee or north Mississippi seemed the best possibility, and this was a sound military move. Union commander Halleck even predicted as much, writing McClellan, "I certainly should [concentrate there] if I were in Johnston's place." Thus, the Federals saw the need to "isolate Johnston from Memphis and Columbus." Still, some historians have made an overblown case that Beauregard literally "drew him [Johnston] out of the central Tennessee Valley into the Mississippi Valley area," some saying he even went so far as to give the senior general orders. These arguments, which contain little to no supporting evidence, are part of a larger contextual thesis that Beauregard was, little by little, taking over control of both Johnston and the western theater.[7]

Others saw the same need to cover the Mississippi Valley, including Secretary of War Benjamin, who argued that "no effort will be spared to save the line of communication between Memphis and Bristol, so vital to our defense." President Davis similarly wrote in early March, "I suppose the Tennessee or Mississippi River will be the object of the enemy's next campaign, and I trust you will be able to concentrate a force which will defeat either attempt." Likewise, Beauregard, as early as February 21, argued for the two wings to "again be brought together." Johnston thus put in motion, as early as February 18—just two days after Fort Donelson fell—a plan to move westward to unite with Beauregard's force moving southward along the Mississippi River from Columbus. It was a logical and obvious conclusion, although Johnston reported that "the movement was deemed too hazardous by the most experienced members of my staff." Mackall and Gilmer, in particular, viewed the plan as unwise. Certainly, the Federals could land troops anywhere they wanted along the Tennessee River, which paralleled the Memphis and Charleston Railroad much of the way through Alabama. But the attempt had to be made, yet another gamble that Johnston was willing to take to try to get on top of the situation. "The object warranted the risk," he explained, ordering on February 24, "this army will move on [the] 26th, by Decatur, for the valley of Mississippi." There was no "fog" that some historians argue Johnston fell into; he knew exactly what he was doing even in the depths of a terrible situation, firmly believing Buell, whose Federal forces were moving south to Nashville, would not act decisively enough to cut him off.[8]

Although a couple of days late in moving out, Johnston's force, augmented with Crittenden's troops, soon slogged southward. But it was hampered by muddy roads and washed-out bridges over which all the supplies of the army had to be transported. Tempers flared as troops raided nearby civilians. Johnston issued orders that such activity was to cease unless a division commander or he himself gave authorization for civilians' goods or wagons and teams to be "temporarily" utilized. General Hindman, with Johnston's approval, even had to declare martial law in places. The bulk of the supplies as well as Floyd's brigade moved to Chattanooga, while Johnston headed southward to Decatur, where the railroad crossed the Tennessee River. Johnston intended the column to make fifteen miles a day. By March 3, headquarters had moved as far as Shelbyville and then Fayetteville by March 5. The general reached Huntsville, Alabama, just a little east of Decatur, that same day. There, the picture was becoming a little clearer, Johnston informing Davis simply, "the bad roads and inclement weather, have made the march slow and laborious and delayed my movements." He added, "I have no fears of a movement through Tennessee on Chattanooga… [but] West Tennessee is menaced by heavy forces."[9]

Some faulted Johnston for not leaving the column under Hardee's command and moving on to consult with Beauregard and others at a central concentration point. But Johnston remained with his wing much like he did through the Fort Donelson affair, realizing the danger it faced and how many thought the effort was suicidal. In fact, he wrote to Davis how "even the most minute detail [was now] requiring my attention for its accomplishment." Consequently, the force slowly plodded along during the middle days of March, reaching the Alabama state line by March 11 and moving on to the railroad bridge at Decatur. More delay came in crossing the Tennessee River, however, as the bridge would have to be planked so that the troops and wheeled vehicles could use it. Johnston at first ordered planking between the rails only so both trains and troops could use the span. But the engineers soon found that the wagons and artillery wheels were too wide, so the planking had to go on the rails too. Rather than stop rail traffic, they simply decided to load everything on cars for transport across, which created a bottleneck and took even more time.[10]

Even while dealing with active army operations, Johnston also had to address personal issues. He still had not heard much from Eliza, although a friend wrote him in early March that he had seen her and the children in California recently and all were well. His son William was sick in Virginia and even wrote his father for advice on what he should do when his regiment was mustered out after a year of service. Certainly, Johnston had little time for giving advice while his department was falling down around him, but he was surely happy to hear his son state that the president had seen him in the hospital and "was very kind & almost fatherly to me." William himself was distraught at the news coming from the West, admitting to his uncle William Preston, "in addition to the loss to the Confederacy, I suffer on account of my father, to whom this must be considered a reverse."[11]

Most of Johnston's personal anguish indeed came from fallout from the twin rivers disaster. Early indications in Richmond had "satisfied [us] that the resistance was glorious," but then details of the tainted comedy began filtering in, painting a very different picture. Congress became involved and started asking pointed questions, which the Davis administration could not answer; a special committee then began an inquiry and contacted Johnston directly with questions that he had no time to answer. Benjamin also wrote him for information on the debacle at the twin rivers, which Johnston did not provide because of stubbornness as well as preoccupation in withdrawing his troops. The war secretary wrote, "Congress is very impatient for it," adding, "in [the] mean time send us your plans, condition, and purposes." Johnston merely sent his staff officer Major Munford to brief authorities in Richmond on the developments.[12]

By early March, President Davis was also wanting answers on the operations personally from Johnston. As more information became known, Davis railed against Floyd and Pillow, including why they did not escape with the entire army as well, why only Floyd's brigade got out, and "upon what authority or principle of action the senior generals abandoned responsibility, by transferring the command to a junior officer." He ordered both generals relieved of their duties, which touched off a long and tiresome crusade by both men to clear their names of what Floyd described as the "greatest injustice." Pillow even published his report of the fighting to, he said, "correct misapprehension and explain necessity which compelled capitulation at Donelson." Secretary Benjamin was not impressed, writing that Pillow "has committed the offense of publishing his report."[13]

Davis's main concern, however, was with his friend Johnston. The department commander had only made matters worse in the West by stubbornly refusing to discuss frankly the events; Johnston's son later related that "his [father's] whole life had been a training for this occasion." As it happened, there was a bill just out of Congress to appoint an overall Confederate commander, and Davis would no doubt have placed Johnston in the position had the general not been under such a cloud at that moment; instead, he simply vetoed the bill to buy time. In fact, the president had to write repeatedly to Johnston, finally sending him a very personal, at times blunt, letter on March 12 assuring him of his confidence but demanding answers. "We have suffered great anxiety because of recent events in Kentucky and Tennessee, and I have been not a little disturbed by the repetition of reflection upon yourself," Davis assured his old friend. Yet without a full report from Johnston, he had been forced to provide blindly "for you such defense as friendship prompted and many years' acquaintance justified, but I needed facts to rebut the wholesale assertions made against you to cover others and to condemn my administration." The president went on: "I respect the generosity which has kept you silent, but would impress upon you that the subject is not personal but public in its nature; that you and I might be content to suffer, but neither of us can willingly permit detriment to the country." Davis still had hope, however, that Johnston could "drive him [the enemy] from the soil as well of Tennessee as of Kentucky" and closed by declaring, "with confidence and regard of many years, I am, very truly, your friend."[14]

Although Johnston had many supporters, among them Brigadier General James R. Chalmers writing how his commander was "most foully and unjustly censured," certainly the theater commander had become the face of the disaster. And such blame ate at the basic tenets of honor that all humans feel: approval of peers. Part of that was certainly Johnston's own doing; his bluff to make the Federals think he was strong and assertive had worked on the Confederate home front just as well, and Southerners now wanted to know why the strong Johnston had suddenly lost all of Kentucky and most of Tennessee. Newspapers even started using the word "incompetent" to describe him. Davis mentioned that "the purpose of your army at Bowling Green [was] wholly misunderstood, and the absence of an effective force at Nashville ignored. You have been held responsible for the fall of Donelson and the capture of Nashville. 'Tis charged that no effort was made to save the stores at Nashville and that the panic of the people was caused by the army. Such representations, with the sad foreboding naturally belonging to them, have been painful to me and injurious to us both; but, worse than this, they have undermined public confidence and damaged our cause."[15]

Such vitriol was evident in newspapers and letters, such as in one Kentucky congressman's diatribe to Davis. On March 11, E. M. Bruce wrote:

> I have been with and near General Johnston's army ever since he was assigned command; have been his admirer and defender; still admire him as a man; but in my judgment his errors of omission, commission, and delay have been greater than any general who ever preceded him in any country; inexcusably and culpably lost us unnecessarily an army of 12,000 men, the Mississippi Valley, comparatively all provision stores, by one dash of the enemy. This is the almost unanimous judgment of officers, soldiers, and citizens. Neither is it mere opinion, but is demonstrable by dates, facts, figures, and disastrous results. He never can reorganize and re-enforce his army with any confidence. The people now look to you [Davis] as their deliverer, and imploringly call upon you to come to the field of our late disasters and assume command, as you promised in a speech to take the field whenever it should become necessary. That necessity is now upon us."[16]

Others pressured Davis to remove Johnston as well, or at the least to supersede him by taking command himself. Kentuckians in the Confederate Congress pushed for Breckinridge's promotion so he could take command, although Breckinridge quashed the idea. Representatives even debated Johnston's competence and the army's confidence in him. Most notably, all but three of the Tennessee delegation wrote to Davis and voiced their disapproval: "right or wrong, confidence is no longer felt in the military skill of Gen. A. S. Johnston." When the congressmen went to the president directly, stating, "we come in the name of the people to demand the removal of Sidney Johnston from command because he is no general," Davis would have none of it and retorted: "Gentlemen, I know Sidney Johnston well. If he is not a general, we had better give up the war, for we have no general."[17]

Unfortunately, there were doubters within the army as well. One soldier noted, "if Old Johnson had have acted as he should have done, we could not only sustained ourselves, but captured and killed all of the enemy, and rid Tenn of the foul invader." Frances Shoup later related that some were "nervous about going into battle with him in command." Braxton Bragg's wife, Elise, was filling her husband with partisan ideas as well, although there is no evidence the general ever displayed them himself: "I have lost the little confidence I ever had in the President's favorite S. Johnston." Hardee had to quell complaints about Johnston among his staff, correctly noting that anything they said "would be regarded as coming from me." He also squashed reports that the theater commander drank heavily, certainly just rumors. But at the same time, Hardee wrote privately that "nothing can save us except the presence of the President, who ought to come here, assume command, and call on people to rally to his standard." There is even evidence that Mackall himself had lost confidence in Johnston. Yet one of Davis's nephews later at Corinth informed the president, "from a few superior officers whom I hear talk, the only ground of complaint that can justly be laid at his [Johnston's] door, is that he is slow, not that he is unworthy of confidence."[18]

His supporters expressed their opinions as well, Colonel John A. Wharton of the Texas Rangers sending his promise, "I desire to fight under no other leadership, and that such is the feeling of the Texas Rangers." And perhaps most importantly, Johnston seemed to have never lost confidence in himself. Captain Gilmer admitted that "the general wears a very anxious face given our reverses: still he expresses confidence that better fortune awaits us." To his friends Johnston confided his opinions, telling one: "Ah! My dear friend, I cannot correspond with the people. What the people want is a battle and a victory. That is the best explanation I can make. I require no vindication. I trust that to the future." To Munford he confided: "You know I anticipated this. It will last no longer than is necessary for me to be in condition to fight a battle. As soon as I get men enough, I have no fear but that this clamor will become praise."[19]

Consequently, Johnston did not respond publicly, which certainly tore at the need to defend his reputation, the most basic need for honor. But in his lifelong pattern of going against commonly held notions of Southern manhood, especially defending one's own reputation, Johnston refused to respond to attacks or lay blame elsewhere. But he did write his friend Davis a long letter of explanation on March 18 from Decatur, delayed because of "the pressure of affairs and the necessity of getting my command across the Tennessee." (He left out an important word and sent a follow up three days later to rectify.) Johnston sent the response by hand with staff officer Thomas M. Jack, who reported to the Confederate White House and was ushered into Davis's office. The president warmly asked, "how is your general—my friend General Johnston?" Jack could only make a brief reply that he was well when another officer entered the room, soon to be introduced as General Robert E. Lee. While Lee took Jack into polite conversation, the president eagerly opened Johnston's letter and read it to himself, Jack keeping one eye on Lee and the present conversation while he "watched, at the same time, with eager interest, the countenance of the President, as he read the clear, strong, and frank expressions of his old friend and comrade." Jack related that "there was a softness then in his face; and, as his eye was raised from the paper, there seemed a tenderness in its expression, bordering on tears." When the staff officer returned to Tennessee, Johnston simply queried "in a playful way, . . . how did the president receive you?" Jack shot back, "as the aide-de-camp of his friend."[20]

In the letter, Johnston politely stated that he had had no time to gather information amid the chaos of the retreat from Nashville and had barely even had time to read, much less gather evidence against, Floyd's and Pillow's reports. But he had sent them on to Richmond with a staff officer, Colonel St. John R. Liddell. As to his silence, he denied generosity but explained, "I observed silence, as it seemed to me the best way to serve the cause and the country," even though he knew full well "it would lead to heavy censures [that] would fall upon me." Yet Johnston answered some of Davis questions now, such as that no reinforcements had been requested by Floyd or the other generals at Fort Donelson. "I was in hopes that such dispositions," he further explained, "would have been made as would have enabled the forces to defend the fort or withdraw without sacrificing the army." Later he admitted that he had anticipated the eventual fall of Fort Donelson but not the loss of the garrison.[21]

Johnston assured the president that he felt no disregard for him: "I have been governed from a deep personal sense of the friendship and confidence you have always shown me and from the conviction that they have not been withdrawn from me in adversity." He even prodded him to come west, which the president had mentioned as a possibility, even to take command of the army. "Were you to assume command, it would afford me the most unfeigned pleasure to help you to victory and the country to independence," Johnston wrote. "Were you to decline still your presence alone would be of inestimable advantage." He argued that a visit by Davis would "encourage my troops, inspire the people, and augment the army."[22]

Excuses or explanations aside, Johnston still seemed upbeat. He declared to Surgeon Yandell that "General Scott's 'Anaconda Scheme'" would not work because the South was too big to be "squeezed to death in that fashion." But there was still a crisis growing in front of him. When he wrote Davis on March 18 from Decatur, Johnston already had reports of Buell's army moving southward from Nashville as well as Grant's forces moving southward along the Tennessee River, "landing at Pittsburg." He had gambled and failed in his original defensive line, but now he was organizing another one, effectively assembling another hand in this game of high-stakes poker. And Johnston intended to win this next game. "The test of merit in my profession with the people is success," he concluded his letter to Davis, which the president actually used later in the war to persuade General Lee not to resign after Gettysburg. "It is a hard rule, but I think it right. If I join this corps to the forces of Beauregard (I confess a hazardous experiment), those who are now declaiming against me will be without an argument." Staff who read the letter were stuck by the "test of merit" sentence and advised against sending it, but Johnston retorted, "well, critically perhaps it is not correct, but, as the world goes, it is true, and I am going to let it stand." He similarly told Munford: "The clamor of to-day is converted into the praises of to-morrow by a simple success. All I require to rectify that is to get in position where I can fight a battle, and I think all will be well."[23]

All the while, Johnston had more tangible actions to take than letter writing. His next major question, after the nonissue of whether to move westward and join with Beauregard's forces, was where to meet. This, too, was largely a nonissue, although historians and especially Johnston's son (but only with noncontemporary sources and memoirs) made it one to emphasize Beauregard's apparent growing dominance over Johnston, even seemingly giving him orders ("send me Gen Bushrod Johnson immediately, also percussion caps to Ruggles at Corinth and to Lovell [at] New Orleans"). Johnston, for instance, informed Davis as early as March 7 that Beauregard "has been urging me to come on." Gilmer similarly wrote his wife that "we hear daily from Genl. Beauregard who is anxious for reinforcements from this army to assist him in the battle he expects to have with the enemy."

And Johnston did indeed defer to him, writing at one point, "where can the troops join you with most effect?" But the Creole was onsite in the area, not Johnston, and time was limited, a sick and flustered Beauregard fearing the Federals would "intercept" Johnston's movement westward. The confusion of writing in cipher also complicated matters to the point that nerves were frayed and fears were blown out of proportion.[24]

Certainly, as early as March 2 Beauregard wrote Johnston, "I think you ought to hurry up your troops to Corinth by RR as soon as practicable, for here or thereabouts will soon be fought the great battle of this controversy." Although at one point Johnston mentioned Bolivar on the Hatchie River, where there was ample defensive ground and a railroad for supply that was "further from [the] enemy's base," there was indeed a growing consensus that Corinth, because of the railroads, was the obvious place to concentrate. The Confederate commander at the town from February 18 onward, Brigadier General Daniel Ruggles just up from New Orleans, loudly proclaimed the importance of the area surrounding the rail-line crossroads. "If General Johnston does not cover the Tennessee River the enemy will get into possession of the Memphis and Charleston Railroad, with open communication to Mobile, Memphis, and New Orleans," he argued to Polk. To Johnston himself he asserted that "if the enemy reaches the Charleston and Memphis Railroad he can move on Mobile, Memphis, and New Orleans." Beauregard also counseled that "the Memphis and Charleston Road, so important on account of its extension through Eastern Tennessee and Virginia, must be properly guarded." Continual reports of Union gunboats patrolling the Tennessee River only intensified the concern.[25]

General Lovell at New Orleans also recommended Corinth as the concentration point as early as February 12, as troops under Ruggles moved northward. These reinforcements had been ordered to Columbus, and Lovell was not at all happy about losing them. "I can illy afford to spare these troops," he wrote, but admitted that "the necessities of the case, however, seem to require that these troops should be sent from here." But if they were to leave, he wanted them to go to where they could make a difference and recommended to Johnston Corinth, "as at that point it would be available for any emergency likely to arise." He explained that the Mississippi town was "an important strategical point, as it is not only connected by rail with all the places above indicated, but is only a day's march from the Tennessee River." Beauregard recommended Corinth as the army's concentration point as early as March 2, and Johnston concurred on the fifth, although he began ordering reinforcing troops there as early as February 12.[26]

The largest factor determining where to meet, however, was the enemy's movements. By the first of March, when Union gunboats assailed a few Louisiana defenders at Pittsburg Landing, just twenty-two miles from Corinth, even landing troops, attention swiftly began to coalesce in that area. Then news came of the Federal surge southward along the river, with a concentration first taking place at Savannah in early March and then a movement on up the river into Mississippi and westward toward Purdy. Johnston thought ahead and by March 11 argued, "it is supposed Buell will concentrate [his] main force there to co-operate with Grant." Johnston and others had cavalry out watching the enemy's movements, especially those of Buell, just as the Federals were keeping track of his own march and trying their best to "separate Johnston from Memphis." Orders also went out from various Confederate commands to "keep a close observation on the river."[27]

The biggest scare came in mid-March, when Union troops actually came ashore at Crump's and Pittsburg Landings, intent on wrecking the two main railroads to the west and south. Breaks on either, of course, would have hindered concentrating Confederate troops, Beauregard's wing still strung out north of Jackson and Johnston's still as far out as Alabama. The main threat was General Sherman's arrival at Tyler's Landing near Yellow Creek in Mississippi, but heavy rains doomed that operation and flooded the river. He turned back without breaking the Memphis and Charleston Railroad and moved northward to the first landing still above water, which was Pittsburg. There, the Union army went into camp just twenty-two miles from Corinth and the railroads.[28]

Johnston and Beauregard kept a firm eye on these movements, thankful for the weather system moving through, although it also terribly devastated Confederate attempts to hurry troops westward. Still, Beauregard called on his commander for help in defending the railroad from Corinth to Iuka and beyond, Johnston sending as many troops as he could to the area. But it was a struggle. "Owing to the condition of the roads and the water," Crittenden wrote from Decatur on March 15 amid the deluge, "I am unable to move my command to-day." Hindman at Courtland similarly wrote that his wheeled vehicles were stuck, and it would probably be two weeks before the roads would dry out. The infantry could still march slowly, but the wagons and artillery needed to be moved by rail. Johnston informed Davis that he was hurrying troops as best he could to fulfill Beauregard's request for support "as he expected battle." But, he added, "the rains have been excessive and yet continue."[29]

As the rains moved out and the Federals went into camp at Pittsburg Landing, Johnston's force slowly slogged westward. "Hurry the forces forward," he ordered Hardee on March 17, although Colonel Bowen, commanding a brigade, had recently described how "the road between here and Decatur is reported utterly impassable." Johnston similarly intoned to Hindman to move "as fast as possible." And he, too, planned to move. "I am glad to hear General Johnston is joining us," Bragg wrote from Bethel Station, Tennessee, on March 16. The theater commander had moved to Decatur by March 17 and made plans to burn the railroad bridge at Florence if necessary to keep the enemy off his flank (he also wanted excess cotton burned to keep it from falling into enemy hands). As he shifted westward, Johnston continually queried the commanders near Corinth about enemy movements and positions. To Bragg's summons to hurry, he replied on the eighteenth, "now moving forward as fast as possible. . . . Ninety-three miles to Corinth." By then, Corinth had certainly coalesced as the logical place to concentrate the high command, if not the army. Bragg, who arrived there by March 19 and expected battle "at any moment," certainly thought so, arguing to Beauregard, "this position is unquestionably the strategic point for this section of country." Johnston's brother-in-law Colonel Preston also similarly advised that "a battle seems not far distant. The chances are for one, bloody and decisive, between Corinth and Jackson, toward Bolivar, covering Memphis."[30]

Of course, concentration meant bringing two full generals into the same army, although Johnston was clearly senior and the commander of the department. Beauregard acknowledged this and even asked, "hence I desire, as far as practicable, specific instructions as to the future movements of the army." Yet Johnston had always had trouble asserting his authority to peers, and as he had with Polk, for example, so he would with Beauregard, the hero of Fort Sumter and Manassas. This was especially the case when the sick Louisianan finally took command of his wing on March 5, declaring, "our mothers and wives, our sisters and children, expect us to do our duty even to the sacrifice of our lives."[31]

In fact, Beauregard was already devising his own schemes as if in independent command, including how the Confederates should adopt a "defensive, active" posture and naming his wing the "Army of the Mississippi."

Johnston allowed the Creole to command for now, he not being on site yet and not even knowing if Beauregard had recovered from his bout of illness; he even was hesitant to issue Polk orders in case "you [Beauregard] have assumed command, and our orders conflict." For his part, Beauregard was immensely worried about the organization of Polk's troops and issued elaborate directives for their order of battle, begging for more general officers to lead the larger units to be created. Secretary of War Benjamin responded that there were only so many generals available, and Joe Johnston, facing what would become onslaughts in both the Shenandoah Valley as well as on the Virginia Peninsula, was "reluctant to allow any of his officers to be withdrawn from his command." Beauregard also called on the governors of Tennessee, Alabama, Mississippi, and Louisiana to send thousands of troops each to join with his force and Van Dorn's army, which he recommended bringing over from Arkansas, to march northward, retake the twin rivers, "assail Cairo, and threaten, if not indeed take, Saint Louis itself." (In a quandary, Richmond now consented to accepting even twelve-month troops provided they were armed—some regiments at this point were armed only with lances). Beauregard emphasized the "dangers accumulating day by day" and warned of the "immediate loss to the Confederate States of the Mississippi River and Valley." To Van Dorn he penned a quick note: "what say you to this brilliant programme[?]" Historian Charles Roland has described these actions as "a breathtakingly broad interpretation of Johnston's statement that he was to act independently."[32]

But Beauregard was not even at Corinth himself at that time and would not move permanently there until late March. There was also no discussion of Johnston's troops actually moving into the Mississippi town either. Beauregard and others frequently counseled their commanding general to leave his column strung out along the Memphis and Charleston Railroad around Burnsville and Iuka, Mississippi, to cover the railroad where it was nearest to the river. In fact, Bragg sent a message on March 20 that some of Johnston's troops had arrived at Corinth, but "the rest of your forces had better concentrate near Burnsville, as indicated by General Beauregard." Still, Corinth itself was the logical place to meet for most of the Confederate forces, strung out as they were from Corinth eastward to Tuscumbia and northward to Union City , and all knew the pressure of time they were under. Polk wrote President Davis directly on March 11, "we hope to concentrate in time to meet him [Grant and his Union army]." Johnston's column thus moved on, albeit slowly, aided by transportation sent out from Corinth to help the men on their way. Such aid included some 160 cars and engines from the Mississippi Central Railroad, diverted over to the Memphis and Charleston at Johnston's request.[33]

Meanwhile, the now-awake Confederate government was doing all it could to help as well. Secretary Benjamin wrote, "if I do not bend every energy to the aid of Beauregard and Sidney Johnston the enemy must, with his overwhelming numbers, pierce our lines into the Lower Mississippi Valley." He described this possibility, with McClellan bearing down on Richmond at the same time, as "our hour of peril." Benjamin did everything he could, finding more troops and sending all the arms he could scrape up, including some seven thousand sent to Corinth in late March.[34]

The generals there were active as well, a more and more assertive Beauregard calling on the governors himself for more troops and even calling on plantation owners to provide their brass bells to be melted and cast into cannon; historian Thomas Connelly has argued that this was "impractical but was excellent propaganda." He and Johnston thought along the same lines in another effort, as Beauregard had already called for Van Dorn, fresh off his defeat at Pea Ridge in early March, to join him in his movement northward. Van Dorn had tried to make a showing in Missouri even during the twin rivers crisis, writing Sterling Price, "this seems to me the movement best calculated to win us Missouri and relieve General Johnston, who is heavily threatened in Kentucky." Beauregard could only request, but Johnston had the authority to order Van Dorn eastward, which he did. Some historians, including biographer Roland, have criticized Johnston for doing this too late; he told Van Dorn only on March 23, "move your command to Memphis by the route in your judgement the best and most expeditious." Van Dorn even came to Corinth for consultations, bringing Johnston's old Texas neighbor Dabney Maury with him.[35]

By that point, Johnston had reached Corinth as well, arriving on March 23. He quickly set up quarters at the William Inge house downtown, close to other generals' quarters, though he kept an office in the nearby Tishomingo Hotel at the crossing of the vital railroads he was so desperate to defend. His hostess in Corinth was Augusta Inge, wife of Major William Inge, who was in service in Virginia but was at that time home on leave. Inge himself volunteered to serve on Mississippi general Charles Clark's staff in the coming operations.[36]

Johnston informed Davis that he was at Corinth and immediately went into conference with Bragg, Polk, and Beauregard, who had come down from Jackson to meet him. He also advised the president that he had called Van Dorn eastward because of the obvious threat building on his front, with Grant at Pittsburg Landing and Buell moving to join him. But not all of Johnston's troops, nor Hardee himself, had arrived as yet. Although some had made it into town by then, the rest were still strung out along the railroad as far east as Tuscumbia.[37]

Much remained to be done even after the high-command concentration was perfected. Paramount on the list, with two full generals on site, was a confirmation of who was in command. Gilmer, his faith in Johnston shaken after Fort Donelson, soon after wrote his wife: "We have here now Genls. A. S. Johnston and Beauregard—Maj. Genls. Bragg and Polk and Hardee—and Brigadier Genls. too numerous to name. Among them all, I fear there is not a Napoleon." Obviously, Johnston was senior, but he was under a cloud, and Beauregard was the hero of Fort Sumter and Manassas. Perhaps surprisingly, and certainly against the manhood code of the day, the departmental commander offered to let Beauregard control the army in battle while he remained overall strategic commander. The Creole refused on the grounds of his health but later wrote that it was "one of the most affecting scenes of my life." Johnston proclaimed, "Well, be it so, General! We two together will do our best to secure success." Whether he fully intended to give up tactical control is arguable, Johnston later telling Munford, who opposed the plan, "I think it but right to make the offer." But then he added, "I will be present at the battle, and will see that nothing goes wrong." Perhaps he also knew Beauregard's health would not allow him to take command. Others also remonstrated loudly against the offer when it began to circulate in rumors among the camps. Kentucky Confederate governor George W. Johnson wrote to Johnston: "It is rumored here that you intend to yield to the senseless clamors of fools and pretenders, and to give up the command of the army at the very crisis of our fate. This, if done, will be fatal to our cause." In the end, Johnston retained full command, but his offer of tactical control only muddied the waters even more, making Beauregard that much more assertive in his second-in-command position. Dire results would follow.[38]

Johnston also received a kind note from another friend, written the same day as George Johnson's.

No one has sympathized with you in the troubles with which you are surrounded more sincerely than myself. I have watched your every movement, and know the difficulties with which you have had to contend. I hope your cares will be diminished, if not removed, when your junction with the other lines of your army has been completed, which must be accomplished by this time. I need not urge you, when your army is united, to deal a blow at the enemy in your front, if possible, before his rear gets up from Nashville. You have him divided, and keep him so, if you can. Wishing you, my dear general, every success and happiness, with my earnest prayers for the safety of your whole army, and that victory may attend your movements, I remain, truly and sincerely your friend.

It was from his old lieutenant colonel in the 2nd U.S. Cavalry, Robert E. Lee.[39]

More tangible efforts also took place in the first few days after Johnston's arrival at Corinth. One was establishing a defense for the town, which Bragg had already started in the form of a line of fortifications that Johnston approved. Another major need was combining the various groups together into a whole. Bragg described the gathering army as "an heterogeneous mass, in which there was more enthusiasm than discipline, more capacity than knowledge, and more valor than instruction." But the army was never fully concentrated until the eve of battle; although the high command eventually gathered at Corinth, the army never fully did. By the end of March, much of Johnston's force was still scattered along the Memphis and Charleston Railroad east of Corinth, with Breckinridge at Burnsville and Crittenden and other brigades as far away as Iuka. Likewise, some of Polk's troops, an entire division under Major General Frank Cheatham, were still as far north along the Mobile and Ohio as Bethel Station, with guards eastward to Purdy to watch the Federals at Crump's Landing and to shield that railroad. Out in front of Johnston's army, on the road to Pittsburg Landing, were two brigades, one under Colonel Randal Gibson at Monterey and another under Brigadier General Chalmers even farther forward. Still, the bulk of the army was now concentrated around Corinth itself.[40]

Efforts to consolidate these units into a coherent whole went forward, largely at the instigation of Beauregard, who thrived on organization, orders of battle, and the minutia of command and control. General orders went out on March 29 creating the organization of the army, which retained the name

Army of the Mississippi, with Johnston in command and Beauregard second to him. Three corps and a reserve were established—effectively four corps. The senior major general, Polk, commanded the First Corps, made up primarily of the troops from Columbus with division and brigade commanders who had mostly been with the bishop all along: Charles Clark, A. P. Stewart, and Cheatham among others. Bragg, next senior in line, took the Second Corps. This was the largest of the three and had two divisions, one under Ruggles mostly made up of troops he had brought northward from New Orleans and the other under Brigadier General Jones Withers, consisting mainly of Bragg's original troops from Pensacola and Mobile. Hardee, being the junior of the three commanders, took the Third Corps, smallest of the three and made up of brigades commanded by his officers from Bowling Green, including Brigadier Generals Hindman, Patrick Cleburne, and Sterling A. M. Wood. The Reserve Corps, under Crittenden, was mostly the forces brought over from East Tennessee. In addition to being Second Corps commander, Bragg was also named chief of staff for the army, and he and the other commanders started making their lists of staff and corps departmental heads. It was a quick coalescing to be sure and logical by taking into consideration the chains of command and the histories of the various corps.[41]

More than just the larger army organization was on Johnston's mind, however, as he and Beauregard had numerous details with which to deal. Supply was critical, with depots established farther south, and martial law instituted at Jackson and Grenada, Mississippi. Johnston also worried over the bridge at Florence, Alabama, telling the commander there to destroy it if the Union gunboats reportedly on the Tennessee came too close. A tougher command problem was what to do with Crittenden, who was under suspicion for drunkenness. Knowing he was nearing battle, Johnston recognized this as a definite problem that needed to be rectified one way or the other. He sent Hardee to Iuka to investigate the situation. Hardee reported on April 1 that, after investigating both Crittenden and Brigadier General William H. Carroll, he had "found sufficient evidence against them to require their arrest." Before returning, he had Crittenden arrested for drunkenness and Carroll for "drunkenness, incompetency, and neglect of his command." Hardee also reported "a most wretched state of discipline and instruction" with the troops under their command. Johnston had no other choice but to promote Breckinridge, the next-ranking commander and the only other general officer in the Reserve, to command that corps.[42]

The biggest decision, of course, was what to do about the growing Federal menace along the Tennessee River. Johnston and company kept cavalry out watching enemy movements, and they knew Grant was at Pittsburg Landing with an army of tens of thousands, although one staff officer arrived at a figure of four divisions and some twenty-five thousand men. The Confederates also knew Buell was on the way to join Grant with a like number of troops. Given their shortage in everything from men to arms to ammunition, Johnston and Beauregard, who moved down to Corinth from Jackson on March 26, realized the top priority was keeping the two large Federal forces apart and dealing with them one at a time. This was a common concept in military theory, but it was also just plain common sense. In addition to General Lee's advice, President Davis, as early as March 26, advised, "if you can meet the division of the enemy moving from the Tennessee before it can make a junction with that advancing from Nashville the future will be brighter." Although he assured Johnston, "my confidence in you has never wavered, and I hope the public will soon give me credit for judgment rather than continue to arraign me for obstinacy," Davis added, "it would be worse than useless to point out to you how much depends upon you." He then ended warmly, "may God bless you, is the sincere prayer of your friend."[43]

Slowly but surely, the obvious need for a preemptive attack on Grant's forces at Pittsburg Landing came into focus, although it had always been in Johnston's mind. It was perhaps the only chance the Confederates had once they were as concentrated as they could possibly be and while the Federals were still separated. It was, in fact, quite possibly the last best chance at major success in the West. It was not necessarily Johnston's or Beauregard's idea but more the result of common sense. Even if Van Dorn's forces arrived in the near future, the whole would be hard pressed to deal with the combined armies of Grant and Buell. Time was now of the essence. As early as April 1, in fact, Beauregard ordered that scouts watching the enemy should be careful: "it would be well not to awaken the enemy's suspicions to any intention on our part of advancing in that direction."[44]

Over the course of the first days in April, matters congealed so well that the army was put on alert to move to the attack. Troops, one order from Johnston read on April 1, "will be placed in readiness for a field movement and to meet the enemy within twenty-four hours." Indications were that Grant was active at Pittsburg and that Buell was nearing, making the time short in which to do anything against the separated Union armies. But was the Army of the Mississippi ready for such a fight? Johnston was about to launch the biggest gamble of his career, an attack with a green and inexperienced army on a veteran enemy army on its own ground. It was definitely a long shot and very risky, Johnston remarking that he had to roll "the 'iron dice' of battle." But while a gamble, it was in reality the only option available for the Confederates to have anything close to parity against their enemy. Johnston's numbers were not apt to rise any time soon, as Van Dorn was still weeks away from arriving with only a few thousand troops at that, while mere days or even hours would see Buell appear with many more thousands of Union troops to roughly double Grant's numbers. This was a gamble, but it was logical—a calculated risk that had to be taken.[45]

But then the schedule was pushed up even more. On the night of April 2, word came from Cheatham at Bethel that the Federals at Crump's Landing were on the march, possibly foreshadowing a larger movement. It was actually a reactionary effort against Cheatham's own probes, but the Tennessean took it as the start of a grand Union offensive. With that word indicating a separation of Grant's forces and the continually approaching Buell, the Confederate high command went into action.[46]

The decision was made that very night. When word from Cheatham came to Polk, he went to Beauregard, who sent a message to Johnston stating, "now is the moment to advance, and strike the enemy at Pittsburg Landing." The principal officers congregated at Bragg's headquarters, where they woke the chief of staff, who participated in his nightshirt. The plan was quickly decided to march out of Corinth early the next morning, April 3, and move the twenty or so miles northeastward to attack Grant at Pittsburg Landing on the fifth. Johnston sent out an army-wide proclamation that morning: "Soldiers of the Army of the Mississippi: I have put you in motion to offer battle to the invaders of your country. . . . Remember the precious stakes involved." He acknowledged the gamble being taken, writing of "all worth living or dying for," and assured them that "with such incentives to brave deeds and with the trust that God is with us, your general will lead you confidently to the combat, assured of success." This proclamation was to be read at the head of every regiment.[47]

But mass confusion actually resulted in the ensuing hours. First verbal orders and then written ones went out, some before midnight and some afterward, causing confusion about terms like "early to-morrow morning." One such order went out late on April 2 but only arrived hours later in some camps on the morning of April 3: "the commander of the forces directs that you hold your command in hand ready to advance upon the enemy in the morning by 6 A.M." There was also confusion among the high command about what type of attack would take place, with Beauregard continuing to take liberties concerning his authority with the army. Johnston sent a quick note to President Davis on April 3 that the attack was going forward, citing Buell's approach as the main reason for the quick advance. He explained that after a concentration of all units from Corinth, Bethel, and Burnsville on the road to Pittsburg, "Confederate forces, 40,000, ordered forward to offer battle near Pittsburg." He then mentioned the deployment he had in mind: "Polk, left; Hardee, center; Bragg, right wing; Breckinridge, reserve." Johnston concluded by saying, "hope engagement [occurs] before Buell can form junction."[48]

Beauregard had other ideas, however. He gathered slips of paper and notes, sometimes even hand-drawn maps on tabletops. The task of putting this all together in the form of written orders fell to the army's new assistant adjutant general, Colonel Thomas Jordan, who had held the same position on Beauregard's staff. He replaced Colonel Mackall, who had been appointed a brigadier general in early March and sent to command at Island No. 10. Jordan now assembled these notes into the famed Special Orders No. 8, sometimes mentioned as being patterned after Napoleon's order of battle at Waterloo. Johnston, who despised minutia and paperwork, whether as the Texas secretary of war or as army commander, had unwisely left it to Beauregard to draft the full orders for the advance, once again not properly overseeing a peer-level subordinate even when in the same town. Instead of the linear formation with a general reserve Johnston had described to Davis, Beauregard and Jordan produced a column of corps in which Hardee held the first line; Bragg, some thousand yards back, manned a second line; and Polk and Breckinridge followed in columns even farther to the rear. It was very different than what Johnston had intended, and historians have wrangled for decades over the reasoning for the disparity. There is little evidence to know what happened, whether Johnston ordered a change or if Beauregard simply did it on his own initiative. There is likewise little evidence whether Johnston approved of Beauregard's change or just had to go along with it due to time constraints. Beauregard himself stated a year later that "the movement ending in the battle of Shiloh was suggested by me. I drew up the plan and order of battle, which I read and explained on the 4th of April to Generals Johnston and Bragg, and these were accepted without the change of one word." In the rush, there is the possibility that Johnston never mentioned the tactical deployment he had in mind, and Beauregard simply devised his own, which Johnston accepted. We do know that the Confederate forces went into action according to Beauregard's orders, however, and the idea that Johnston acquiesced was consistent with his pattern of behavior of not standing up to friends or equals. Still, Johnston evidently had some say in the matter, he issuing the same day additional orders that "in the approaching battle every effort should be made to turn the left flank of the enemy so as to cut off his line of retreat to the Tennessee River and throw him back on Owl Creek, where he will be obliged to surrender." There is the distinct possibility that once Johnston accepted Beauregard's plan due to a lack of time to change it, he issued the left-flank order to clean up the plan and bring it more in line with his original thoughts, which had placed his largest corps (Bragg's) on the army's right flank in order to turn that critical Union left.[49]

Johnston would have been much better served by taking firm control of the operation (and Beauregard), because Beauregard had produced an extremely complicated process to even get to the battlefield, much less to attack the enemy army. The orders called for two corps, Hardee's and Polk's, to move along the westward-running Ridge Road while the other two, Bragg's and Breckinridge's, would move along the main road that ran through Monterey, Tennessee. Splitting the corps on different roads was not a bad idea certainly, given the state of the pathways and the greenness of the troops. But to meld the four corps together prior to the assault, Beauregard called for a complicated maneuver in which they would weave together while on the march near a ridge called Mickey's, a mere three or four miles southwest of the Union camps. Hardee was to go forward and deploy, whereupon Bragg was to take the road next before Polk moved forward, with Breckinridge following in rear. Guides selected from locally raised companies were detailed to help in the complicated maneuvers.[50]

Because of their general confusion and the complex methodology of the orders, the troops began their moves late, not until the afternoon of April 3. Johnston himself watched some of the soldiers file by his quarters; flags were given to those units without any. Not surprisingly, the march quickly turned into a fiasco. It was simply more than the inexperienced troops, and more importantly their inexperienced officers, could perform. Some units did not go along, being simply too unfit for duty, and were left at Corinth. While

Hardee, Polk, and Bragg were all on hand, they had enormous problems keeping their columns moving and in correct position. Making the situation even worse was a severe weather system moving through the area on April 4 and 5, bringing torrents of rain that confused the troops and muddied the roads into seemingly bottomless mud pits. Thus, the moving army lurched to an almost standstill as April 4 became April 5, the day of the proposed attack. Hardee was behind schedule but managed to get into his assigned position by midmorning, from which he could still have launched the assault, if only a few hours later than originally planned. But he could not advance without support, and that is where the major problems emerged, as Bragg's and Polk's columns slogged along the quagmires churned up by Hardee's leading troops. And the more rain that fell, the muddier the roads became.[51]

Making matters even worse were impromptu changes in the marching plan, forced by nature and circumstances. The army was terribly fractured and had to be amalgamated together. Part of the advance forces near Monterey had been alerted to be ready, but others were surprised on the fourth to find their army marching forward. Likewise, Cheatham's arriving division from Bethel had to be incorporated into the First Corps before moving forward, so Polk had to halt and let Bragg's entire corps move on ahead of him. Breckinridge's advance in the rear was less problematic, although he faced the longest route of march, starting from Burnsville, and increasingly had to contend, the closer he came to Mickey's, with the roads churned up by the other commands. As would be expected, the intricate timetable of the plan went off track, with Bragg pushing one of his divisions through Mickey's on the morning of April 5 while Polk waited. Bragg had changed the route of his other division, so when no more troops appeared, Polk concluded that the entire Second Corps was through the junction, which it was not. The bishop moved ahead, only to find out that Bragg's other division was now behind him. It was a perfect storm of chaos, and Polk's men had to move to the side of the road to let Bragg's division pass. Mix in hundreds of artillery pieces and wagons accompanying the foot soldiers, and it was a recipe for disaster. The army, even by dark on April 5, was not anywhere near the position it was supposed to hold at daylight that morning.[52]

Another part of the problem was the lack of the top commanders on the field to direct the march. Neither Beauregard nor Johnston left Corinth until the morning of April 4, indicating, in opposition to what some historians have claimed, that the attack was scheduled to begin on April 5, not the

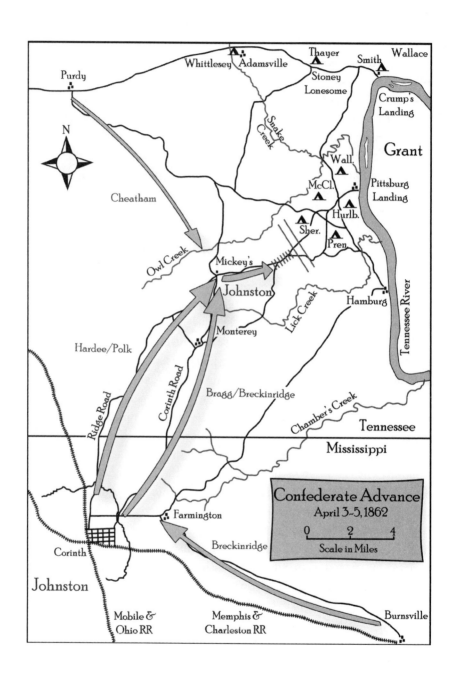

Purdy

Whittlesey Adamsville Thayer Smith Wallace
Stoney Lonesome
Crump's Landing

Snake Creek

N

Grant

Cheatham

Wall.
McCl.
Pittsburg Landing
Hurlb.
Sher.
Pren.

Owl Creek

Mickey's
Johnston

Hamburg

Lick Creek

Monterey

Hardee/Polk

Tennessee River

Corinth Road

Ridge Road

Bragg/Breckinridge

Chamber's Creek

Tennessee

Mississippi

Confederate Advance
April 3-5, 1862

0   2   4
Scale in Miles

Farmington

Corinth

Johnston

Breckinridge

Burnsville

Mobile &
Ohio RR

Memphis &
Charleston RR

day before. Certainly, there would be no attack launched without the army commanders on the ground. Most convincingly, Polk wrote, "it was resolved by our commander-in-chief (General Johnston) to attack the enemy in his position on the Tennessee River, if possible, at daybreak on April 5." Beauregard should have been at the head of the columns to direct traffic considering his complicated plan, but he was sick at the time and traveled in an ambulance, leaving Corinth after Johnston and catching up with him at Monterey. In fact, he later related, "I only went to the battle at the urgent request of General Johnston, for I was so unwell at the time."[53]

Johnston also moved forward amid the chaos. He left his headquarters at the Inge house in downtown Corinth on the morning of April 4, stopping at the doorway on his way out. Munford later described this scene: "I will ever remember his pause on the door-step, lost in thought, and how, looking up, he muttered, half aloud, 'Yes, I believe I have overlooked nothing.'" Mrs. Inge had prepared him as best she could, slipping two sandwiches and a piece of cake into his coat pocket before his departure. He and Beauregard slept at Monterey that night, still confident of an attack the next morning. In fact, Johnston was up early the next morning and hurried Polk forward to aid in the still-planned attack. But as the wee hours of the morning unfolded, Johnston began to experience the daunting circumstances his troops had faced amid the torrents of rain.[54]

Johnston nevertheless moved northward, accompanied by the members of his staff who he had grown accustomed to since arriving in Tennessee. Captains H. P. Brewster and Nathaniel Wickliffe were still with him, as were Lieutenant George Baylor and Thomas Jack. Majors Dudley M. Hayden, Munford, and Calhoun Benham and quartermasters Major Albert J. Smith and Captain W. L. Wickham all saw to the army's needs. Captain Theodore O'Hara (of "The Bivouac of the Dead" fame) had joined as well as acting inspector general, and, of course, Johnston's brother-in-law Colonel Preston was there too. Governor Harris, now with no capital and pitifully little parts of his state left under his control, had made good on his promise to go to the army with his troops and now served as a volunteer aide. The army's medical director, Dr. David W. Yandell, was also with Johnston personally. The general told Yandell to stay with him and turn over field command of the army's medical staff to another surgeon. "I want you to see a battle—a big battle," he told the doctor, adding, "and then, besides, I want you with me, for some of us will be hurt." Also along was his former slave Randolph, who had been with Johnston the entire time. The night before at Monterey, Johnston briefed his staff on the lay of the land so they would be well prepared for action the next day.[55]

Hoping for the battle to begin that morning, Johnston rode forward before daylight on April 5 toward the junction at Mickey's. There he found total chaos amid the confusion of Bragg's and Polk's corps. Beauregard had joined him by this time and also viewed the utter chaos there. Bragg had informed Johnston the day before that "bad roads, inefficient transportation badly managed, and the usual delay of a first move of new troops have caused the delay." He later admitted, "but few regiments of my command had ever made a day's march." The heavy rains did not help matters, but Johnston pushed on ahead to the rear of Hardee's line, which was soon assembled in its prearranged place. There, he waited for the Second Corps to take position so he could start the assault. Bragg's right division soon arrived and went into line behind Hardee, but his left division was nowhere to be seen. Minutes and then hours passed. Staff officer Munford remembered that, as the hours moved on, "General Johnston began to show signs of impatience." Finally in the early afternoon, tired of waiting, the situation was so chaotic that the normally even-tempered Johnston lost his cool, barking, "This is perfectly puerile! This is not war!" He rode rearward to find out what was wrong and at Mickey's set to work sorting out the various corps. But this took time, and he agonizingly watched as the hours ticked by on the fifth, the very day he was supposed to be fighting the great battle for the Mississippi Valley. Johnston also realized that Buell was inching closer and closer throughout the day, but there was just no way he could attack Grant with an army in such confusion. With matters finally sorted out, Johnston and Beauregard both again moved forward as far as the Bark Road entrance to the Corinth Road, just a half mile behind Hardee's front line. There, they mulled over the developments and decided to postpone the attack. Fortunately, by the time the sun began to sink in the clearing skies, the mess was almost completely sorted out. Delayed a day, the assault would take place the next morning.[56]

Johnston and his staff made their camp that afternoon just off the main road toward the rear of the army, between the bivouacking troops of Polk's and Breckinridge's corps. But Johnston wanted to see more of his army and again went forward that evening to make sure all was in hand and ready for the advance the next morning. As he rode along the lines, the men cheered him, but he quieted them and simply told them to "look along your guns, and fire low." One brigade commander wrote that, as Johnston rode by, "he looked like a hero of the antique type, and his very appearance on the field was a tower of more than kingly strength."[57]

But additional trouble arose as Johnston approached Beauregard's headquarters, set up a few thousand yards forward on a tall ridge where the Bark Road joined the main Corinth Road, just to the rear of Bragg's corps line. He rode up to a group of officers discussing the next day's attack, Beauregard evidently explaining the plan to them "on the ground." Johnston, in Polk's words, stepped up and "asked what was the matter." The discussion grew fervent as the general officers debated their options. Beauregard, though ill, was vehemently counseling a withdrawal, saying that the march took so long and the approach was so haphazard and loud that the enemy was bound to be alerted to their presence. Indeed, Hardee's advance had even contacted probing Federals on April 3 and then met others more forcefully the next day, resulting in a small skirmish and even firing of cannon. Beauregard envisioned a nightmarish situation in which the enemy would be "intrenched to the eyes" as the Confederates charged forward. Indications only a day or two old from prisoners captured by the army's advance elements suggested that there were no fortifications, but the Creole argued that they could not be sure since fortifications could go up in only a matter of hours. Hardee was not present, being at the front with his most-forward troops, but Bragg seemed to agree with Beauregard. Breckinridge did not say much. He was not even a military man but merely a politician in uniform, having just assumed his current command position three or four days earlier. He simply responded that his provisions were adequate, bracing Johnston even more. Polk was for continuing the attack, a stance Johnston argued long and forcibly for at this impromptu council of war. He exclaimed that "this [withdrawal] would never do, and proceeded to assign reasons for that opinion."[58]

It was at this point that Johnston chose to finally break with his peer Beauregard, who had been almost running things for a while now. Johnston had time and again allowed his subordinates to run amok, but this was where it ended. Later that night he confided to Dr. Yandell: "Beauregard is sick . . . I don't think much of the opinions of a sick man in matters that require action." Johnston argued that withdrawing would be worse than even a defeat and took his stand in what biographer Charles Roland has described as a Clausewitzian moment when a commander had to make a firm decision on the eve of battle. Johnston did so. Historian Thomas Connelly has called it "a rare moment of decision" for Johnston before proceeding to disparage that decision. Nevertheless, Johnston was firm. "Gentlemen, we shall attack at daylight to-morrow," he barked, disbanding the meeting "a little abruptly," Munford admitted. As he walked away, Johnston muttered to a staff officer, "I would fight them if they were a million," not only using hyperbole but also indicating the great gamble that he knew he was ordering. He had made similar comments to others, including Governor Harris. Knowing the lay of the land, he added, "they can present no greater front between these two creeks than we can, and the more men they crowd in there the worse we can make it for them." Another meeting of the high command that evening at Johnston's headquarters resulted in the same determination.[59]

Yet behind the bold show, there was a sense of uneasiness for the meek Johnston, perhaps even second-guessing, illustrating his apprehension of bucking a peer like Beauregard. Munford explained that "despite the exterior calm, I saw that he was deeply moved." Johnston walked over to him and admitted: "I want to tell you something which I desire remembered. I shall tell nobody but you and Preston . . . they wish me to withdraw the army without a battle; what is your opinion?" Munford backed him wholly, and Johnston's spirits seemed to revive some, he adding, "I have ordered a battle for to-morrow at daylight, and I intend to 'hammer 'em'!" Former secretary of the interior Jacob Thompson, a member of Beauregard's staff, similarly related that "General Johnston took my arm, and remarked, 'I perceive that General Beauregard is averse to bringing on the attack on the enemy in the morning. . . . Don't you think it is better to fight, and run the chances of defeat rather that retreat? . . . [A]n order to retreat . . . I fear . . . would have the same effect as a defeat.'" Johnston further argued: "Don't you think we had better try and fight the two armies in detail? The junction is not yet made, and it is probable will not be made to-morrow." And while Johnston never reported or wrote about the battle, his brother-in-law Colonel Preston gave just a week or two later what possibly is the closest we have to Johnston's innermost thinking at the time: "He appreciated the disadvantage of attacking the enemy so near the river, where the gunboats and transports gave the resources of retreat or reinforcement as emergency might demand, but he also felt the necessity of reinspiring confidence, after the loss of Henry & Donelson and of destroying the temporary prestige of the enemy."[60]

So the die was cast. Johnston would roll the "iron dice of battle" in what was certainly his greatest gamble to date. Throwing his green and inexperienced army, led by generals nearly as inexperienced, into a battle against a more veteran enemy army that could very well be alerted to his presence and even entrenched, all in a heavily wooded wilderness, was indeed a gamble. Still worse, the enemy army was about to receive reinforcements, which nevertheless made the risky attempt all the more necessary. Johnston realized what Beauregard did not, that withdrawing now and fighting later would only put the Confederate army in a worse position in the future. If a battle was to be fought, it had to be here, now. With Van Dorn nowhere near arriving east of the Mississippi River while Buell was approaching rapidly, this was the only time when Johnston would have odds this good. The simple truth was that the unfavorable odds confronting the Confederate army on the night of April 5 would only become more dire if the attack was called off. It was a high-stakes gamble to be sure, and not just for the army—Johnston's entire reputation as a soldier, cracked already, largely hung on the outcome of this battle. His best friend in the army, Leonidas Polk, admitted shortly after Shiloh that Johnston also saw this effort as "an opportunity which he had coveted for vindicating his claims to the confidence of his countrymen against the inconsiderate and unjust reproaches which had been heaped upon him." While a military gamble of the highest order, the assault on Pittsburg Landing would also be an effort to regain the honor his reputation had lost.[61]

Johnston apparently had his reputation and honor on his mind frequently that evening and night. He talked freely with Assistant Adjutant General Jordan about his old days in California. The colonel had been stationed there for years, although he was in Washington during "the momentous winter of 1860–61." Johnston admitted that he was taken aback at the duplicity he felt the government had utilized against him, on one hand writing that he was being offered a top Union generalship while at the same time sending his replacement under cover, fearing Johnston would turn against the United States and do something treasonous. "He had evidently been deeply hurt," Jordan concluded, "that his personal character had not shielded him from the suspicion of doing aught while holding a commission that could lead his superiors to suppose it necessary to undertake his supersedure by stealth."[62]

But Johnston could not brood on the past, having proven willing on numerous occasions to let affronts pass by the wayside. Now, rather, it was time to mold the future, and he was confident. He later confided to Yandell, "I do it, not because, as some people have said, I must fight, or be relieved of command, but because I can whip him." Subservient to the Southern cause was the rekindling of Johnston's reputation if victorious, but most importantly, the fate of two nations perhaps hung in the balance of this truly magnificent gamble Johnston was about to make. Jefferson Davis certainly realized as much. Apprised of Johnston's plans, he wrote a quick note back to him on April 5, even as the Confederate army was slogging its way northward toward Pittsburg Landing. "Your dispatch of yesterday received," it began. "I hope you will be able to close with the enemy before his two columns unite. I anticipate victory."[63]

— 6 —

WE MUST THIS DAY CONQUER OR PERISH

SHILOH

The morning of the 6th of April was remarkably bright and beautiful," Colonel Preston reflected; some believed that the bright sun was "the sun of Austerlitz," a good omen. Johnston himself had spent the night before in an ambulance at his headquarters near the rear of his deployed army. He had continued the conversations about the need for battle with his officers and staff for a while, but he ultimately lay down for a few hours' sleep. Even the next morning, however, Beauregard was still advising a retreat. He had declined Johnston's offer of tactical command but apparently thought that the mere offer entitled him to make some of the decisions anyway. Yet as the generals talked around daybreak, the sounds of shots fired came from the front. "There," Preston interrupted, "the first gun of the battle!" Johnston immediately turned to his staff: "note the hour, if you please, gentlemen." Major Munford recorded the time as 5:14 A.M. Johnston again declared that the army would attack: "The battle has opened gentlemen; it is too late to change our dispositions." As the confident general mounted Fire Eater to ride to the front, he alerted his staff: "To-night, we will water our horses in the Tennessee River."[1]

With the obvious sounds of battle intensifying, Johnston rode forward with his staff into the calculated risk he had launched. He left the still-ailing Beauregard in the rear to oversee the entire effort, an error that would defy the "unity of command" principle of war and would see Beauregard largely work at cross-purposes to Johnston's plan of turning the Union left flank. Nevertheless, as Johnston reached the front the battle continued to pick

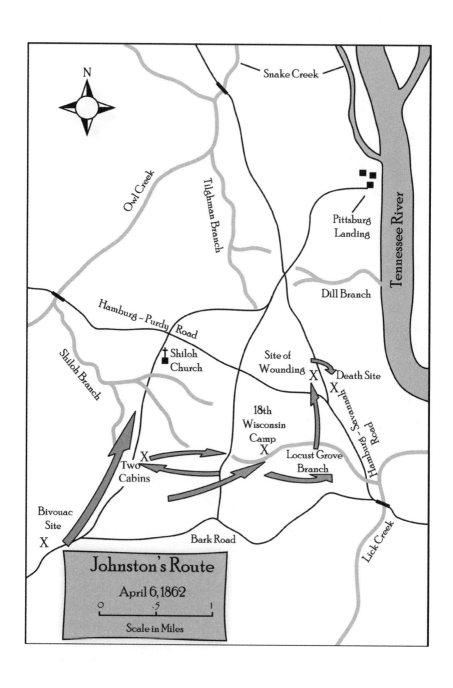

N

Snake Creek

Owl Creek

Tilghman Branch

Pittsburg
Landing

Tennessee River

Dill Branch

Hamburg ~ Purdy Road

Shiloh Branch

† Shiloh
Church

Site of
Wounding

X Death Site

X

Hamburg ~ Savannah Road

18th
Wisconsin
Camp
X

Locust Grove
Branch

X
Two
Cabins

Bivouac
Site
X

Bark Road

Lick Creek

Johnston's Route

April 6, 1862

0   .5   1

Scale in Miles

up all along the initial line of Hardee's corps. Moving forward by the guide of marks blazed on trees, Hardee had not yet met the stiffest opposition at the Union camps but was already battling a fair number of skirmishers and pickets, augmented by reinforcements sent out to delay the Confederates. This small band of Federals did their job well, falling back from position to position but offering at least a semblance of resistance. The effect among the green Confederates was stark. New to battle, the soldiers of Hardee's front line stopped and started, delaying often to dress ranks, even independently at the brigade level. These Confederates were not used to operating together in such large numbers, and what later in the war would have been a whirlwind movement against minimal resistance was rather a major delay for the Confederates in the early hours of the battle that became known as Shiloh. Nevertheless, Johnston pushed them forward, at one point telling brigade commander Hindman: "You have earned your spurs as major-general. Let this day's work win them." He also met up again with Beauregard around 6:30 A.M. and, according to Beauregard staff officer Jacob Thompson, "expressed himself satisfied with the manner in which the battle had been opened."[2]

As the battle continued to unfold, Johnston followed the slowly progressing lines of his extreme right flank, moving up behind Brigadier General Adley Gladden's and Colonel Robert Shaver's brigades. A few casualties resulted from this initial fighting, but the green Confederates were more confused than bloodied. When he heard that a portion of the line had broken near Seay Field, Johnston galloped back to the area and rallied a portion of Shaver's brigade that had come unhinged at the first shock of battle. Moving forward as his troops met increasing resistance, Johnston continued to command from the front. Preston remembered that the general dove into the fight and reformed his lines. "There were many dead and wounded, and some stragglers breaking ranks," he noted, "whom General Johnston rallied in person." A member of Johnston's escort company verified this. "Instantly he quickened to a gallop, with the staff and escort following, and right into the *melee* we plunged." A staff member cautioned Johnston about exposing himself, but, as Dudley Haydon explained, "he smilingly rode to the brow of the hill where we could distinctly see the enemy retreating." Yet obviously chagrined at the confusion already appearing and the resulting lack of momentum, all caused by what could only be described as light Federal resistance, Johnston chose to leave nothing to chance. He sent Preston to the rear to bring up his second line, Bragg's corps of around ten thousand men. Surely, Bragg's weight in numbers would take care of whatever was in front.[3]

While the Second Corps moved forward and entered the battle, Johnston rode to the west to observe the fighting in that sector. There, he watched as Brigadier General Patrick Cleburne's brigade engaged the Federals near Shiloh Church. He sat near two cabins that stood on the eastern side of the Corinth–Pittsburg Landing Road and watched the action across Rhea Field; Preston recorded in his diary, "loud cheers and handsome advance of our troops over 150 acre field." One eyewitness described the scene: "through this field General Cleburne's brigade moved in fine order, with loud and inspiring cheers, to attack the camp." Unfortunately, Cleburne was not successful, and neither would the next two lines be able to break the Shiloh Church position held by General Sherman. The ground was extremely good for the defense, and the Confederate brigades made charge after futile charge up the ridge, only to come back down each time in defeat.[4]

To make matters worse, the Confederate line in this area seemed to be outflanked on the left, which caused Johnston to call on Beauregard for reinforcements for that sector. Colonel Thompson had ridden forward and found the commanding general squarely amid the fighting. He described the scene, the epitome of the fog of war that Johnston and the other commanders were operating within: "The battle was then raging furiously. General Johnston was sitting on his horse where the bullets were flying like hailstones. I galloped up to him amid the fire, and found him cool, collected, self-possessed, but still animated and in fine spirits." Yet Johnston was obviously bothered by news he had just received that the enemy was "sending forward strong re-enforcements to our left." This report probably described the convoluted antics of Colonel John McDowell's Federal brigade, as there were no Union reinforcements heading to the extreme Confederate left. Still, Johnston thought it deserved attention and ordered Thompson to make his way to Beauregard and report the situation. "Say to General Beauregard," he ordered, "we are sweeping the field before us, and in less than half an hour we shall be in possession of their camps, and I think we shall press them to the river. Say, also, I have just learned from a scout, or messenger, that the enemy is moving up in force on our left, and that General Breckinridge had better move to our left to meet him." Thompson later remembered that as he turned his horse to gallop away, Johnston stopped him. "Do not say to General Beauregard that this is an order, but he must act on what additional information he may receive. The reports to him are more to be relied on than to me." Obviously, Johnston was amid the thick of the raging battle and could not have a comprehensive view of the happenings, having left Beauregard in the rear for that exact purpose. Beauregard started Breckinridge to the left, but when news arrived that Sherman had retired, the Creole recalled him and sent his troops to the right, where he deemed the greatest need to rest.[5]

After addressing this perceived threat to the left, Johnston started to ride back to the right of his line, the critical area in his mind where he would turn Grant's left flank. New threats were emerging there as well. Johnston had apparently always been concerned about his right flank, with which he hoped to drive the enemy into the swamps and destruction. Spying Colonel George Maney with five companies of the 1st Tennessee Infantry, Johnston ordered him to move to Lick Creek and watch that flank for any Federal movement from the direction of Hamburg. Maney remembered with apparent satisfaction, "General Johnston, commanding in person, directed me to change my course." There also occurred here a humorous episode, during which Johnston told the Tennesseans, "I have selected you for the post of honor to-day," asking rhetorically if each man had his requisite forty rounds of ammunition. "No, General, I 'ain't got but thirty-eight!" came the reply from one of them, whereupon a smiling general told the soldier to see his orderly sergeant for two more rounds.[6]

The most pressing problem Johnston uncovered, however, was not a phantom threat like the one from Hamburg, but an all-out Federal defense on his right flank. By this time, Shaver's and Gladden's brigades had run into Brigadier General Benjamin Prentiss's division at his camps. The Federals, at least for the moment, were offering stiff resistance. Gladden's brigade was particularly hit hard, and Gladden himself was down with a nasty shoulder wound that would eventually take his life. Bragg's second-line brigades had to move forward to help break this position; most notably, Chalmers's Mississippi brigade was fighting in the large ravines that bordered Locust Grove Branch. With foreboding reports from that sector, including one from a civilian caught between the lines and who testified that there were upward of a hundred thousand Federals on the battlefield, Johnston saw the need for additional weight on this wing as well. He nevertheless dismissed the scared civilian with a smile and a proclamation that "they won't be a mouthful for us!"[7]

Breckinridge, Johnston thought, was moving to the left, which left Polk's corps, the third in line, to move to the right. Johnston rode about behind his temporarily stalled lines, soon finding Polk himself. The bishop was impressed with what he saw, remarking that Johnston, "as commander-in-chief, seemed deeply impressed with the responsibilities of his position." He added, "it was observed that he entered upon his work with the ardor and energy of the true soldier, and the vigor with which he pressed forward his troops gave assurance that his persistent determination would close the day with a glorious victory." Johnston quickly ordered him to send a brigade to the right. Polk ordered his lead division commander, Brigadier General Charles Clark—apparently with him—to send the requested brigade. Johnston then personally ordered Clark to send Brigadier General Alexander P. Stewart's unit. Clark sent the orders, and going that way anyway, Johnston personally led Stewart forward.[8]

Stewart brought his brigade up and was no doubt awe inspired when he saw who would guide him into position. "We continued to advance," Stewart later remembered, "until General A. S. Johnston came up and directed me to move my brigade to the right, to support of General Bragg." Then just as quickly, Stewart related, Johnston was gone. After moving through open woods, a field, and up to an abandoned enemy camp, Stewart reported: "General Johnston having gone to some other part of the field, and finding no one to give me directions, after halting a few minutes I moved the brigade forward." He would never see Johnston again, but his few minutes with the army commander made a lasting impression. "No one who saw him on the field of battle on that fateful morning of April sixth could fail to be struck by his bearing. His whole mien was singularly noble and soldierly, characterized by a calm dignity that was inspired by a consciousness of power and confidence." Unknown to Stewart, Johnston had not ridden far away, just over the hill to the camp of the 18th Wisconsin, which sat on some of the highest ground on the battlefield. From there, he would direct the battle for several hours.[9]

By this time, around 9:30 A.M., Johnston was beginning to get his bearings amid this fog of battle. He had admittedly spent most of the morning riding back and forth behind his lines in a reactionary posture. A member of his escort company later remembered, "always at a gallop, we traversed a great part of the field. [But] he seemed cool and collected all the time." Indeed, Johnston at times outran his escort. He also encountered Union prisoners, who begged to be spared being shot. Johnston retorted: "Why men, you don't suppose we kill prisoners, do you? Go to the rear and you will be safe there." Looking at the overall progress concerned Johnston, however, as the initial attack had ground down to a slow trudge at best, with heavy resistance having developed the closer the Confederates came to the initial Federal camp line. "The sight was a painful one," Surgeon Yandell admitted of viewing the heavy covering of dead and wounded already on the ground. Indeed, by this time, at least two shot-up brigades, Cleburne's and Gladden's, were all but out of the action for several hours. Johnston even came across Gladden's bloodied brigade and ordered it to charge, but he quickly realized its true condition and countermanded the order. Other units, particularly those in the first wave of attack, had been hit hard as well.[10]

Now, however, Johnston began to direct the battle with more organization. To be sure, he had not lacked confidence throughout the morning, and his ability to inspire his men had never left him. One must only look at the comments of Thompson, Polk, and Stewart to see the inspiration that was Johnston on the field of Shiloh. And even amid the floundering confusion of the opening actions, his Confederates had managed to drive Prentiss's entire division from the field and were preparing to outflank the tremendously heavy resistance Sherman was offering at Shiloh Church. Temporarily bewildered and staggered in the early morning hours, Johnston would now use that dogged attitude, his do-or-die mentality, and take control of the situation.[11]

Johnston was indeed beginning to see a clearer picture. As he rode into the first captured Union camps, those of Colonel Madison Miller's brigade, he observed what had obviously been a chaotic situation, with breakfasts still cooking and all indications that surprise had been achieved. Apparently, the Federals were neither alerted to nor fortified against the Confederate army's presence; Beauregard's fears had been unfounded and Johnston's determination proven correct. But now was no time to stop. Always intending to hook around the enemy's left flank and press it away from the river, he spent much of the next few hours on the Confederate right. Witnessing the hard fighting near Spain Field, which had cost him General Gladden and many soldiers of lower rank, Johnston surmised that his right far outflanked the enemy left in this area. In fact, the sounds of battle were heard far to the west, all the way to and past Shiloh Church, while absolutely nothing was heard to the east. Johnston evidently decided he had located the enemy flank, and, according to his plan, he began to turn it.[12]

From the high ground around the 18th Wisconsin camp, Johnston directed a large-scale movement that shifted a major portion of his army from a northward posture to a northwestward slant, hoping to push Grant's army into the swamps of Owl and Snake Creeks to the northwest of Pittsburg Landing. Major Munford remembered that the general "was in the act of swinging his troops round on his left as a pivot," noting that "the completion of this movement faced the troops at an angle of about 45° toward the left, when the forward movement became uniform." Hardee was also there, and the two senior officers and their staffs rode forward to reconnoiter a second line of camps in the distance, perhaps eight hundred yards to the front. The large assemblage of mounted officers caught the enemy's eye, and Federal batteries soon opened up on the group. Shells from the gunboat *Tyler* in the Tennessee River also fell nearby, although these could not have been fired in response to the generals' presence. Despite the danger, Johnston was very much hands-on in moving troops in this sector. Hardee later reported that he was satisfied that Johnston was "in person directing the battle" here and moved off to the left in response to a large cannonade that had developed there. Although taking some refuge from the artillery fire (Preston later remembered that "General Johnston rode down the hill to escape the shells"), Johnston nevertheless continued to direct events on the right, putting himself in danger at times in order to do what had to be done.[13]

Unfortunately, Johnston had made a severe misjudgment amid this confusing action. The silence he had heard to the east was not because of a lack of Federals in that direction. There were indeed no Federals for a half a mile to the east, which Chalmers's right did not reach beyond. Farther in that direction, however, was the Union brigade of Colonel David Stuart. A gap a half a mile wide existed in the Federal line here, which was to be plugged by Prentiss's third brigade, which had not yet formed. Consequently, much of Chalmers's brigade hit unoccupied space, evidently prompting Johnston to think he had located the enemy flank. In reality, that flank rested on Lick Creek, another mile to the east.[14]

Just such crushing news arrived as Johnston meandered around the captured Union camps: word of a major enemy force to the east from an engineer sent out early that morning to scout the Federal left. Samuel Lockett approached the general, who, after inquiring about the man's identity, calmly directed: "well, sir, tell me as briefly and quickly as possible what you have to say." Lockett explained that an entire Federal division was farther to the east. Although it was in actuality merely a badly scared brigade of only three regiments, this intelligence obviously took Johnston aback. Preston remembered him "pondering [the situation] a little while." Munford related that "again glancing at his watch, he remarked, 'It is now time to move forward.'" Johnston made up his mind that something had to be done to counter this new threat, this extended flank. Obviously, it was too late to call back the majority of the troops he had sent bounding off to the northwest to drive the enemy army into the swamps. He could, however, recall two of the far-right brigades. Chalmers had proceeded northward toward the Peach Orchard and was even then trading some long-range fire with Union troops of Brigadier General Stephen Hurlbut's division, yet another Union division in the eastern sector of the battlefield. Brigadier General John K. Jackson's Alabamians were also nearby, having just begun their move to the northwest. Both were part of Brigadier General Jones Withers's division. Johnston thus ordered Withers to recall these two brigades and send them on a flanking march along the Bark Road to the rear and attack the new enemy flank on the Hamburg–Savannah Road. Withers remembered, "General A. S. Johnston, who was present, immediately ordered the division to move to the right." Chalmers similarly explained, "we were about to engage them [Hurlbut's men] again, when we were ordered by General Johnston to fall back, which was done." To take Withers's place in line, Johnston called on Beauregard to send two of Breckinridge's brigades to fill the resulting gap. Obviously, he had gotten word that these units had not been sent into action on the left and were still available; he thus sent his brother-in-law Colonel Preston and Captain Wickliffe to guide Colonel John Bowen's and Colonel Walter Statham's brigades into line. Johnston was moving his brigades like chess pieces, shifting two farther to the right and filling the empty space with reserve units. Shuffling so many troops around the battlefield, especially on an undefended flank, was not ideal, but it had to be done—yet another calculated risk that was certainly not an extravagant decision at this point.[15]

With the decision made, Johnston patiently waited as his new right flank developed, spurring on the troops when he met them. Coming to a brigade with Arkansas soldiers, he spoke to them: "Men of Arkansas! They say you boast of your prowess with the bowie-knife. To-day you wield a nobler weapon—the bayonet. Employ it well." He had the same effect all over the battlefield that day, numerous commanders receiving his orders and no less than seven getting them from him personally. For the army commander to be issuing orders to even division but certainly to brigade and especially regimental commanders during a fight was absolutely breaking the chain of command, especially when he had a second in command to the rear who was managing the overall battle. On top of that, the fact that Beauregard and the corps and division commanders were all giving orders too, as well as untold staff officers who were roaming the field and giving orders in the name of their commanders, made for an especially confusing operation. It is a wonder that the Confederates achieved as much command and control as there was, although Johnston's presence all over the battlefield at first and then concentrated on the right later in the day seemed to be the defining feature of command, with the corps and division commanders largely invisible or simply acting out his larger desires. It is also a wonder that Johnston was not in more personal danger, being at the front for much of the day. He was hit by an expended round at one point, playfully joking with staff officer Thomas Jack, "slapping his [own] thigh and smiling, upon a spent ball which had struck and stung him."[16]

Sensing the victory, Johnston continued directing the battle from the vicinity of the 18th Wisconsin camp for around two hours, until about noon. But while there he witnessed what was becoming a problem with the Confederates all over the battlefield: soldiers breaking ranks and looting the enemy's camps. One officer burst from a captured Union tent holding several valuable items. Spying the general, the guilty officer held up his loot in victory. Johnston was not amused. "None of that, sir; we are not here for plunder!" Perhaps feeling he had overreacted, Johnston then took a single tin cup between his fingers and remarked, "let this be my share of the spoils to-day."[17]

It was also in the 18th Wisconsin camp that Johnston made a fateful decision that would soon affect him personally. Seeing there a number of wounded of both sides from the earlier action, he ordered his surgeon, Dr. Yandell, to set up a hospital and care for them. Johnston told him, "these were our enemies a moment ago, they are prisoners now." Yandell tried to make the point that he should stay with his commander. But Johnston was adamant that he would call for the surgeon if he left the area, although he later left the scene without telling him. The surgeon would be of no more use to him that day.[18]

While Johnston tarried near the Federal camp, the battle raged on. By noon or a little before, Breckinridge's two reserve brigades arrived on the scene, and Johnston personally helped guide them into position. In fact, he moved forward over the gullies and ravines with the soldiers, coming up directly to the rear of Bowen's brigade. There, just on the high ground over-looking a tributary of Locust Grove Branch, Johnston found another point from which he could direct the movements of his right wing. Governor Harris, having temporarily attached himself to the staff for the battle, remembered Johnston's activities. Visiting the spot decades afterward, in 1896, Harris remembered: "Here, within ten steps of the place where I am, General Johnston sat on his horse for over an hour and a half or two hours from about noon on Sunday, putting his Reserve in position. Everything is perfectly natural just as I remember it. There is the stream where our orderlies went for water and where soldiers were filling their canteens, over there was the camp that we passed through in coming here."[19]

Johnston also ranged to the right of his line, on the tall bluffs overlooking Locust Grove Branch. From there, he continued to direct the battle on the far right flank, Colonel Joseph Wheeler of the 19th Alabama relating that Johnston pushed Jackson's brigade forward toward Stuart's Federals "with his own lips." Watching the rightmost unit in the army, Chalmers's brigade, trudge forward, Johnston was obviously happy with this move he had made, having basically unfolded a new right wing of the Confederate army. He was perfectly confident that these four brigades could handle this newly discovered Union division, turn it, and then join in on the effort to drive the Federals into the swamps to the northwest. Johnston was so confident, in fact, that he expressed to Major Munford that this was the key stroke of the battle. The staff officer later remembered: "We sat on our horses, side by side, watching that brigade [Chalmers] as it swept over the ridge; and, as the colors dipped out of sight, the general said to me, 'That checkmates them.' I told him I was glad to hear him announce 'checkmate,' but that 'he must excuse so poor a player for saying he could not see it.' He laughed, and said, 'Yes, sir, that mates them.'"[20]

Yet there was little real success. From his elevated position, Johnston watched as his reserve brigades tried in vain to push the enemy line out of the Peach Orchard. Fierce fighting took place as the Confederates assaulted the Federal position several times. Finally seeing his units were not making progress, Johnston made his fatal gamble, one that, as was his custom in difficult places, carried him past the level of calculated risk to the realm of desperate gambler. His troops were currently unable, under the leadership of Breckinridge and Withers, to drive on to victory. And with no more reserves to call forward like he had done on several occasions earlier in the day, the only option left was to wade into the melee himself and inspire his troops to greater efforts. Certainly, the army commander's place was not on the front line leading charges, but this was the critical point in Johnston's critical gamble. It all came down to this effort at turning the enemy flank. He had to lead personally—to conquer or perish. And so it was here that Johnston crossed the line between calculated risk and betting everything he had, even life itself, in an attempt to win it all.[21]

Positioned well behind Bowen's brigade, Johnston rode forward through the rear areas of the fighting around 1:00 P.M., coming under fire as he did. Taking refuge with his men in a small hollow in which sat a "mule lot," Johnston continued to direct the battle. Munford remembered Johnston sitting in "a depression about thirty yards behind our front line, where the bullets passed over our heads; but he could see more than half of his line, and, if an emergency arose, could meet it promptly." The major also related how "the general passed his eye from the right of the line to his extreme point of vision in the direction of the left, and slowly back again." Johnston sent various staff officers on errands to position certain brigades and batteries, and at times he rode up and down the line itself. At one point a shell came incredibly close to him, passing over the heads of the men in the first line and landing a little to the left. Governor Harris remembered: "Here the firing was kept up with great energy by both armies for, perhaps, an hour, during the whole of which time the general remained upon the line, more exposed to the fire of the enemy than any soldier in the line. After the firing had been thus continued for near an hour, the general said to me: 'They are offering stubborn resistance here. I shall have to put the bayonet to them.'"[22]

When Breckinridge received word of the pending assault, he rode to Johnston and admitted that he could not get his men to charge, particularly one Tennessee regiment. Overhearing the conversation, Governor Harris took exception to the slight. "Let the Governor go to them," was Johnston's reply. When Breckinridge further reported he could not get his troops to advance, Johnston replied, "Oh, yes, general; I think you can." When Breckinridge responded that he had tried and failed, Johnston calmly said: "Then, I will help you. . . . We can get them to make the charge." Harris remembered that the Confederate line at this time "slightly wavered with a backward tendency." Johnston told him, "I will go to the front, order, and lead the charge." Harris later remembered, "just as he was in the act of passing through the line to the front, he said to me, 'Go to the extreme right and lead the Tennessee regiment stationed there." The governor did so, moving forward on foot with the troops, "pistol in hand." Back near the center, Johnston began to ride along the line, whipping up the emotions of the men in prelude to the bayonet charge. To the infantry of Bowen's brigade, he "told us a few more charges and the day was ours." Moving down the line of soldiers with fixed bayonets, Johnston tapped each bayonet with the little tin cup he had claimed as his spoils in the Wisconsin camp. "These must do the work," he implored. "Men! They are stubborn; we must use the bayonet." A Tennessean remembered him announcing that this place was the key to the battlefield, and they had to "unlock it" with their bayonets.[23]

It was increasingly evident that Johnston was going to lead this charge himself; he had worked with raw volunteers much of his life and knew they had to be led personally. And this was the crisis point of the great gamble. At the climax of emotion, for both general and soldiers, Johnston yelled, "I will lead you!" He wheeled Fire Eater around and moved forward, followed immediately by the men of Bowen's battle line, "thrilling and trembling with that tremendous and irresistible ardor." The soldiers nearest the general moved forward with him "as if drawn to him by some overmastering magnetic force." Colonel Preston noted that Johnston "advanced with Bowen's brigade in person." All along the line, the other Confederate brigades, the men wildly cheering, joined the advance that Johnston led across Sarah Bell's cotton field. One of Bowen's colonels, John D. Martin, reported that Johnston "halted in 200 or 300 yards, and told us to charge ahead; the enemy were before us."[24]

The attack was successful, Colonel Preston writing the next day that Johnston "had just led a splendid charge taking the third camp of the enemy." And it was due in large part to his personal leadership. A vast number of officers and soldiers later remembered how majestic and knightly Johnston had appeared that day. One of his brigade commanders declared that he "looked like a hero of the antique type, and his very appearance on the field was a tower of more than kingly strength." Bragg remembered being "inspired by his coolness, confidence, and determination. Few men have equaled him in the possession and display at the proper time of these great qualities of the soldier." Johnston's personal leadership, even amid great danger, was on full display, persuading reluctant men to attack even when a former vice president and senator could not. Yet historians have argued endlessly about whether Johnston's true role was that of leading troops personally. Biographer Charles Roland has defended Johnston's frontline leadership against accusations that he had no business being there, writing that "Johnston was where he ought to have been at Shiloh." Indeed, the commander knew by this point that he had to risk his life just then to make the most critical tactical action of the most critical strategic effort successful, which it would not have been any other way. He accordingly placed himself at the point of most danger, certainly a place he had no business being as army commander were it not for the critical nature of the moment.[25]

Hurlbut's Federals withdrew to another line of defense, which Johnston soon began to press by repositioning his units and sending them onward. Rather than again lead the assault, however, he rode back a short distance behind his line to use a small knoll to get the best view possible of the ongoing attack. There Harris found him. "I had never, in my life, seen him looking more bright, joyous, and happy, than he looked at the moment that I approached him. The charge he had led was heroic. It had been successful, and his face expressed a soldier's joy and a patriot's hope." Apparently, Johnston was also in a playful mood. Showing him a cut in his boot caused by enemy fire, Johnston remarked, "Governor, they came very near putting me *hors de combat* in that charge." To another man, he flopped the boot sole and exclaimed, "they didn't trip me up that time." A concerned Harris then asked if he was wounded, but Johnston replied in the negative.[26]

But his gamble had cost him dearly, although no one, not even Johnston himself, recognized it at the time. As the fighting raged on and Johnston and Governor Harris sat on the knoll talking, a Federal battery opened up on the new Confederate line. Harris remembered that Johnston "paused in the middle of a sentence to say, 'Order Colonel Statham to wheel his regiment to the left, charge, and take that battery.'" The governor rode the two hundred yards, delivered the order, and made his way back. As he reported the order delivered and the troops in motion, Harris sadly remembered, "the General sank down in his saddle, leaning over to the left." The startled governor remembered it was "in a manner that indicated he was falling from his horse." Stopping midsentence, Harris grabbed Johnston by the collar and held him on the horse. He bent forward and looked him in the face and asked, "General, are you wounded?" With what Harris described as "a very deliberate and emphatic tone," Johnston answered, "Yes, and I fear seriously."[27]

A horrified Harris yelled to nearby Captain Wickham of Johnston's staff to go find Dr. Yandell but to send the first surgeon he saw on the way. Yet just in that short amount of time, Johnston was obviously getting worse. Harris remembered, "the general's hold upon his reigns relaxed, and it dropped from his hand." Taking the reigns with his own in one hand and supporting Johnston with the other, Harris and Wickham guided the horses into a small ravine behind the lines and out of the line of fire. The governor slipped off his horse and pulled Johnston "over upon me, and eased him to the ground as gently as I could." Wickham then galloped away to find a doctor. Harris spied a nearby soldier and sent him to locate any staff officer he could and bring him there quickly. But by this time, Johnston was hardly conscious, and a horrified Harris, now with Johnston's head in his lap, was alone with the dying general. "With eager anxiety I asked many questions about his wounds," he sadly remembered, "to which he gave no answer, not even a look of intelligence."[28]

As Harris unloosed Johnston's cravat and searched for a torso wound, other staff officers arrived, including Colonel Preston. He related that he was nearby when Captain O'Hara rode up in haste, "informing me that General Johnston was wounded and lying in the ravine." Although the staff would later find out that he had been hit as many as four times, only one bullet penetrated the skin. No other wound could be found besides a liberally bleeding gash in his right leg. Johnston had been hit in the popliteal artery and was dying from a loss of blood. Dr. Yandell perhaps could have treated the wound successfully with a tourniquet, but Johnston had ridden forward without him earlier in the battle. Moreover, earlier detection possibly could have saved him, but endless debate has raged ever since over whether Johnston's sciatic injury from the Texas duel had deprived him of feeling the wound in his leg; if it did, the result of an unfortunate earlier gamble came back to doom him in a later gamble. Harris tried to pour brandy into his mouth, and Johnston swallowed the first dose, but upon a second a few moments later, the governor remembered, "he made no effort to swallow; it gurgled in his throat in his effort to breathe, and I turned his head so as to relieve him." An obviously grieving Preston, kneeling beside his brother-in-law, cried, "Johnston, do you know me?" Some thought they saw a faint smile in response, but Preston reasoned that "he breathed for a few minutes after my arrival, but he did not recognize me." Then it happened. "I searched but found no wound upon his body. I attempted to revive him, but he expired without pain a few moments after," Preston miserably noted. "In a few moments he ceased to breathe," Harris recalled. "He died calmly, and, to all appearances, free from pain—indeed so calmly, that the only evidence I had that he had passed from life was the fact that he ceased to breathe, and the heart ceased to throb. There was not the slightest struggle, nor the contortion of a muscle; his features were as calm and as natural as at any time in life and health." It was around 2:30 P.M., April 6, 1862.[29]

Despite the enormity of the disaster playing out before their very eyes, the shocked staff kept their heads. Preston requested that Harris go inform Beauregard he now commanded the army. Despite the emotion of the loss of Johnston in addition to his own brother and nephew that day, Harris mounted Fire Eater because his own horse had run off. He remembered that he "found him so badly crippled that I dismounted and examined him, and found upon examination that he was wounded in three legs by musket balls." He rode Fire Eater only to where Johnston had left an orderly and more horses. The governor took a fresh mount and made his way to Beauregard, who took the news stoically, expressing regret but adding, "everything else seems to be going on well on the right"; while showing little emotion with the battle still raging, Beauregard admitted a year later that he took charge of the army "to my very great regret." Harris agreed that the Confederates were enjoying success on the right, so Beauregard simply stated, "then, the battle may as well go on." And it did, largely the way it had been going since Beauregard was more in command of the army overall than Johnston had been. Meanwhile, Preston and the rest of Johnston's staff took the body, wrapped in a blanket, by ambulance to his headquarters site of the night before, where a couple of staff officers, John W. Throckmorton and Captain Wickham, remained with it. Beauregard's surgeon, Dr. Samuel P. Choppin, examined the body and found a bullet had entered the back of the leg. This sparked some wild speculation that the general was shot from the rear by one of his own men, despite the fact that a horseman could at any time be facing any direction on a spirited and excited mount that was also in the process of being wounded multiple times. The doctor also found that Johnston had actually been hit four times. Once was by a spent ball on the thigh, a second by a piece of shell above the right hip, and a third that cut his boot sole. Munford surmised that "but one bullet broke the skin—and that, alas! Was fatal." The rest of the staff, full of knowledge of the battle and battlefield, served Beauregard the rest of the day, the Creole telling Dr. Yandell, who also wanted to examine the body immediately, "no, Dr. you can do him no good now, stay with me, maybe some of us may need you presently." But that night Beauregard allowed the staff to transport Johnston's body back to Corinth.[30]

Albert Sidney Johnston had entered the Battle of Shiloh a desperate man. Reeling from defeat and calls for his removal and facing an imminent combination of enemy armies on his front, he had to win a victory on April 6. It was his last gamble. Over and above the ramifications surrounding his own honor, if this gambit failed, then Corinth and probably the entire Mississippi Valley was doomed—and with them the Confederacy. Johnston had to win a victory, and he was determined to do everything in his power to achieve it. But at 2:00 P.M. on the sixth, Johnston ran out of options. He had sent in his last reserves, and they were stalled. The only choice he had left was to wade into the battle himself and hopefully inspire his men to greater efforts.[31]

Unbeknown to Johnston, however, his last earthly success was only temporary. His army would not win the victory at Shiloh, his successors would not defend the Mississippi Valley, and his region would not win its independence. Perhaps he died for nothing, but Johnston probably would not have looked at it that way. He had done everything he humanly could, even making the ultimate sacrifice. His declaration was "conquer or perish." He did the latter, the highest-ranking officer to be killed in the entire war, and the highest-ranking American military officer ever to die in combat.[32]

It is arguable that, entering the battle, Johnston knew that he would die, or at least realized the vivid possibility that he would not live through the fighting. His son William explained how Johnston "had often expressed to the writer a preference for this death of the soldier." He had to win if the South had any chance of stemming the vast blue tide that was even then surging into its heartland. This was the line he had drawn; Shiloh had to be a victory. And Johnston was perfectly willing to die gaining that victory, if that is what it cost. In a statement given out to the troops upon their march to Pittsburg Landing, he had declared that they were fighting "for all worth living or dying for." Likewise, even a cursory look at Johnston's rhetoric on the evening of April 5 and even during the battle itself reveals that his mind was on one concept: victory or death. Johnston's remark that he would "fight them if they were a million" does not show bluster and conceit as was the case with some younger Civil War generals such as John Pope or Joseph Hooker, but rather it reveals Johnston's desperation, a gamble he would have to make even when the odds greatly disfavored him. He made a similar comment about rolling the "iron dice of battle," which betrayed his view that this attack was a high-stakes gamble, even if a necessary one. Similarly, when he met his son's best college friend, brigade commander Randal Gibson, he noted: "Randal, I never see you but I think of William. I hope you may get through safely to-day" yet then added significantly, "but we must win a victory." As heartrending as it would be to sacrifice his son's best friend, Johnston realized the situation justified it if necessary. Perhaps most telling, he remarked to Colonel John S. Marmaduke, who had been with him in Utah as well as Kentucky, "my son, we must this day conquer or perish." Johnston had to win this gamble, even if it required entering the fight on the front lines himself and dying. If he did not win, he truly would die trying.[33]

Despite efforts to keep it secret, word of Johnston's death spread quickly. Even the Federals understood its significance. Many of them even thought they had the general's body itself, although it was actually a distant relative of his first wife, Thomas Preston. McClernand erroneously declared that Johnston fell "within 30 yards of my tent," while Sherman mistakenly placed the death near his troops at Shiloh Church. One of Buell's division commanders, Brigadier General Alexander M. McCook, even put Johnston's death on the second day of battle, while fellow division commander Brigadier General Thomas J. Wood boasted that his men had also recovered a field desk with Johnston's order of battle and proclamation to his troops inside. At one point an Alabama lieutenant, sent with dispatches and bearing a flag of truce, talked with General McCook while a courier went ahead inside Union lines. They discussed the location of Johnston's body, McCook saying "an officer was found dead on the field who was said by many to be General Johnston." The lieutenant "reassured him that we [the Confederates] certainly had the body of General Johnston." Incidentally, McCook also asked about Union division commander Prentiss. When told he was captured and in Confederate hands, McCook "remarked with much profanity that he hoped we would keep him."[34]

But Johnston's remains were safely in the hands of his staff. Even better, one of them was, of course, his brother-in-law William Preston, thus offering some family participation in the initial mourning. Beauregard gave Johnston's staff "the last sad duty of accompanying the remains of their lamented chief from the field." They left headquarters at 6:00 A.M. on April 7, making the sad journey back to Corinth. Word spread throughout the Confederacy as soon as they arrived in town. Beauregard already had sent the news to Richmond on the night of April 6, stating that he had won a victory but that Johnston "fell gallantly leading his troops into the thickest of the fight." Colonel Preston himself sent President Davis an account of the event when he arrived at Corinth, writing: "General Johnston fell yesterday at 2.30 while leading a successful charge, turning the enemy's right [left], and gaining a brilliant victory. A minie-ball cut the artery of his leg, but he rode on till, from loss of blood, he fell exhausted, and died without pain in a few moments. His body has been intrusted to me by General Beauregard to be taken to New Orleans, and remain there until directions are received from his family." He later related that Beauregard gave him *"carte blanche . . .* as to General Johnston's remains."[35]

But the staff first took the remains to his headquarters house in Corinth, where Mrs. Inge sadly watched as Johnston's lifeless body, wrapped in army blankets, was placed in his room. "It was lifted tenderly and carried to his room in Corinth and placed on an improvised bier amid silence and tears," she recalled. Mrs. Inge could only lament, "three days before he had left this room in all the vigor of mature manhood; now he was asleep in the same room, a martyr to his country's cause." She and several other ladies took over the funerary process by cleaning the body and uniform and wrapping him in a Confederate flag. While doing so, she found half of her cake and one of the sandwiches still in Johnston's pocket. The ladies also cut locks of his hair before laying him in a simple white pine coffin that cost eight dollars, which the Confederate government paid. Johnston lay in state for several hours while many Corinth residents came to mourn. Soon after, the staff put the coffin on board a train bound for New Orleans.[36]

Preston also played the part of kinsman after Shiloh. As soon as he returned to Corinth and telegraphic connection on April 7, he notified Johnston's son of the death: "your father died in my arms yesterday at half past two on the field of battle." He later wrote a more lengthy and heartfelt description of Johnston's command on April 18. Preston also took care of several of his brother-in-law's unpaid bills and financial matters, including his estate, which was owed by the Confederate government $524 for services up through his death. William Johnston eventually arrived and assumed the estate, taking most of Johnston's personal effects, including two saddles and bridles, his sword, gold watch, compass, yellow sash, and gold ring. Also found among his items were four keys and a corkscrew. He gave his uncle Johnston's field glass, cot, canteen, and revolver and sold him the gray horse sent from Mississippi. William sent Fire Eater back to the Flournoy plantation in Arkansas to recover from his wounds, later taking him as his own horse. He also kept Umpire for the time being as his own, although later selling him for a thousand dollars. To Johnston's servant Randolph he gave one of his father's blankets. Unfortunately, word took longer to reach Eliza and the children out in California; cruelly, the initial account they received on April 15 was "General all right." Obviously, the devastating news that she was now a widow arrived shortly thereafter.[37]

In Richmond, Jefferson Davis was distraught at the first news from Beauregard and Preston, hoping against hope that his friend and near-idol Johnston was still alive. The president had been concerned earlier at the lack of news, telling his wife Varina, "I know Johnston, and if he is alive either good or bad news would have been communicated at once." When news of the victory arrived that also included notice of Johnston's death, Davis admitted, "victory however great cannot cheer me in the face of such a loss, and God grant that it may not be true and that he yet lives." Confirmation arrived later, at which time the president wept over his perished friend.[38]

The news was indeed shocking. President Davis informed the Confederate Congress on April 8 that the army had won, "but an all-wise Creator has been pleased, while vouchsafing to us His countenance in battle, to afflict us with a severe dispensation, to which we must bow in humble submission. The last lingering hope has disappeared, and it is but too true that General Albert Sidney Johnston is no more." He went on to add a personal note.

> My long and close friendship with this department chieftain and patriot forbids me to trust myself giving vent to the feelings which this sad intelligence has evoked. Without doing injustice to the living, it may safely be asserted that our loss is irreparable, and that among the shining hosts of the great and the good who now cluster around the banner of our country there exists no purer spirit, no more heroic soul, than that of the illustrious man whose death I join you in lamenting. In his death he has illustrated the character for which through life he was conspicuous—that of singleness of purpose and devotion to duty. With his whole energies bent on attaining the victory which he deemed essential to his country's cause, he rode on to the accomplishment of his object, forgetful of self, while his very life-blood was fast ebbing away. His last breath cheered his comrades to victory; the last sound

he heard was their shout of triumph; his last thought was his country's; and long and deeply will his country mourn his loss.[39]

Congress responded with a declaration of thanks for the victory but expressed its "profound sorrow" at Johnston's loss; both houses adjourned out of respect. One Louisianan objected during the debate on the adjournment in the House of Representatives—"we could best evince our regret for the fall of our heroes by imitating their examples in discharging the duties which devolve upon us"—but he soon withdrew his objection. Another praised Johnston but admitted that his death "has dissipated every cloud which momentarily marred the splendor of his glorious name." A Mississippi representative read Johnston's March explanatory letter to President Davis on the floor, after which one of the Tennessee representatives who had called for Johnston's removal admitted that he had now "alter[ed] his opinion."[40]

Once back in Corinth, Beauregard also announced the news to his army. "Soldiers: Your late commander-in-chief, General A. S. Johnston, is dead. A fearless soldier, a sagacious captain, a reproachless man, has fallen; one who in his devotion to our cause shrank from no sacrifice; one who, animated by a sense of duty and sustained by a sublime courage, challenged danger and perished gallantly for his country whilst leading forward his brave columns to victory. His signal example of heroism and patriotism, if imitated, would make this army invincible. A grateful country will mourn his loss, revere his name, and cherish his manly virtues." Ironically, letters to Johnston continued to arrive for days following his death.[41]

Meanwhile, Colonel Preston and the rest of the staff accompanied Johnston's remains southward to New Orleans, intending to eventually transport them to Texas. Dignitaries were on hand in the Crescent City to meet the body, including the Louisiana governor and his staff as well as Confederate commander Mansfield Lovell and his staff. One of Johnston's staff officers, Thomas Jack, noted, "the streets were thronged with citizens, and, as the procession moved slowly along, I saw tears silently flowing from the eyes of young, middle-aged, and old." Soon, the coffin took its temporary abode at St. Louis Cemetery in the tomb of the city's mayor, John T. Monroe. Someone simply wrote in pencil on the tomb: "General A. S. Johnston, C.S.A., Shiloh, April 6, 1862." Another scribbled: "Texas weeps over her noblest son. A Texas soldier."[42]

But the pain did not subside thereafter. Southerners memorialized Johnston in verse all across the Confederacy. The loss especially lingered for Jefferson Davis. It was a difficult day when a lock of Johnston's hair arrived, Major Munford having sent it "not to the President, but to the Friend." It was also difficult when William Johnston arrived in Richmond, Davis admitting, "I felt an emotion stranger when I saw him than I have felt since Shiloh, after the first shock." The pains of loss also affected William, of course, particularly on May 13, 1862. Now an aide to the president, who was gone all that day visiting the army then confronting McClellan on the Peninsula, he sat much of the day in Davis's office reading his father's correspondence and grieving over his loss. Perhaps worst of all for those mourning Johnston's death was the realization that, once the Federals captured New Orleans on April 25, just a few weeks after Shiloh, Albert Sidney Johnston lay in an occupied city. He would do so for the remainder of the war.[43]

General Johnston had initiated battle at Shiloh as a responsible calculated risk that had to be taken; there was no other option left the Confederate high command in the West. But throughout the day on April 6, amid the fog of war and confusion the battlefield became known for, he drifted closer and closer to crossing the line of acceptable risk to the point of desperate gambler. Johnston had already shifted from his own mentality of leniency, appeasement, and forbearance he had shown his subordinates in the Forts Henry and Donelson campaign to taking firm stands against those who wanted to take different paths, such as Beauregard's desire to call off the attack on Grant's army and return to Corinth. But as he continued his drift toward firmness and resolve, Johnston crossed the line to gamble himself in order to win the battle. The wager cost him his life, but perhaps it also cost the Confederacy to a greater degree than most anyone could have envisioned at the time.

WE HAD NO OTHER HAND TO TAKE UP HIS WORK

THE WEST AFTER JOHNSTON

In the center of Shiloh National Military Park stands one of the most impressive monuments on the battlefield. The United Daughters of the Confederacy (UDC) Monument, erected in 1917 at a cost of $50,000 and dedicated in front of a crowd of fifteen thousand, is very impressive in its elegant lines, moving statuary, and symbolism. Erected with money raised by schoolchildren and the women of the South to mark a battlefield at that time (and still today) sharply tilted toward Union memorialization, the UDC Monument boldly proclaims the honor and duty of Confederate soldiers at Shiloh.[1]

Besides the beauty, elegance, and size of the monument, its symbolism is perhaps most important. Placed on the battlefield in the heyday of the Lost Cause, wherein proud Southerners sought to explain their defeat in the Civil War and their reasons for fighting, the monument in its imagery is a classic example of that movement. The bronze figures adorning each flank represent the four branches of the Confederate army (infantry, artillery, cavalry, and the officer corps), with each providing its own view of the fighting. The cameos on each side between the figures and the central statue represent the two days of battle, with eleven (for the number of Confederate states) on the right denoting the first day's fighting and lifted up in victory, whereas the ten (fewer because of casualties) on the left are bowed in defeat, reflecting the result of the second day. Even the placement of the monument, at the high-water mark of the Confederate struggle on the first day where the Hornet's Nest defenders surrendered, speaks volumes.[2]

Most importantly, the three bronze figures in the center portray a seeming dance of defeat. Death and Night, portrayed as two veiled figures, stand on either side and just behind a front feminine figure, her head bowed. The two are symbolically taking the laurel wreath of victory from the South, represented by the central figure in front. In effect, the Lost Cause argument was that Death and Night had stolen victory from the Confederates at Shiloh. Many Southerners claimed that nightfall on April 6, 1862, came too quickly, that if they just had a few more hours of daylight their victory over Grant would have been complete. Similarly, and most importantly, Death helped snatch victory from the Confederacy by taking General Albert Sidney Johnston, whose likeness appears directly below the three central figures. Many Southerners have argued that had Johnston not perished when he did, he would have won the battle while his successor Beauregard threw away the triumph. As a result, speculative questions have long raged over what would have happened had Johnston not died or if his successor had not squandered the victory nearly won by calling off the assaults because of looming darkness. It was thus at Shiloh that Johnston, somewhat as a martyr despite the obvious cloud he was under until his death, "became immortal." But in the larger context, Johnston's death and the compulsive gamble that caused it had larger ramifications well beyond the outcome of Shiloh.[3]

Johnston died amid the still-raging battle, and debate over the effects of that death on the rest of the fighting afterward has raged ever since. Yet had he lived, it is hard to imagine he could have done any more than Beauregard did. Johnston would have faced the same daunting defense and terrain his successor met. And had Beauregard not called off the attacks as night fell on the sixth, it is equally evident that they would not have succeeded, those tasked with making the assaults having already decided among themselves to stop for the day. Accordingly, Beauregard did not throw away Johnston's victory; in fact, there was no victory to throw away. Thus, there is no basis for the Lost Cause argument that death and night stole victory from the Confederates at Shiloh, although the idea does make for a provocative and beautiful monument.[4]

But Johnston did not just affect the Civil War in the West while he was alive and in command. In fact, his death also had broad and lasting ramifications that played out for years while his bullet-torn body lay in the grave in New Orleans. While it is debatable how much of a difference his death made on the field of Shiloh itself, it is actually in the future command of the western Confederacy that Johnston's absence was most significant. Consequently, his personal gamble with his life affected the larger Confederacy and the millions of people seeking independence. Perhaps Johnston's admirer Jefferson Davis himself said it best when he explained, "when Sidney Johnston fell, it was the turning-point of our fate; for we had no other hand to take up his work in the West."[5]

Davis's statement was bold but true, at least in part. Eastern-theater partisans might take umbrage that Johnston's death sealed the Confederacy's fate; arguments between the importance of the eastern versus the western theater have raged for decades and will continue into the future. On the assertion that there was no other general to take Johnston's place, however, Davis was entirely correct. An early West Point history incisively related that "in the death of Gen. Albert Sidney Johnston the Confederates suffered a loss from which it seems their army in the West never recovered, and this for the reason that there apparently never was a leader thereafter in that section who had at once the full confidence of its people and of the Confederate government." Historian Steven Woodworth has argued that "with Johnston removed from the scene, Davis's interaction with his generals would become vastly more complex and problematical."[6]

Just who could take Johnston's place in the West? First, there were the four remaining full generals in Confederate service at the time, one of whom was Beauregard, the logical successor on the field of battle. But given his current poor health plus his differences with the Davis administration and the president himself—one of his staff officers called Davis "your arch enemy" as early as July 1862—Beauregard was not the permanent solution, at least not in Davis's mind. In fact, he was relieved of command just a couple of months after Shiloh, ostensibly for going on sick leave without authorization. Later when the president found out that Beauregard was implying anti–Sidney Johnston feeling, there was no chance of the Creole's reinstatement. Davis's biographer William C. Davis, in fact, has surmised that the president's "prejudice toward Beauregard after he failed Sidney Johnston's memory kept the fourth-ranking officer in the Confederacy virtually out of the war for its last three years." Significantly, Davis confidentially wrote his brother just two weeks after Shiloh, "Beauregard may possess courage & as an Engineer skill but he wants character to command respect." Beauregard would not tactically command another major army for the rest of the war.[7]

The other remaining full generals were no more candidates either. The ranking Confederate general, Samuel Cooper, was simply not an option for field command since he was never going to leave his desk in the War Department in Richmond. That left Robert E. Lee and Joseph E. Johnston, whose fates were intertwined. Someone had to lead what most considered the Confederacy's first army (Department No. 1, while Sidney Johnston commanded Department No. 2), what would eventually become known as the Army of Northern Virginia. Joe Johnston commanded in Virginia at the time of Shiloh, with Lee, having previously held commands in western Virginia and South Carolina, now serving as an advisor to Davis. But Joe Johnston fell with an artillery wound in the shoulder at Seven Pines, just miles from Richmond, in late May; his wound was still bothering him even during the Vicksburg Campaign the next summer, a full year later. As a result, Joe Johnston could not be the replacement for the perished Sidney Johnston until much later in the war. Even then, because of his own differences with Davis, he would actually command the western army only a few months in two stints, the first during the Atlanta Campaign and the second at the end of the war, when it no longer made any real difference. Like Beauregard, Joe Johnston was never Davis's go-to general either. And his wounding at Seven Pines also affected Lee, whom Davis sent to command the Virginia army. Once Lee took over in early June, he would never give up command of the foremost Confederate army. In fact, he would only leave Virginia twice during the remainder of the war, both times on ill-fated invasions of the North, first in September 1862 and then in the summer of 1863.[8]

Since all four remaining Confederate full generals were unavailable for various reasons, command of the western army required someone else. As a result, Davis dipped down into the next tier of generals to find a replacement for Sidney Johnston. And that created chaos. The crux of the problem was elevating one of many equals to the command of his former colleagues. Each perhaps inwardly thought he would do better than the others of the same tier in rank, but they had accepted Johnston as one of the original full generals and gave him (and Beauregard for that matter) the necessary respect and deference. But elevating one of several equals to a new rank of superiority in the middle of the war stood the chance of leaving the others unsatisfied. Making matters more problematic was the thorny issue of seniority, whereby it would cause even greater animosity if someone junior was elevated over others.[9]

And that is exactly what happened. The next tier in rank were the major generals commanding corps in the Confederate armies. Accordingly, it seemed best to choose a new leader from among the four corps commanders of the Army of the Mississippi. The senior major general, and hence commander of the army's first numbered corps, was Leonidas Polk. He outranked the next-senior corps commander at Shiloh, Braxton Bragg, by two and a half months. Making the situation even more tense, Bragg outranked the next corps commander in line, William J. Hardee, by a mere three and a half weeks. The fourth commander, John C. Breckinridge, was still a brigadier general and a politician (later being Confederate secretary of war) and so was not really considered as Johnston's replacement. But being the former U.S. vice president, he had plenty of clout. The same held basically true for one of the two transplant generals from the trans-Mississippi. Sterling Price did not become a major general until a month before Shiloh, but Earl Van Dorn was senior by date to Hardee, although falling behind Polk and Bragg, trailing the latter by only seven days. That said, it became evident quickly that Bragg, with the urging of Beauregard, was the anointed one; he was promoted to full general immediately after Shiloh, with the new opening for a full general. Bragg expressed his own doubts, wiring the secretary of war: "I feel greatly honored at my selection by the President to succeed Sidney Johnston—no one can fill the vacancy." Others doubted, too; William Preston, now a brigadier general and brigade commander in the army at Corinth, wrote his nephew William on May 30: "We miss your father. The Double Bees [Beauregard and Bragg] do not rise to the exigency."[10]

The ascension, upon Beauregard's dismissal, of one of these equals caused a sharp reaction from the others, and it continued to fester throughout Bragg's tenure as commander of the Army of Tennessee. This year and a half is often seen as one of the most critical eras of the army's history and the western Confederacy's existence. Some argue that the war in the West was lost by the time of Shiloh, while others argue for Atlanta's importance in the charged geopolitical year of 1864. Still, one would be hard pressed to find a more critical period in the West than Bragg's tenure in command from June 1862 to December 1863, encompassing the Kentucky, Stones River, Tullahoma, Chickamauga, and Chattanooga Campaigns. The fate of the Southern nation was perhaps on the line, and the new army commander needed all the support he could get from his subordinates.[11]

But the next eighteen months were a disaster for both Bragg and the

Confederacy, in large part because of the backbiting from the new general's former equals, now his subordinates. No three more bitter enemies of General Bragg emerged than the three highest-ranking officers initially under him, Polk, Hardee, and Breckinridge. Historian Steven Woodworth argues that "Davis . . . allowed Polk and his cronies to destroy the effectiveness of Bragg as an army commander." Bragg himself wrote of his own efforts being "most distasteful to many of my senior generals, and they wince under the blows. Breckinridge, Polk & Hardee especially." At one point Hardee wrote Polk: "I have been thinking seriously of the condition of affairs with this army. . . . What shall we do? What is best to be done to save this army and its honor? I think we ought to counsel together." And Bragg certainly thought Hardee wanted his spot, writing a friend of his potential "retirement": "I must say there is no man here to command an army. The one who aspires to it is a good drill master, but no more, except that he is gallant." But by far, Polk was the most obnoxious opponent of Bragg, the differences between them stemming from the Shiloh concentration, with open hostility emerging in the Kentucky Campaign and ballooning thereafter. After being relieved by Bragg, the bishop wrote: "The poor man who is the author of this trouble is I am informed as much to be pitied or more than the object of his ill-feeling. I certainly feel a lofty contempt for his puny effort to inflict injury upon a man who has dry nursed him for the whole period of his connection with him and has kept him from ruining the cause of the country by the sacrifice of its armies." Certainly, Bragg continually seeking their approval, even in the form of asking whether he still retained the confidence of the army, did not help. Hardee wrote a blistering response to one inquiry: "I feel that frankness compels me to say that the general officers, whose judgment you have invoked, are unanimous in the opinion that a change in the command of this army is necessary. In this opinion I concur."[12]

There is no way to know if Albert Sidney Johnston, had he lived, would have performed any better than Bragg or if any of the other original full generals would have either. Still, many thought so. Randal L. Gibson, a brigade commander and avowed Bragg hater to be sure, related that "the West perished with Albert Sidney Johnston, and the Southern country followed." Yet the reality is that none of the available alternatives were good options to Davis, who truly believed there was "no other hand to take up his work in the West." Johnston's demise thus left command of the western Confederacy's most formidable defending army in the hands of a general pulled up from equals to command those equals who never quite accepted him. While the situation deteriorated quickly thereafter, the snowball effect started rolling that mild April day when Johnston gambled away his life and perished instead of conquered at Shiloh.[13]

Yet Johnston was long in a new grave by the time these effects became obvious. "When I die," he once told his brother-in-law William Preston, "I want a handful of Texas earth on my breast." He similarly told staff officer Thomas Jack that "he desired of his country six feet of Texas soil." It was obvious Johnston was a Texan and desired to rest there at the end of his life, so Texas authorities began the process of bringing his remains "home" soon after the war. They formed a committee of veterans to remove the body, the event taking place in January 1867. New Orleans citizens flocked to the grave, although no specific events were planned, and one newspaper reported that "a spontaneous procession was formed" as the hearse made its way through the streets of the city to the railroad station. Pallbearers were the elite of former Confederate generals, including Beauregard, Bragg, and Buckner as well as James Longstreet, John Bell Hood, Richard Taylor, and Gibson. After leaving New Orleans by rail, the casket was soon transferred to a steamer for the journey to Texas.[14]

Problems emerged as the vessel neared Galveston, however. The Federal commander of the city, Major General Charles Griffin, just two years removed from civil war, declined to allow any procession or other events relating to Johnston's arrival or departure. He saw it as his duty, "owing to the position that General Johnston occupied toward the United States Government, during the latter period of his life, to forbid the funeral procession." (The people of Galveston showed no remorse when Griffin himself succumbed to yellow fever just a year later.) Appeals went to higher-ups, with one allegedly returning a "very coarse and cynical" reply and Major General Philip Sheridan responding, "I have too much regard for the memory of the brave men who died to preserve our Government, to authorize Confederate demonstrations over the remains of any one who attempted to destroy it." An impromptu assembly occurred nevertheless before the body was moved on to Houston, where the same rules were in effect but, according to Johnston's son, were "not strictly enforced." Ultimately, the remains arrived at Austin, where Governor James W. Throckmorton presided over the ceremonies. After lying in state at the capitol, Johnston's remains were interred at the Texas State Cemetery, the title of his staff officer Theodore

O'Hara's famous Mexican War poem inscribed on the coffin: "The Bivouac of the Dead."[15]

Now a widow with several young children to raise, Eliza remained in California during the war, and much of the family remained there for generations. President Davis ensured the government looked after Eliza throughout the conflict, although she later came on hard times. And Davis always paid special homage to his friend as well. A particularly touching moment was when Preston gave the president Johnston's pistol worn at Shiloh. After the war, Davis helped dedicate a monument to Johnston in New Orleans on Shiloh's anniversary in 1887. William Johnston also took special care of his father's memory, writing extensively, including a large biography entitled *The Life of General Albert Sidney Johnston*.[16]

But Johnston's memory has morphed into divergent strands since that time. Many Civil War enthusiasts and casual commentators on the war, particularly in the South, still attest to the "had Johnston lived the South would have won Shiloh and maybe the war" line. On the other hand, many, if not most, academic historians fault him for what was really a miserable and costly several months in command. While there are certainly Johnston apologists, most notably historian Charles Roland, there are also detractors such as historian Thomas Connelly, who picked apart every single possibility of wrongdoing whether factual or interpreted that way. But the truth lies somewhere in the middle.

The most oft-asked question has been whether Sidney Johnston could have rendered the kind of leadership his peers such as Joe Johnston or more importantly Lee provided after their own initial missteps. For instance, many wonder if he could have become the Confederacy's western Lee if he had lived, whether he could have learned from his mistakes and developed into a first-rate commander. Certainly, Lee had his own missteps early in command, mainly in the Seven Days' Battles when coordination, timing, and the determination of his subordinates were nowhere like that displayed later in the war. Joe Johnston, prior to Lee, had the same kinds of troubles at Seven Pines and even earlier in 1861 in northern Virginia. Obviously, there was a learning curve when commanding these unprecedented numbers of troops and untried subordinates, but Lee's and Joe Johnston's missteps did not lead to the loss of significant amounts of territory or the loss of large chunks of their forces. And given his competing personality traits of overboard mildness in some cases and overboard rashness in others, the answer to the question of whether Sidney Johnston could have become another Lee is likely no.

Due mainly to those personality conflicts, it is obvious that, unlike Lee in particular or even Grant—his peer on the other side—Johnston did not have the makings to be the "genius" that Napoleonic military theorist Carl von Clausewitz described. Both he and the other famed theorist of the day, Henri Jomini, dwelled at length on the ideal commander and the needed coup d'oeil. But Jomini more tangibly emphasized the selection and utilization of a good chief of staff and command staff and most importantly specified the actions a military commander should employ, such as massing against an inferior force of the enemy and acquiring decisive points. He also delved into the makeup of the ideal commander somewhat as well, writing that two main attributes were necessary, "a high moral courage, capable of great resolutions," and "a physical courage which takes no account of danger." Jomini summed up that a good general "must know how to arrange a good plan of operations, and how to carry it to a successful termination." Certainly, Johnston had the courage Jomini required and, after months of planning but not producing, was on the cusp of carrying out the new operational plan he had decided upon. Whether that idea would have succeeded even had he lived was an altogether different matter.[17]

Clausewitz went further in examining what he termed military "genius" and looked at the makeup of the commander. He provided a wide range of attributes, what he called "a harmonious combination of elements," that were essential to success. These are courage, intellect, presence of mind, strength of will, energy, staunchness, character, and an ability for quick understanding of terrain and situations, the "coup d'oeil" Jomini also describes. But there are significant common denominators in Clausewitz's discussions of these attributes, all of them having to do with steadiness, quickness, and boldness, which Sidney Johnston was admittedly not blessed with. And despite Roland's use of Clausewitz to emphasize Johnston's decisive stance to continue the Shiloh offensive, which was true and indicated a growing maturity of his military command ideas, it is abundantly clear that Johnston did not have many of the attributes Clausewitz requires for the military genius, among them firmness, quick understanding, or steadiness. While he possessed some of the Clausewitzian attributes, he did not possess them all, and the uneven results followed in his command tenure. Indeed, Johnston was no military genius as defined by either Clausewitz or Jomini, he lacking the basic tenets of the famed Napoleonic coup d'oeil. Jeremy Gilmer, himself not a genius of a staff officer as required by Jomini, perhaps said it best when he decided that, among all the Confederates generals at Corinth—Johnston included, "among them all, I fear there is not a Napoleon."[18]

It is clear that both Jomini and Clausewitz emphasize the strength of a commander's mind, Clausewitz more than Jomini, and have determined that a man of firm belief in a plan and the ability to execute that plan, even with adaptations, is very much a key. Obviously, so many Civil War commanders, from George McClellan to John Pemberton, did not make the mark, but Grant and Lee were among those few who, in much more Clausewitzian form, made a decision even if it was risky and unpopular and stuck by it. Johnston showed signs of doing so at the end of his tenure, which leads to some speculation that he had begun to learn from his mistakes, but it was far too late to remedy the significant losses he had already endured by being so unsteady, methodical, and meek.

Obviously, Johnston made mistakes. But rather than enumerate all of them, large and small (some debatable), as historians have done through the decades since the war, it is perhaps more instructive to look at his life as a whole and see the patterns of problematic command mentalities that caused those individual mistakes. Examining flaws in Johnston's military command mentality may yield more clues as to why he made certain decisions and not others, and it can readily explain why his command of Department No. 2 was marred with so many perceived mistakes.

In essence, Johnston did not have the personality to be a great commander. There are three major detrimental personality/lifestyle traits that led him to be the general he was. One was that Johnston was slow to make decisions, events often overtaking him in the fast-paced poker style of warfare he was engaged in, especially as active operations began in mid-January 1862. A chess player who preferred a slow, methodical thinking-man's game, he simply could not keep up with events and they overwhelmed him while he increasingly concentrated on single individual parts while neglecting the whole. And this was a lifelong issue he faced, whether in response to the wave of deaths in the early 1830s, his military issues in Texas in the late 1830s, his financial problems his entire life, or his Confederate career.

Johnston himself remarked on his preference for slow, methodical decision making. In writing his son, he noted: "I have occasionally offered you a little of my experience, of which I have a large stock, purchased at high prices (which men of strong will have always to pay), to save you expense; but I doubt if it is a transferable article. It does not do to deal too much in expenditures; the means will not hold out. Caution and reflection are a cheap and safe substitute. It is better to make a survey, and sound where you intend to dive, than buy the same information by heedlessly plunging in and breaking your head." But caution and hesitation in war was not a great recipe, especially when confronted with the likes of the aggressive Grant. Johnston realized as much, even once ironically writing in reference to the Mexican War activities waged by others that "war like any other business cannot progress prosperously in the hands of pidlers." Still, he could rarely raise himself from the "piddling" mentality, even if he knew he needed to.[19]

Others readily picked up on Johnston's slowness of thought and action. His chief engineer, Captain Gilmer, for instance, noted in 1861 that he "is a cautious man & will not move until he feels confident of success." Even Johnston's archenemy Grant reflected on this, writing that Johnston was "vacillating and undecided in his actions." Many historians have agreed, Woodworth arguing that Johnston often "seemed to be one step behind." Connelly, admittedly hypernegative toward all things Johnston, observed that "he seemed able to grasp only one area of thought at a time, and unable to view the total command picture of his department."[20]

A second major issue was that Johnston was too gentlemanly and too lenient with his subordinates, not overseeing them properly and assuming their competence at face value with their rank. His self-confessed "repugnance to writing" did not help in keeping up with these subordinates, contributing to little coordination within his overall department, especially between his districts, until the concentration prior to Shiloh. Johnston simply let his subordinates largely command in their specific areas.[21]

But that was obviously a problem, as Johnston was seemingly a poor judge of character and never really seemed to have a grasp on reality when it came to his subordinates' ability. An example of this was his continual defense of Floyd and Pillow. Remarkably, the latter even met with Johnston the night before he left for Shiloh, at which time, according to Pillow's biographers, he even attempted to put Pillow back into the command structure. Johnston's dependence on mediocre-at-best and oftentimes downright-incompetent commanders such as Polk, Zollicoffer, Crittenden, Floyd, and Pillow caused enormous problems when they failed both Johnston and the Confederacy, leading to major disasters. But no error was so large as his insistence on allowing Floyd to command during the critical days of Fort Donelson. Significantly, Johnston seemed never to be able to command lackluster subordinates who were either his equals or superiors in past years. Men such as Polk (his roommate at West Point), Pillow (a major general in the Mexican War, during which Johnston was a mere colonel), or Floyd (governor of Virginia and U.S. secretary of war while Johnston still was a colonel) were all incompetent but seemed to garner his respect and deference because of their previous status and current rank.

Historians have also written extensively on this aspect of Johnston's command mentality. Beauregard's biographer T. Harry Williams has concluded: "Johnston refused to go to Donelson. He seemed obsessed with the idea that he personally had to conduct the column at Bowling Green to safety. His actions almost defy rational analysis." Connelly has argued that "his gentle tone and childlike faith in others made him an easy mark for an insubordinate lieutenant," adding that this mildness and trust "in human goodness [also] brought him much grief." Woodworth has even asserted that "his best course, viewed in the abstract, would have been to ensure that he was personally present at whatever position Polk commanded." Ultimately, Johnston was responsible for his subordinates' actions, but he did not monitor them closely or go himself to the critical scenes of action.[22]

Yet perhaps Johnston's greatest weakness was his frequent crossing of the line between acceptable risk taking to irrational behavior in the fast-moving poker game his life became, both personally and especially as Confederate theater commander. Certainly, he often took gambles, many of them acceptable and required by the terrible hand he had admittedly been dealt. Even in his Confederate command, many of his decisions that were truly risky were the correct and indeed only choice available. Given his lack of men and arms and the lengthy stretch of territory he was required to defend in 1861, he had no choice but to gamble that he could bluff the enemy until winter and more resources came along. And then after that gambit failed and he decided on the concentration at Corinth, there was no doubt that the gamble of an attack on Grant's forces at Pittsburg Landing, perilous though it was, represented the only real option Johnston had at the time. It was an acceptable risk.

But all too often, Johnston found himself caught up in the fury of command and making unwise decisions that more times than not exacerbated the already negative situation—in the end, even costing him his life. Crossing over from calculated risk-taker to obsessed gambler intent on one final hand that would win everything back often proved near-fatal to Johnston throughout his life. Certainly, his duel in Texas, his assumption of huge debt on China Grove, and finally his wading into battle himself at Shiloh were obviously detrimental to his own well-being, the last actually resulting in his death. Again, Johnston probably knew better; in slower times (such as during the Mexican War when, significantly, he was not in charge), he again ironically wrote that "the glory of the American arms ought not depend upon the hazard of the die" and that, in reference to cutting loose from a supply line, it was "foolishness to run the risks they have done from the beginning of the war." But once in command in a swift-moving game of war, Johnston simply could not help himself. Instead, he bet everything, even his life, and lost. And in a larger context, Johnston's death was not just consequential for himself and his family or even for his army at Shiloh. His death had ramifications that reverberated for the entire Civil War and negatively affected the South's chances for success.[23]

That said, there were, of course, mitigating circumstances that any commander, Lee and Grant included, would have been hard pressed to overcome. The length of the territorial line Johnston was tasked with defending; the geographic challenges of having three rivers piercing that line; a lack of adequate or even remotely adequate troops, arms, and supplies; a lack of competent subordinates; political influences; an administration in Richmond that would not support him until it was too late; and an aggressive opponent in Grant were all problems under which, combined, almost any commander would have wilted. And there were times when a considerable gamble had to be taken, the calculated risks that every commander faces. But Johnston's command mentality, alternating between too little oversight and too many overly risky gambles, made these issues entirely unsurpassable. That he was methodical and lenient while at the same time prone to overplaying his hand seems to argue that Johnston was not a good fit for the western (or any major) command under such circumstances.

Yet under these conditions of too much ground to cover, too few resources, and a prickly civilian administration that never forgave enemies, the question must be asked: could anyone have done better or even as good? Initially upon first appointment, perhaps one of the three full field generals in Virginia could have been spared to go out west. But given their later experiences in the war, there is no indication that Joe Johnston or Beauregard could have made any more progress in the dismal situation than Sidney Johnston did. A bolder, firmer, and more resolute Lee perhaps could have, yet he, too, stumbled in the war's first year and had to learn from his mistakes. Such stumbles in the perhaps more important and vulnerable Confederate West would likely have netted the same reverses for Lee that Johnston endured. Yet given what happened later in the conflict as well, perhaps Lee was the only one who could have made a difference in that theater, but he was tied up for the remainder of the war in Virginia. The net result was that, despite Sidney Johnston's personality flaws that grated away at his effectiveness in command, the problems outside his own personal makeup were just as glaring and likely insurmountable for anyone expect possibly Lee. In this case, historian Richard McMurry was entirely correct in his assessment of the problem of there being only one Lee for the entire Confederacy.[24]

Yet the major emphasis here is on Johnston, not Lee, although numerous historians have tried to make it a comparison. Roland, for instance, has argued that Johnston was "the one man who might have given the Confederates of the western theater a leadership comparable to that of Robert E. Lee in the east." Others obviously have disagreed, T. Harry Williams writing: "Nothing that Johnston did in his brief career justifies the belief that he had the elements of greatness. Many things that he did suggest that he was not qualified for high command." Perhaps Albert Castel has summed it up best in stating that Johnston "had been noble and gallant but indecisive and (the worse defect in any general according to Napoleon) unlucky." Given his standing in mid-1861 (perhaps unfounded as some argue), there was logic behind Davis's appointment, but as his command over the next few months showed, Johnston was not all that was advertised. The plain fact is that he was simply too methodical, too accommodating, and too lenient to be a good general, and his tenure in command of the Confederate army in the West showed as much. When these attributes caused him to get into crisis situations, he overcompensated and crossed the line from calculated risk to high-stakes gamble to regain his equilibrium. Certainly, with these personality and command traits, there is no indication that Johnston would have risen to the level of Lee in the East. Still, given how the events of the western theater played out for the rest of the war, there was probably no better choice to continue commanding the army had he lived.[25]

But we will never know exactly what Albert Sidney Johnston would have done or become because of his death on the field of Shiloh, the result of rolling the "iron dice" of battle and his own final gamble with his life—a high-stakes bet he lost in full.

NOTES

•———•

ABBREVIATIONS

ASJ   Albert Sidney Johnston

FHS   Filson Historical Society, Louisville, KY

MDAH   Mississippi Department of Archives and History, Jackson

NARA   National Archives and Records Administration, Washington DC

OR   *War of the Rebellion: A Compilation of the Official Records of the Union and Confederate Armies* (Washington, DC: U.S. Government Printing Office, 1880–1901). All citations to series 1 unless otherwise stated.

SNMP   Shiloh National Military Park, Shiloh, TN

TSLA   Tennessee State Library and Archives, Nashville

TU   Tulane University, New Orleans, LA

UNC   University of North Carolina, Chapel Hill

UTA   University of Texas at Arlington

WP   William Preston

WPJ   William Preston Johnston

YU   Yale University, New Haven, CT

PREFACE

1. William Preston Johnston, *The Life of Gen. Albert Sidney Johnston: His Service in the Armies of the United States, the Republic of Texas, and the Confederate States* (New York: D. Appleton, 1879), 608 (hereafter cited as Johnston, *Life*).

2. Johnston, *Life*, 14–15, 151–52.

3. Johnston, *Life*, 54; Charles P. Roland, *Albert Sidney Johnston: Soldier of Three Republics* (Austin: University of Texas Press, 1964), 116 (hereafter cited as Roland, *Johnson: Soldier*).

4. Johnston, *Life*, 54; Roland, *Johnston: Soldier*, 116; Bertram Wyatt-Brown, *Southern*

Honor: Ethics and Behavior in the Old South (New York: Oxford University Press, 1982), 343. For more context on gambling, see ibid., 327–61; and Everett Dick, *The Dixie Frontier: A Social History* (New York: Knopf, 1948), 164–69.

5. Rhys Isaac, *The Transformation of Virginia: 1740–1790* (Chapel Hill: University of North Carolina Press, 1980), 119; Kenneth S. Greenberg, *Honor and Slavery* (Princeton, NJ: Princeton University Press, 2020), 88. For Nimitz, see E. B. Potter, *Nimitz* (Annapolis: Naval Institute Press, 1976), 87; and Craig L. Symonds, *Nimitz at War: Command Leadership from Pearl Harbor to Tokyo Bay* (New York: Oxford University Press, 2022), 106, 111, 121, 166, 175, 246, 267, 277. Admiral Chester Nimitz, prior to the Battle of Midway in June 1942, had given his commanders orders for "the principle of calculated risk": "the avoidance of exposure of your force to attack by superior enemy forces without prospect of inflicting, as a result of such exposure, greater damage to the enemy."

6. James J. Broomall, *Private Confederacies: The Emotional Worlds of Southern Men as Citizens and Soldiers* (Chapel Hill: University of North Carolina Press, 2019), 2.

7. Robert Elder, *The Sacred Mirror: Evangelicalism, Honor, and Identity in the Deep South, 1790–1860* (Chapel Hill: University of North Carolina Press, 2016), 4; Johnston, *Life,* 71–72; Thomas L. Connelly, "The Johnston Mystique," *Civil War Times Illustrated,* no. 5 (October 1967):14–23; Bertram Wyatt-Brown, *Southern Honor: Ethics and Behavior in the Old South,* 25th anniv. ed. (New York: Oxford University Press, 2007), xxxv, 14.

8. Johnston, *Life,* 122, 164; Roland, *Johnston: Soldier,* 17, 107; Wyatt-Brown, *Southern Honor* (1982), 353; ASJ to George Hancock, October 24, 1839, Johnston Papers, TU. For context on dueling, see Wyatt-Brown, *Southern Honor* (1982), 350–61; and Dickson D. Bruce Jr., *Violence and Culture in the Antebellum South* (Austin: University of Texas Press, 1979).

9. Connelly, "Johnston Mystique," 14–23.

10. Roland, *Johnston: Soldier;* Roland, *Albert Sidney Johnston: Jefferson Davis' Greatest General* (Abilene, TX: McWhiney Foundation Press, 2000) (hereafter cited as Roland, *Johnston: General*); Johnston, *Life.*

11. John R. Lundberg, "'I Must Save This Army': Albert Sidney Johnston and the Shiloh Campaign," in *The Shiloh Campaign,* ed. Steven E. Woodworth (Carbondale: Southern Illinois University Press, 2009), 8.

12. Albert Castel, "Dead on Arrival," *Civil War Times Illustrated* 36, no. 1 (March 1997): 35; Connelly, "Johnston Mystique," 14–23; Connelly, *Army of the Heartland* (Baton Rouge: Louisiana State University Press, 1967), 62, 103, 112, 126–27; Larry J. Daniel, *Conquered: Why the Army of the Tennessee Failed* (Chapel Hill: University of North Carolina Press, 2019), 14.

I. TO A GENTLEMAN THIS TASTE IS ESSENTIAL

1. Johnston, *Life,* 1–2; Mrs. Ball to Miss Benton, undated, ASJ Genealogy Letter, Kentucky Historical Society, Frankfort.

2. Johnston, *Life,* 2.

3. Johnston, *Life,* 2–3, 9.

4. Johnston, *Life,* 2–5, 8–9.

5. Johnston, *Life,* 4, 9.

6. Johnston, *Life,* 3–5; William C. Davis, *Jefferson Davis: The Man and His Hour* (New York: HarperCollins, 1991), 128, 199.

7. Johnston, *Life*, 1–25. For more context on kinship, see Carolyn Earle Billingsley, *Communities of Kinship: Antebellum Families and the Settlement of the Cotton Frontier* (Athens: University of Georgia Press, 2004).

8. Johnston, *Life*, 7–8.

9. Johnston, *Life*, 6. For Josiah Stoddard Johnston, see "Johnston, Josiah Stoddard (1784–1833)", *Biographical Directory of the United States Congress*, https://bioguideretro.congress.gov/Home/MemberDetails?memIndex=j000194; and the Josiah Stoddard Johnston Papers, Historical Society of Pennsylvania, Philadelphia.

10. Johnston, *Life*, 6–7.

11. Johnston, *Life*, 2, 8–9; Eliza Johnston to ASJ, November 28, 1827, ASJ Papers, FHS.

12. Johnston, *Life*, 2–3; Edward Harris to Postmaster General, June 4, 1800, ASJ Papers, FHS.

13. Johnston, *Life*, 1–25. For context on Southern manhood, see Lorri Glover, *Southern Sons: Becoming Men in the New Nation* (Baltimore: Johns Hopkins University Press, 2007). For the relationship between statesmanship and slavery among Southern gentlemen, see Kenneth S. Greenberg, *Masters and Statesmen: The Political Culture of American Slavery* (Baltimore: Johns Hopkins University Press, 1988).

14. Johnston, *Life*, 2, 6.

15. Stephen E. Ambrose, *Duty, Honor, Country: A History of West Point* (Baltimore: Johns Hopkins University Press, 1966).

16. Johnston, *Life*, 10; Nathaniel Eaton to WPJ, January 1, 1873, Johnston Papers, TU.

17. Name Index to U.S. Military Academy Cadet Application Papers, 1805–66, undated, 215; and ASJ to John Calhoun, May 18, 1822, E 243—U.S. Military Academy Cadet Application Papers, 1805–66, RG 94, NARA.

18. *Register of the Officers and Cadets of the U.S. Military Academy, June, 1823* (New York: U.S. Military Academy Printing Office, 1823), 12, 15; *Register of the Officers and Cadets of the U.S. Military Academy, June, 1824* (New York: U.S. Military Academy Printing Office, 1824), 10, 12; *Register of the Officers and Cadets of the U.S. Military Academy, June, 1825* (New York: U.S. Military Academy Printing Office, 1825), 8–9; *Register of the Officers and Cadets of the U.S. Military Academy, June, 1826* (New York: U.S. Military Academy Printing Office, 1826), 6–7; *Roll of the Cadets Arranged According to Merit in Conduct for the Year Ending 30th June, 1826* (New York: U.S. Military Academy Printing Office, 1826), 3–6; Roland, *Johnston: Soldier*, 13–14; Edward White to WPJ, March 3, 1873, Johnston Papers, TU.

19. Johnston, *Life*, 12–13; Davis, *Jefferson Davis*, 28; Edward White to WPJ, March 3, 1873, Johnston Papers, TU.

20. Johnston, *Life*, 12–13.

21. George W. Cullum, *Biographical Register of the Officers and Graduates of the U.S. Military Academy at West Point, N.Y., from Its Establishment, in 1802, to 1890, with the Early History of the United States Military Academy*, 10 vols. (Boston: Houghton, Mifflin, 1891), 1:367–68; Johnston, *Life*, 13–14; Joseph H. Parks, *General Leonidas Polk, C.S.A.: The Fighting Bishop* (Baton Rouge: Louisiana State University Press, 1962), 24.

22. Johnston, *Life*, 17; Henry Clay Invitation, October 25, 1826, Johnston Papers, TU; Eliza Johnston to ASJ, December 26, 1826, ASJ Papers, FHS.

23. Johnston, *Life*, 18.

24. Johnston, *Life*, 18; ASJ to William Bickley, October 10, 1827, Johnston Papers, TU; ASJ

to Roger Jones, October 21, 1831, ASJ Papers, FHS; ASJ to Colonel Towson, July 11, 1827, ASJ Letter, Chicago History Museum.

25. Johnston, *Life,* 21.

26. Johnston, *Life,* 22–23, 45; Stephen W. Berry, *All That Makes a Man: Love and Ambition in the Civil War South* (New York: Oxford University Press, 2004), 12. For more on Southern family honor, see Wyatt-Brown, *Southern Honor* (1982), 117–326; and James J. Broomall, "Wartime Masculinities," in *The Cambridge History of the American Civil War,* 3 vols., ed. Aaron Sheehan-Dean (Cambridge: Cambridge University Press, 2019), 3:4. See also Steven M. Stowe, *Intimacy and Power in the Old South: Ritual in the Lives of Planters* (Baltimore: Johns Hopkins University Press, 1987).

27. Johnston, *Life,* 24–25; Henrietta Johnston to Caroline Preston, April 15, 1831, ASJ Papers, FHS.

28. Johnston, *Life,* 24–25; Rock Island Conference Notes, April 13, 1832, Johnston Papers, TU.

29. James M. McPherson, *For Cause & Comrades: Why Men Fought in the Civil War* (New York: Oxford University Press, 1997), 31, 78; Berry, *All That Makes a Man,* 9; ASJ to William Bickley, October 10, 1827; and ASJ Diaries, 1832, Johnston Papers, TU. For the Black Hawk War, see Kerry A. Trask, *Black Hawk: The Battle for the Heart of America* (New York: Henry Holt, 2005).

30. Johnston, *Life,* 21, 27, 36; Davis, *Jefferson Davis,* 40; Nathaniel Eaton to WPJ, January 1, 1873, Johnston Papers, TU. For the antebellum army and operations on the frontier, see Samuel J. Watson, *Peacekeepers and Conquerors: The Army Officer Corps on the American Frontier, 1821–1846* (Lawrence: University Press of Kansas, 2013).

31. Johnston, *Life,* 1–25.

32. Johnston, *Life,* 46; Nathaniel Eaton to WPJ, January 1, 1873, Johnston Papers, TU.

33. Johnston, *Life,* 12.

34. Johnston, *Life,* 50–55.

35. Johnston, *Life,* 47.

36. Cullum, *Biographical Register,* 1:367–68; Johnston, *Life,* 1.

37. Berry, *All That Makes a Man,* 21; Johnston, *Life,* 48–49; Caroline Preston to Edward Hobbs, June 21, 1832, ASJ Papers, FHS.

38. Johnston, *Life,* 50–51.

39. Johnston, *Life,* 47.

40. Johnston, *Life,* 47; Roland, *Johnston: Soldier,* 48.

41. Johnston, *Life,* 48–49.

42. Johnston, *Life,* 52; Cullum, *Biographical Register,* 1:368; John Davidson to WPJ, January 16, 1873, Johnston Papers, TU.

43. Johnston, *Life,* 51–53; Roland, *Johnston: Soldier,* 51; Henrietta Johnston to George Hancock, September 15, 1834, ASJ Papers, FHS.

44. Johnston, *Life,* 53–54.

45. Johnston, *Life,* 54.

46. Johnston, *Life,* 54–55; ASJ to WP, April 20, 1836, Johnston Papers, TU.

47. Johnston, *Life,* 55.

1. Johnston, *Life,* 717.

2. H. W. Brands, *Lone Star Nation: The Epic Story of the Battle for Texas Independence* (New York: Anchor, 2005).

3. Johnston, *Life,* 54–55.

4. Johnston, *Life,* 57, 68.

5. Johnston, *Life,* 63–64, 68–69. See also the Sam Houston Papers at Rice University and at the University of Texas, Austin.

6. Johnston, *Life,* 69, 72–73.

7. Johnston, *Life,* 73.

8. Johnston, *Life,* 74–76, 79–80; Felix Huston to ASJ, February 4, 1837, Johnston Papers, TU. For Huston, see the Felix Huston Papers, MDAH; and Wyatt-Brown, *Southern Honor* (1982), 356–57.

9. Johnston, *Life,* 75–77; ASJ to Felix Huston, February 4, 1837, Johnston Papers, TU.

10. Johnston, *Life,* 76–78; Nathaniel Eaton to WPJ, January 1, 1873, Johnston Papers, TU.

11. Johnston, *Life,* 78–79; George W. Morgan Autobiography, 1883, George W. Morgan Papers, Library of Congress, Washington, DC.

12. Johnston, *Life,* 78–79.

13. Johnston, *Life,* 80–81, 83–85.

14. Johnston, *Life,* 80–81, 83–85; ASJ to Secretary of War, April 22, 1837, Johnston Papers, TU.

15. Sam Houston to ASJ, February 7, 1837; and William Fisher to ASJ, February 7, 1837, Johnston Papers, TU. For Houston, see James L. Haley, *Sam Houston* (Norman: University of Oklahoma Press, 2002).

16. Johnston, *Life,* 84–87, 91; Roland, *Johnston: Soldier,* 64, 79; ASJ Order Book, 1837–38, Johnston Papers, TU.

17. Johnston, *Life,* 90–96, 114. For examples of letters of recommendations during 1839, see ASJ Papers, FHS.

18. Johnston, *Life,* 95–98; ASJ to President Lamar, December 18, 1838, Johnston Papers, TU.

19. Johnston, *Life,* 113, 119–21; ASJ to Sam Houston, January 5, 1840, Johnston Papers, TU. See also Folders 1–4, ASJ Collection, UTA.

20. Johnston, *Life,* 122–23; Roland, *Johnston: Soldier,* 105; ASJ to George Hancock, October 24, 1839, Johnston Papers, TU.

21. Johnston, *Life,* 123; Roland, *Johnston: Soldier,* 112.

22. Johnston, *Life,* 123; Lease, March 28, 1850, ASJ Papers, FHS.

23. Johnston, *Life,* 128.

24. Johnston, *Life,* 129.

25. Johnston, *Life,* 129; Roland, *Johnston: Soldier,* 101, 119; "Copy of Opinion of the Supreme Court," *Texas Republican* (Marshall), June 12, 1858; Land Documents, 1839–88, ASJ Papers, YU; Wyatt-Brown, *Southern Honor* (1982), 360, 373; Broomall, "Wartime Masculinities," 5.

26. Johnston, *Life,* 155, 165.

27. Johnston, *Life,* 147, 159; ASJ to George Hancock, February 28, 1847; and ASJ to Edward Hobbs, June 10, 1849, Johnston Papers, TU; Wyatt-Brown, *Southern Honor* (1982), 360, 373; Greenberg, *Honor and Slavery,* 62.

28. Johnston, *Life,* 146–48, 151–53, 158; Roland, *Johnston: Soldier,* 141; ASJ to WPJ, August 3, 1847, Johnston Papers, TU.

29. Johnston, *Life,* 129–30, 156, 165.

30. Johnston, *Life,* 155, 157, 159, 165, 182; ASJ to George Hancock, March 22, 1848; and ASJ to Edward Hobbs, June 10, 1849, Johnston Papers, TU.

31. Johnston, *Life,* 145; Roland, *Johnston: Soldier,* 121, 164.

32. Johnston, *Life,* 131–36, 142, 145; Zachary Taylor to George Hancock, February 8, 1846; and ASJ to George Hancock, February 28, July 10, 1846, Johnston Papers, TU. See also Folder 5, ASJ Collection, UTA.

33. Johnston, *Life,* 138–42; ASJ Receipt Book, 1847, ASJ Papers, FHS; ASJ to WPJ, September 28, 1846; and Joseph Hooker to WPJ, June 3, 1875, Johnston Papers, TU.

34. Johnston, *Life,* 142–45; Davis, *Jefferson Davis,* 145; Roland, *Johnston: Soldier,* 138.

35. Johnston, *Life,* 143–46, 152.

36. Johnston, *Life,* 160; Roland, *Johnston: Soldier,* 126.

37. Johnston, *Life,* 167–69.

38. Johnston, *Life,* 167–69; ASJ to R. Jones, December 2, 1849, ASJ Letter, University of Southern Mississippi, Hattiesburg. For the regular army prior to the Civil War, see Robert Wooster, *The United States Army and the Making of America: From Confederation to Empire, 1775–1903* (Lawrence: University Press of Kansas, 2021).

39. Johnston, *Life,* 170, 182; ASJ to George Hancock, December 14, 1850, Johnston Papers, TU. See also Folder 6, ASJ Collection, UTA.

40. Johnston, *Life,* 171–73, 175, 181; ASJ Diary, 1850, Johnston Papers, TU; Roland, *Johnston: Soldier,* 158; ASJ Trip Diary, 1850; ASJ to daughter, August 10, 1854; ASJ to WPJ, December 23, 1854; and WPJ Trip Diary, 1855, Johnston Papers, TU.

41. Johnston, *Life,* 178–79; Roland, *Johnston: Soldier,* 152–53, 163, 166; H. McCulloch to ASJ, August 10, 1851, ASJ Papers, FHS.

42. Roland, *Johnston: Soldier,* 165; Thomas Wood to ASJ, July 8, 1852, ASJ Papers, FHS; Davis, *Jefferson Davis,* 119; Linda Lasswell Crist et al., eds., *The Papers of Jefferson Davis,* 14 vols. (Baton Rouge: Louisiana State University Press, 1971–2015), 8:597 (hereafter cited as Christ, *Davis Papers*).

43. Johnston, *Life,* 183–84; ASJ to WPJ, January 1, 1855, Johnston Papers, TU.

44. Johnston, *Life,* 184; Samuel Cooper to ASJ, May 19, 1855, Johnston Papers, TU.

45. ASJ Commission, March 9, 1855, Johnston Papers, TU; Davis, *Jefferson Davis,* 231; Brian Steel Wills, *George Henry Thomas: As True as Steel* (Lawrence: University Press of Kansas, 2012), 78–79; Robert G. Hartje, *Van Dorn: The Life and Times of a Confederate General* (Nashville: Vanderbilt University Press, 1967), 59; Nathaniel Cheairs Hughes Jr., *General William J. Hardee: Old Reliable* (Baton Rouge: Louisiana State University Press, 1965), 52; Johnston, *Life,* 185; Joseph Johnston to ASJ, March 10, 1855, Johnston Papers, TU. The real 2nd Cavalry would be somewhat synonymous to a fictional pre–World War II regiment in which George Marshall, Douglas McArthur, Dwight Eisenhower, George Patton, Mark Clark, Hap Arnold, and Omar Bradley all served.

46. Roland, *Johnston: Soldier,* 171–73; Emory M. Thomas, *Robert E. Lee: A Biography* (New York: Norton, 1995), 163–64; Johnston, *Life,* 186; Hughes, *Hardee,* 53; ASJ to Samuel Cooper, October 12, 1855, YU; ASJ to daughter, September 21, 1855; William Hardee to ASJ, September 26, 1855; and ASJ to WPJ, September 29, 1855, Johnston Papers, TU.

47. Johnston, *Life*, 187–89; Eliza Johnston to WPJ, November 9, 1855; and Eliza Johnston Diary, 1855–56, Johnston Papers, TU.

48. Johnston, *Life*, 189, 191; Roland, *Johnston: Soldier*, 93, 177–78; Dabney H. Maury, *Recollections of a Virginian in the Mexican, Indian, and Civil Wars* (New York: Charles Scribner's Sons, 1894), 103; Stephen D. Engle, *Don Carlos Buell: Most Promising of All* (Chapel Hill: University of North Carolina Press, 1999), 51; ASJ to Samuel Cooper, December 5, 1856, YU; ASJ to Samuel Cooper, January 4, 1857, ASJ Letter, University of Kentucky, Lexington; ASJ to Samuel Cooper, May 27, 1856; and ASJ to WPJ, May 7, 1856, Johnston Papers, TU. See also Folders 7–9, ASJ Collection, UTA.

49. Johnston, *Life*, 189–90; Roland, *Johnston: Soldier*, 182, 242; ASJ to George Hancock, October 24, 1839; ASJ to WPJ, June 15, 1849; and ASJ to WPJ, August 21, September 12, November 23, 1856, Johnston Papers, TU; James B. McPherson, *Battle Cry of Freedom: The Civil War Era* (New York: Oxford University Press, 1988), 153–62.

50. Roland, *Johnston: Soldier*, 184; ASJ Letters, University of Utah, Salt Lake City; "Col. A. Sidney Johnston," *Louisville Courier*, February 1, 1858. See also Folder 10, ASJ Collection, UTA. For the Mormon Rebellion, see David L. Bigler and Will Bagley, *The Mormon Rebellion: America's First Civil War, 1857–1858* (Norman: University of Oklahoma Press, 2011).

51. Johnston, *Life*, 208–9; ASJ to Amos Eaton, September 24, 1857, YU; George Lay to William Harney, June 29, 1857; and Robert E. Lee to ASJ, August 1, 1857, Johnston Papers, TU.

52. Johnston, *Life*, 208–13, 215, 217–20, 222–23; ASJ Military Orders Book, 1857–58, Johnston Papers, TU; ASJ to Assistant Adjutant General, September 11, 1857; and ASJ to Fitz John Porter, September 12, 1857, YU; Fitz John Porter Diary, 1857–58, Johnston Papers, TU; ASJ to Major, January 4, 1858, YU.

53. Johnston, *Life*, 221, 223–24. See also the Alfred Cumming Papers at Duke University and at the University of California, Berkeley.

54. Johnston, *Life*, 226–30, 233, 235, 240; ASJ Military Orders Book, 1858–59; and Military Correspondence, 1858–59, Johnston Papers, TU; ASJ Military Pay Record, December 3, 1858, Brigham Young University, Salt Lake City.

55. Johnston, *Life*, 235–38, 241, 243; Roland, *Johnston: Soldier*, 204; Engle, *Buell*, 53; "Late and Interesting from the Army in Utah," *Buffalo (NY) Daily Courier*, December 9, 1859. See also ASJ Letters, 1857–59, YU; and ASJ to WPJ, August 27, 1859, ASJ Papers, FHS.

56. Johnston, *Life*, 241, 243; *OR*, 50(1):449; ASJ Military Orders Book, 1859–60; and Military Correspondence Book, 1859–60, Johnston Papers, TU.

57. Johnston, *Life*, 246–48; Roland, *Johnston: Soldier*, 238; ASJ to WPJ, August 27, 1859, Johnston Papers, TU.

58. Johnston, *Life*, 248; *OR*, 50(1):433; Roland, *Johnston: Soldier*, 241–42; ASJ to WPJ, January 17, 1861 (mislabeled 1860); and Johnston Memo, November 15, 1860 (filed under 1861), Johnston Papers, TU.

59. Johnston, *Life*, 256–61, 265, 271–72; *OR*, 50(1):433, 437–39, 444, 449, 451–52, 454–58, 462–63, 465; ASJ to Lorenzo Thomas, April 9, 1861; and unknown to WPJ, April 27, 1861, Johnston Papers, TU; Jeremy Gilmer to wife, October 23, 1862, Jeremy F. Gilmer Papers, UNC; ASJ to Abraham Rencher, March 5, 1860, Huntington Library, San Marino, CA, digital copy at University of New Mexico, Albuquerque.

60. Johnston, *Life*, 234, 260–64, 266; *OR*, 50(1):447–48, 455, 463–64, 469, 471–72; ASJ to WPJ, September 23, 1858; unknown to WPJ, April 27, 1861; E. V. Sumner to Colonel, April 28,

1861; and Fitz Porter to Major, May 6, 1861, Johnston Papers, TU; C. P. Gaukles to ASJ, May 6, 1861, RG 109, chap. 2, vol. 217, NARA.

61. Johnston, *Life,* 159; ASJ to Edward Hobbs, June 10, 1849, Johnston Papers, TU.

62. ASJ to WPJ, February 25, 1861, Johnston Papers, TU.

3. THAT IS SIDNEY JOHNSTON'S STEP

1. Johnston, *Life,* 194; Eliza Gilpin to ASJ, February 9, 1858, ASJ Papers, FHS. For Seward, see Walter Stahr, *Seward: Lincoln's Indispensable Man* (New York: Simon and Shuster, 2013).

2. Johnston, *Life,* 266, 271–72, 274, 276–77, 279.

3. Johnston, *Life,* 266, 271–72, 274, 276–77, 279; Fitz Porter to ASJ, April 18, May 1, 1861; and Fitz Porter to Major, May 6, 1861, Johnston Papers, TU; William Mackall to WPJ, January 7, 1876, Johnston Papers, TU.

4. Johnston, *Life,* 273; *OR,* 50(1):456; Eliza Gilpin to ASJ, April 15, 1861; and ASJ to Eliza Gilpin, June 1, 1861, Johnston Papers, TU.

5. Johnston, *Life,* 267, 272; Fitz Porter to ASJ, April 18, 1861, Johnston Papers, TU.

6. *OR,* Ser. 2, 2:358–62; Johnston, *Life,* 269, 274, 276, 291; Davis, *Jefferson Davis,* 306; Roland, *Johnston: Soldier,* 235.

7. *OR,* Ser. 2, 2:9, 258–59, 362; Johnston, *Life,* 279, 282–83 268, 272–73, 277–79, 280–86, 289; *OR,* 4:19, 50(1):496; Crist, *Davis Papers,* 7:128; Roland, *Johnston: Soldier,* 252, 256; ASJ to Eliza, June 26, July 1, 5, 21, 1861, Johnston Papers, TU.

8. Johnston, *Life,* 289–91; ASJ to Eliza, August 7, 1861, Johnston Papers, TU; *OR,* 2:752, 50(1):566, 629–30, 639, 879; Parks, *Polk,* 166–67; Steven E. Woodworth, *Jefferson Davis and His Generals: The Failure of Confederate Command in the West* (Lawrence: University Press of Kansas, 1990), 50; Huston Horn, *Leonidas Polk: Warrior Bishop of the Confederacy* (Lawrence: University Press of Kansas, 2019), 8; Crist, *Davis Papers,* 7:329.

9. *OR,* Ser. 4, 1:127–31, 607; Davis, *Jefferson Davis,* 357–61, 377; Crist, *Davis Papers,* 7:314; J. B. Jones, *A Rebel War Clerk's Diary: At the Confederate States Capital, Volume 1: April 1861–July 1863,* 2 vols., ed. James I. Robertson Jr. (Lawrence: University Press of Kansas, 2015), 1:37; ASJ to Leroy Walker, September 11, 1861, Johnston Papers, TU; L. P. Walker to ASJ, August 31, 1861; and ASJ Oath, September 4, 1861, RG 109, chap. 2, vol. 217, NARA; Johnston Commission, August 31, 1861; Acceptance, September 11, 1861; and Oath, ASJ Papers, Library of Congress, Washington, DC.

10. *OR,* 3:688, 4:188, 193, 395–96, 405, 5:830, 52(2):140; Johnston, *Life,* 732; Hughes, *Hardee,* 80; Parks, *Polk,* 167; Crist, *Davis Papers,* 7:292, 313, 320, 323, 330.

11. *OR,* 3:688, 4:188, 193, 395–96, 405, 5:830, 52(2):140; Johnston, *Life,* 732; Hughes, *Hardee,* 80; Parks, *Polk,* 167; Crist, *Davis Papers,* 7:292, 313, 320, 323, 330.

12. *OR,* 3:688, 4:188, 193, 395–96, 405, 5:830, 52(2):140; Johnston, *Life,* 732; Crist, *Davis Papers,* 7:292, 313, 320, 323, 330; Hughes, *Hardee,* 80; Parks, *Polk,* 167.

13. *OR,* 6:788.

14. *OR,* 3:703, 4:188–89, 193, 407, 476, 5:834; Johnston, *Life,* 306.

15. Johnston, *Life,* 307; WPJ to Rosa Johnston, September 18, 1861, ASJ Papers, FHS.

16. *OR,* 4:193–94; ASJ to Davis, September 16, 1861, Johnston Papers, TU.

17. *OR,* 4:405; Roland, *Johnston: General,* 25.

18. *OR,* 3:498, 501; Johnston, *Life,* 314, 379; Timothy B. Smith, *Grant Invades Tennessee: The 1862 Battles for Forts Henry and Donelson* (Lawrence: University Press of Kansas, 2016), 1–41.

19. *OR,* 4:189–90, 408, 52(2):145; Daniel, *Conquered,* 13; ASJ to Samuel Cooper, October 5, 1861, RG 109, E 103, NARA.

20. *OR,* 4:193–94, 418, 7:258; Johnston, *Life,* 316; Woodworth, *Davis and His Generals,* 52.

21. *OR,* 4:193–94; Connelly, *Army of the Heartland,* 68; ASJ to Davis, September 16, 1861, Johnston Papers, TU.

22. *OR,* 4:408, 413, 437; William C. Davis, *Breckinridge: Statesman, Soldier, Symbol* (Baton Rouge: Louisiana State University Press, 1974), 298; ASJ Memos and Answers to Inquiry, undated, RG 109, E 101/193, NARA.

23. *OR,* 4:411–13, 420–21, 7:258–59, 52(2):152; *OR,* Ser. 2, 2:1410–11; Roland, *Johnston: Soldier,* 274; Daniel, *Conquered,* 15.

24. Woodworth, *Davis and His Generals,* 53, 61; *OR,* 3:224–25, 707, 720, 4:193–94, 418, 420, 424, 461, 485, 53:748; ASJ to Price, October 31, 1861, Johnston Papers, TU.

25. *OR,* 3:224–25, 707, 720, 4:193–94, 418, 420, 424, 485, 461, 53:748; Woodworth, *Davis and His Generals,* 53, 61; ASJ to Price, October 31, 1861, Johnston Papers, TU.

26. *OR,* 3:708, 4:412–13, 418, 421–23, 432, 434, 442, 468–69; Johnston, *Life,* 337, 340, 410; ASJ to Benjamin, October 22, 1861, Johnston Papers, TU.

27. Davis, *Jefferson Davis,* 396–97; *OR,* 4:408, 410, 416–17, 423, 436, 441, 455, 52(2):192, 228–29, 53:190; ASJ to Cooper, October 4, 1861, Johnston Papers, TU; ASJ to Davis, January 9, 1862, RG 109, chap. 2, vol. 217, NARA; David Yandell to WPJ, November 11, 1877, Johnston Papers, TU.

28. *OR,* 4:408, 410, 416–17, 423, 436, 441, 455, 52(2):192, 228–29, 53:190; ASJ to Cooper, October 4, 1861; and A. B. Moore to ASJ, September 23, 1861, Johnston Papers, TU.

29. *OR,* 4:407, 426, 430, 432, 445, 453, 459, 472, 490; Johnston, *Life,* 380.

30. *OR,* Ser. 2, 1:541, 543, 2:1398–99, 3:231, 242–43, 273, 309, 771, 791, 793.

31. Johnston, *Life,* 389, 720.

32. ASJ to Eliza, December 29, 1861; Bill of Sale, September 30, 1861; and Unknown to ASJ, October 29, 1861, Johnston Papers, TU.

33. *OR,* 52(2):145, 154, 156; Johnston, *Life,* 317; Orders No. 2, September 26, 1861; and Orders No. 4, October 21, 1861, RG 109, chap. 2, vol. 217, NARA; Blanton Duncan to ASJ, January 10, 1862; ASJ to Eliza, January 6, 1862; and Yandell to ASJ, November 4, 1861, Johnston Papers, TU; Jeremy Gilmer to wife, October 13, November 4, December 20, 1862, Jeremy F. Gilmer Papers, UNC.

34. L. Woolfolk to ASJ, September 4, 1861; P. Gray to ASJ, September 8, 1861; Alex Cowan to ASJ, September 13, 1861; James Meriweather to ASJ, September 5, 19, October 4, 1861; F. Royster to ASJ, October 1861; Umpire Pedigree, December 29, 1857; Alexander Clayton to ASJ, September 20, 1861; Pettus to ASJ, December 5, 1861; and Harris to ASJ, December 14, 1861, Johnston Papers, TU.

35. Arthur Marvin Shaw Jr., "General Albert Sidney Johnston's Horses at Shiloh," *Arkansas Historical Quarterly* 8, no. 3 (Autumn 1949): 206–10; L. Blackburn to ASJ, October 18, 1861; and D. Cockrell to ASJ, October 19, 1861, Johnston Papers, TU.

36. *OR,* 4:409, 417, 430, 444, 452–53, 459, 468, 474, 6:773, 7:807; ASJ to Benjamin, October 22, 1861, Johnston Papers, TU.

37. *OR,* 4:426; Johnston, *Life,* 415.

38. *OR*, 4:416, 436; ASJ to Cooper, October 4, 1861; and Gustavus Henry to ASJ, October 10, 1861, Johnston Papers, TU; William Jackson to Ma, September 18, 1861, William H. Jackson Papers, TSLA.

39. Johnston, *Life*, 326.

40. *OR*, 4:209, 437–38, 441, 444, 7:922; Fisher Hannum to ASJ, 1861, New-York Historical Society.

41. *OR*, 4:433, 440, 446, 453–54, 456–59, 461, 6:783; Johnston, *Life*, 411; William Mackall to Lieutenant Dixon, September 17, 1861; and Mackall to Sir, September 17, 1861, RG 109, chap. 2, vol. 217, NARA.

42. *OR*, 3:535, 4:444–45, 454, 7:922; Johnston, *Life*, 327; William Mackall to F. W. Leland, October 10, 1861, RG 109, chap. 2, vol. 217, NARA; "Memorandum," November 1861; and WP to WPJ, April 18, 1862, Johnston Papers, TU; Jeremy Gilmer to wife, October 21, 1862, Jeremy F. Gilmer Papers, UNC. For Preston, see Peter J. Sehlinger, *Kentucky's Last Cavalier: General William Preston, 1816–1887* (Lexington: University Press of Kentucky, 2004).

43. *OR*, 4:448, 455.

44. *OR*, 4:448, 455, 6:661, 7:259; Johnston, *Life*, 308; Woodworth, *Davis and His Generals*, 55; WP to WPJ, April 18, 1862, Johnston Papers, TU.

45. *OR*, 4:462, 466–67, 473; Johnston, *Life*, 315, 493; Roland, *Johnston: Soldier*, 271; John F. Marszalek, *Sherman: A Soldier's Passion for Order* (New York: Free Press, 1993), 158–59; James Lee McDonough, *William Tecumseh Sherman: In the Service of My Country: A Life* (New York: Norton, 2016), 283–84; Engle, *Buell*, 87.

46. *OR*, 4:463, 484; Jeremy Gilmer to wife, October 17, 1862, Jeremy F. Gilmer Papers, UNC.

47. *OR*, 4:446, 448, 455, 469, 478, 481, 488, 491–92, 552, 560, 7:689, 719, 723, 731, 52(2):239, 246.

48. *OR*, 3:310–11. For Belmont, see Nathaniel Cheairs Hughes Jr., *The Battle of Belmont: Grant Strikes South* (Chapel Hill: University of North Carolina Press, 1991).

49. *OR*, 4:230–31, 7:700–701, 726, 759; *OR*, Ser. 4, 1:838, 929; Johnston, *Life*, 359.

50. *OR*, 4:498, 504, 533, 538, 552, 556, 559, 7:706; *OR*, Ser. 4, 1:855; Woodworth, *Davis and His Generals*, 62–63.

51. *OR*, 4:244, 505, 509, 551, 558, 564, 702, 6:320–21, 327, 390, 398, 400, 403–4, 406, 411, 413, 417–18, 427, 646, 769, 7:688, 690, 694, 738, 749; ASJ to Moore, December 2, 1861, Johnston Papers, TU.

52. *OR*, 3:306, 4:513–14, 517, 522, 529, 532, 539, 543, 550, 554; Nathaniel Cheairs Hughes Jr. and Roy P. Stonesifer Jr., *The Life and Wars of Gideon J. Pillow* (Chapel Hill: University of North Carolina Press, 1993), 196; Connelly, *Army of the Heartland*, 80.

53. *OR*, 4:513–14, 517, 522, 532, 539, 543, 550, 7:692, 705, 747, 52(2):222.

54. *OR*, 7:773–74; Johnston, *Life*, 323.

55. *OR*, 7:699, 710; Larry J. Daniel, *Engineering in the Confederate Heartland* (Baton Rouge: Louisiana State University Press, 2022), 31.

56. *OR*, 3:739, 4:353, 484, 515–16, 524, 530–31, 553–54, 560–63, 7:691, 718, 727–28; Johnston, *Life*, 362; John Davidson to WPJ, January 16, 1873, Johnston Papers, TU.

57. *OR*, 7:746, 759, 779, 809; Crist, *Davis Papers*, 7:441; Connelly, *Army of the Heartland*, 104; David Yandell to WPJ, November 11, 1877, Johnston Papers, TU.

58. *OR*, 3:720, 735, 5:1000, 7:725, 746, 753, 779; Johnston, *Life*, 396; Roland, *Johnston: Soldier*, 280.

59. *OR,* 7:781.

60. *OR,* 4:496, 501, 506, 514, 519, 526–28, 7:692, 709, 752; Daniel, *Engineering in the Confederate Heartland,* 32; Connelly, *Army of the Heartland,* 80, 85; G. W. Woolfork to ASJ, December 5, 1861, Johnston Papers, TU; Jeremy Gilmer to wife, October 23, 25, 1861, January 7, 1862, Jeremy F. Gilmer Papers, UNC.

61. Roland, *Johnston: Soldier,* 281, 285; Connelly, *Army of the Heartland,* 86–87. Connelly actually defends Zollicoffer as "a capable strategist."

62. Connelly, *Army of the Heartland,* 64; *OR,* 4:419–20, 6:823, 826, 7:880.

63. Connelly, *Army of the Heartland,* 60.

4. IF BLAME THERE BE

1. *OR,* 7:788, 814–15.

2. *OR,* 7:788, 814–15; *OR,* Ser. 4, 1:822; Richard M. McMurry, *Two Great Rebel Armies: An Essay in Confederate Military History* (Chapel Hill: University of North Carolina Press, 1989), 58.

3. *OR,* 7:820, 822, 826, 843, 8:734; *OR,* 13:830; Hartje, *Van Dorn,* 60; Jeremy Gilmer to wife, January 5, 1862, Jeremy F. Gilmer Papers, UNC.

4. ASJ to Eliza, January 6, 1862; and Financial Documents and Estate, February–April, 1862, Johnston Papers, TU.

5. *OR,* 7:821, 52(2):622–23; *OR,* Ser. 4, 1:871, 1038.

6. *OR,* 7:822–23, 825; Benjamin Franklin Cooling, *Forts Henry and Donelson: The Key to the Confederate Heartland* (Knoxville: University of Tennessee Press, 1987), 44; McMurry, *Two Great Rebel Armies,* 66.

7. *OR,* 7:757–58, 788, 792–95, 828; Connelly, *Army of the Heartland,* 90.

8. *OR,* 7:757–58, 788, 792–95; Johnston, *Life,* 491; Smith, *Grant Invades Tennessee,* 21.

9. *OR,* 7:817, 825, 52(2):246; Johnston, *Life,* 428–29; Horn, *Polk,* 214; Connelly, "Johnston Mystique," 14–23.

10. *OR,* 7:788, 828–29.

11. *OR,* 7:831–36; Connelly, *Army of the Heartland,* 95.

12. *OR,* 7:528; D. C. Buell to ASJ, February 2, 1862, and following, Johnston Papers, TU; Smith, *Grant Invades Tennessee,* 54–60.

13. Smith, *Grant Invades Tennessee,* 57.

14. Smith, *Grant Invades Tennessee,* 57–58.

15. *OR,* 7:837, 839, 846.

16. *OR,* 7:835, 837–38, 847.

17. *OR,* 7:840–41, 849–51, 852–55.

18. *OR,* 7:103, 838; George Crittenden to ASJ, January 20, 1862, Johnston Papers, TU.

19. *OR,* 7:845; Mackall to Robert Johnson, January 26, 1862, W. W. Mackall Letter, Chicago History Museum.

20. *OR,* 7:102–3; Woodworth, *Davis and His Generals,* 69; Alexander McCook to ASJ January 30, 1862; and Daniel Cliffe to ASJ, January 20, 1862, Johnston Papers, TU. For Mill Springs, see Kenneth A. Hafendorfer, *Mill Springs: Campaign and Battle of Mill Springs, Kentucky* (Louisville: KH Press, 2001).

21. *OR,* 7:844–45.

22. Larry J. Daniel, "'The Assaults of the Demagogues in Congress': General Albert Sidney Johnston and the Politics of Command," *Civil War History* 37, no. 4 (1991): 332.

23. *OR,* 7:846, 849–50, 855, 871.

24. *OR,* 7:858.

25. Smith, *Grant Invades Tennessee,* 66–89.

26. *OR,* 7:358, 859–60, 922.

27. *OR,* 7:860; Smith, *Grant Invades Tennessee,* 90–128.

28. *OR,* 7:860–61.

29. Johnston, *Life,* 432; Timothy B. Smith, "A Frolic up the Tennessee," *America's Civil War* (March 2017): 44–49; Operator to ASJ, February 7, 1862, RG 109, E 101, NARA; Mackall to Bushrod Johnson, February 6, 1862, RG 109, chap. 2, vol. 218, NARA.

30. *OR,* 7:865, 888.

31. Smith, *Grant Invades Tennessee,* 129–53.

32. Daniel, *Conquered,* 15; Smith, *Grant Invades Tennessee,* 129–53.

33. *OR,* 5:1048; Daniel, *Conquered,* 16; Special Orders No. 25, February 5, 1862, RG 109, chap. 2, vol. 220, NARA; Judah Benjamin to Beauregard, January 26, 1862, Johnston Papers, TU. For Beauregard, see T. Harry Williams, *P. G. T. Beauregard: Napoleon in Gray* (Baton Rouge: Louisiana State University Press, 1954).

34. *OR,* 7:259, 895; Alfred Roman, *The Military Operations of General Beauregard,* 2 vols. (New York: Harper and Brothers, 1884), 1:214.

35. *OR,* 7:861.

36. *OR,* 7:861; Johnston, *Life,* 492; Memorandum, February 7, 1862, Johnston Papers, TU; ASJ to Harris and ASJ to Shorter, February 8, 1862, RG 109, chap. 2, vol. 218, NARA.

37. *OR,* 7:861, 15:810, 52(2):171.

38. *OR,* 7:862, 879, 908; Cooper to ASJ, March 8, 1862, RG 109, E 101/193, NARA.

39. *OR,* 7:863.

40. *OR,* 5:1068, 6:408, 823–24, 761–62, 817, 823, 833, 835, 837, 847, 7:863, 867, 53:203, 230–31; Earl J. Hess, *Braxton Bragg: The Most Hated Man in the Confederacy* (Chapel Hill: University of North Carolina Press, 2016), 30.

41. *OR,* 7:863–64; ASJ to Benjamin, February 8, 1862, Johnston Papers, TU.

42. *OR,* 7:259, 861–62, 864; R. Brodie to ASJ, February 8, 1862; Mackall to Colonel Stevenson, February 12, 1862; and Mackall to Captain Lindsay, February 9, 1862, Johnston Papers, TU; Mackall to Captain Skeliha, February 10, 1862; and Mackall to V. K. Stevenson, February 11, 1862, RG 109, chap. 2, vol. 218, NARA.

43. *OR,* 7:272, 278, 366, 863, 865, 867–68; Johnston, *Life,* 437–38; Hughes, *Battle of Belmont,* 228n12; Hughes and Stonesifer, *Pillow,* 196, 216; Mackall to Pillow, February 7, 1862; and ASJ to Clark, February 7, 1862, RG 109, chap. 2, vol. 218, NARA.

44. *OR,* 7:865, 880; Steven E. Woodworth, "When Merit Was Not Enough: Albert Sidney Johnston and Confederate Defeat in the West, 1862," in *Civil War Generals in Defeat,* ed. Steven E. Woodworth (Lawrence: University Press of Kansas, 1999), 20; Woodworth, *Davis and His Generals,* 80–81; Stephen D. Engle, "'Thank God, He Has Rescued His Character': Albert Sidney Johnston, Southern Hamlet of the Confederacy," in *Leaders of the Lost Cause: New Perspectives on the Confederate High Command,* ed. Gary W. Gallagher and Joseph T. Glatthaar (Mechanicsburg, PA: Stackpole Books, 2004), 146; ASJ to Floyd, February 7 and undated, 1862, RG 109, chap. 2, vol. 218, NARA.

45. *OR,* 7:865, 880; Woodworth, "When Merit Was Not Enough," 20; Woodworth, *Davis and His Generals,* 80–81; Engle, "'Thank God, He Has Rescued His Character," 146; ASJ to Floyd, February 7 and undated, 1862, RG 109, chap. 2, vol. 218, NARA.

46. *OR,* 52(2):266, 269; Johnston, *Life,* 455; ASJ to Floyd, February 11, 1862, RG 109, chap. 2, vol. 218, NARA; John Bradford to Captain, February 12, 1862; and Purchase Order, February 14, 1862, Johnston Papers, TU.

47. *OR,* 7:259, 431, 867, 869–70, 872; Roland, *Johnston: Soldier,* 300; ASJ to Floyd, February 13, 1862, RG 109, chap. 2, vol. 218, NARA; Beauregard to ASJ, February 14, 1862, Johnston Papers, TU.

48. *OR,* 7:366, 878–79, 52(2):271–72; Connelly, *Army of the Heartland,* 113.

49. *OR,* 7:255, 880–82, 52(2):274; Johnston, *Life,* 493–94.

50. *OR,* 7:255, 880–82, 52(2):274; Johnston, *Life,* 493–94.

51. *OR,* 7:161, 303, 334, 52(2):273; Hughes and Stonesifer, *Pillow,* 234; Connelly, "Johnston Mystique," 14–23; Connelly, *Army of the Heartland,* 111–12; Woodworth, "When Merit Was Not Enough," 21; Smith, *Grant Invades Tennessee,* 264–350.

52. *OR,* 7:255, 883, 52(2):815.

53. *OR,* 7:256, 259, 418–19, 431, 887; Johnston, *Life,* 495; Special Orders No. 31, February 15, 1862, RG 109, chap. 2, vol. 220, NARA; ASJ to Colonel Bowen, February 15, 1862, RG 109, chap. 2, vol. 218, NARA.

54. *OR,* 7:256, 259, 419.

55. *OR,* 7:418, 426–33.

56. *OR,* 7:260; Crist, *Davis Papers,* 8:51.

57. *OR,* 7:140; Woodworth, *Davis and His Generals,* 84; Pillow to Mackall, February 7, 1862, RG 109, E 101, NARA.

58. Stephen D. Engle, *Struggle for the Heartland: The Campaign from Fort Henry to Corinth* (Lincoln: University of Nebraska Press, 2001), 65; Roland, *Johnston: General,* 29; Hughes and Stonesifer, *Pillow,* 241, 326; Woodworth, *Davis and His Generals,* 60, 70; Johnston Memo, undated, RG 109, E 101/193, NARA.

59. *OR,* Ser. 2, 3:276; Roman, *Military Operations of General Beauregard,* 1:229, 231; Roland, *Johnston: Soldier,* 287, 294; Daniel, *Conquered,* 17–18; ASJ to son, June 26, 1856; and WP to WPJ, April 18, 1862, Johnston Papers, TU.

60. *OR,* Ser. 2, 3:276; Roman, *Military Operations of General Beauregard,* 1:229, 231; Roland, *Johnston: Soldier,* 287, 294; Daniel, *Conquered,* 17–18; Allen Nevins, ed., *Diary of the Civil War* (New York: Macmillan, 1962), 207–8; ASJ to son, June 26, 1856; and WP to WPJ, April 18, 1862, Johnston Papers, TU; "General Albert Sidney Johnston," *New York Herald,* February 17, 1862.

61. *OR,* 7:254, 259; Roland, *Johnston: Soldier,* 290–91, 295; ASJ to Pillow, February 7, 1862; and ASJ to Floyd, February 8, 1862, RG 109, chap. 2, vol. 218, NARA.

62. *OR,* 7:260; Roland, *Johnston: General,* 35, 37, 84.

5. THE IRON DICE OF BATTLE

1. *OR,* 7:259, 432, 887, 52(2):275; *OR,* Ser. 4, 2:281; Johnston, *Life,* 496, 498; Sam Davis Elliott, *Isham G. Harris of Tennessee: Confederate Governor and United States Senator* (Baton Rouge: Louisiana State University Press, 2010), 104; Roland, *Johnston: Soldier,* 298; Harris to ASJ, February 17, 1862, RG 109, E 101, NARA.

2. *OR*, 6:828, 7:880, 889–90.

3. *OR*, 6:828, 7:889–90; Daniel, "Assaults of the Demagogues," 328–29.

4. *OR*, 7:418, 427, 889–90; *OR*, Ser. 2, 3:802–4; Johnston, *Life*, 499, 506; Connelly, *Army of the Heartland*, 133. For Gilmer's orders regarding Nashville's defenses, see RG 109, chap. 3, vol. 8, NARA; and Mackall to Hardee, February 22, 1862, RG 109, chap. 2, vol. 218, NARA.

5. *OR*, 7:418, 427, 889–90; *OR*, Ser. 2, 3:802–4; Johnston, *Life*, 499, 506; Connelly, *Army of the Heartland*, 133.

6. *OR*, 7:890, 892–94, 896, 912, 10(2):311; Johnston, *Life*, 506.

7. *OR*, 7:427, 647, 678; Connelly, *Army of the Heartland*, 138–39, 146.

8. *OR*, 7:258–59, 894, 896, 905; Johnston, *Life*, 505; Roland, *Johnston: Soldier*, 303; WP to WPJ, April 18, 1862; and David Yandell to WPJ, November 11, 1877, Johnston Papers, TU; ASJ to Davis, February 22 1862, RG 109, chap. 2, vol. 218, NARA; Jeremy Gilmer to wife, March 5, 1862, Jeremy F. Gilmer Papers, UNC.

9. *OR*, 7:903, 905, 911–12, 916–17, 10(2):297, 302–3, 13:40.

10. *OR*, 10(2):310; Roland, *Johnston: General*, 48; ASJ to Davis, March 18, 1862, Johnston Papers, TU.

11. J. Brent to ASJ, March 9, 1862; WPJ to ASJ, February 14, 18, 1862; and WPJ to WP, February 19, 1862, Johnston Papers, TU.

12. *OR*, 7:254, 894, 908, 917, 921–22; Crist, *Davis Papers*, 8:52; Henry Foote to ASJ, March 10, 1862, Johnston Papers, TU; ASJ to Henry Foote, March 17, 1862, RG 109, chap. 2, vol. 217, NARA; ASJ to Sir, March 17, 1862, RG 109, E 101/193, NARA.

13. *OR*, 7:254, 894, 908, 917, 921–22; Crist, *Davis Papers*, 8:52; Henry Foote to ASJ, March 10, 1862, Johnston Papers, TU; ASJ to Henry Foote, March 17, 1862, RG 109, chap. 2, vol. 217, NARA; ASJ to Sir, March 17, 1862, RG 109, E 101/193, NARA; Pillow to Hardee, February 20, 1862, RG 109, E 132, NARA; Floyd to Buckner, August 15, 1862, RG 109, E 119, NARA.

14. *OR*, 7:257–58, 10(2):299; Johnston, *Life*, 513; Davis, *Jefferson Davis*, 400; Davis to ASJ, March 12, 1862, Johnston Papers, TU.

15. *OR*, 7:257, 10(2):314, 24(3):940; Johnston, *Life*, 511; Daniel, *Conquered*, 18; Woodworth, *Davis and His Generals*, 85; Daniel, "Assaults of the Demagogues," 329.

16. *OR*, 7:257, 10(2):314, 24(3):940; Woodworth, *Davis and His Generals*, 85; Daniel, "Assaults of the Demagogues," 329; Johnston, *Life*, 511; Daniel, *Conquered*, 18.

17. Daniel, "Assaults of the Demagogues," 329–32; Gustavus A. Henry et al. to Jefferson Davis, March 8, 1862, Gustavus A. Henry Papers, TSLA; Johnston, *Life*, 496, 511–12; Daniel, *Conquered*, 19; Davis, *Breckinridge*, 302; Woodworth, *Davis and His Generals*, 398; Crist, *Davis Papers*, 8:58, 64, 87–89.

18. James Pope to mother, February 24, 1862, Pope-Carter Family Papers, Duke University, Durham, NC; F. A. Shoup, "How We Went to Shiloh," *Confederate Veteran* 2, no. 5 (May 1894): 137; Grady McWhiney, *Braxton Bragg and Confederate Defeat: Volume 1: Field Command* (New York: Columbia University Press, 1969), 207; Hughes, *Hardee*, 95; Roland, *Johnston: Soldier*, 300; Crist, *Davis Papers*, 8:113; Connelly, *Army of the Heartland*, 137.

19. Johnston, *Life*, 515; Jeremy Gilmer to wife, March 6, 1862, Jeremy F. Gilmer Papers, UNC.

20. Johnston, *Life*, 521–22; ASJ to Davis, March 18, 21, 1862, Johnston Papers, TU.

21. *OR*, 6:825, 7:258–60, 419, 10(2):302; Johnston, *Life*, 516; ASJ to Benjamin, March 5, 1862; and ASJ to Davis, March 18, 1862, Johnston Papers, TU.

22. *OR,* 7:260; ASJ to Davis, March 18, 1862, Johnston Papers, TU.

23. *OR,* 7:260–61, 10(1):567, 29(2):639; Johnston, *Life,* 491, 725; ASJ to Davis, March 18, 1862; Davis to ASJ, March 26, 1862; and David Yandell to WPJ, November 11, 1877, Johnston Papers, TU; Special Orders No. 47, March 16, 1862, RG 109, chap. 2, vol. 220, NARA; ASJ to Sir, April 1862, RG 109, E 101/193, NARA.

24. *OR,* 7:890–91, 894, 897, 907, 909–10, 918, 10(2):302, 310; Williams, *Beauregard,* 124; Roman, *Military Operations of General Beauregard,* 1:258; Johnston, *Life,* 506–7; Jeremy Gilmer to wife, March 15, 1862, Jeremy F. Gilmer Papers, UNC; ASJ to Beauregard, March 15, 1862, RG 109, chap. 2, vol. 217, NARA; "Notes of Reference," March 4, 1862; and Beauregard to ASJ, March 2, 6, 8, 11, 13, 21, 1862, Johnston Papers, TU.

25. *OR,* 7:890–91, 894, 897, 910; Johnston, *Life,* 506–7; Williams, *Beauregard,* 124; Roman, *Military Operations of General Beauregard,* 1:258; Beauregard to ASJ, March 2, 8, 1862, Johnston Papers, TU; ASJ to Beauregard, March 15, 1862, RG 109, chap. 2, vol. 217, NARA.

26. *OR,* 7:878; Johnston, *Life,* 541; ASJ to Mansfield Lovell, February 12, 1862; and ASJ to Davis, March 5, 1862, RG 109, chap. 2, vol. 218, NARA.

27. *OR,* 10(2):8, 10–11, 16, 37, 42–43, 58–59, 299, 305, 310, 362, 614, 11(3):8; Memo, March 7, 1862, Johnston Papers, TU.

28. Timothy B. Smith, *Shiloh: Conquer or Perish* (Lawrence: University Press of Kansas, 2014), 8–20.

29. *OR,* 10(2):317, 319, 326–29, 332.

30. *OR,* 10(2):332, 334, 338–39, 340–43, 52(2):288; Mackall to Hindman, March 14, 1862, RG 109, chap. 2, vol. 218, NARA; John Bowen to ASJ, March 13, 1862, Johnston Papers, TU.

31. *OR,* 7:896–97, 899–900, 906, 908–9, 915, 918, 921, 10(2):297; "Notes of Reference," March 3, 4, 1862; and General Orders No. 1, March 6, 1862, Johnston Papers, TU; ASJ to Beauregard, undated, RG 109, chap. 2, vol. 218, NARA.

32. *OR,* 7:896–97, 899–900, 906, 908–9, 915, 918, 921, 10(2):297; Roland, *Johnston: General,* 51; "Notes of Reference," March 3, 4, 1862; and General Orders No. 1, March 6, 1862, Johnston Papers, TU; ASJ to Beauregard, undated, RG 109, chap. 2, vol. 218, NARA.

33. *OR,* 10(2):302, 312, 349, 351, 363; ASJ to Beauregard, March 17, 1862, RG 109, chap. 2, vol. 217, NARA; Beauregard to ASJ, March 19, 1862, Johnston Papers, TU.

34. *OR,* 10(2):334, 350, 53:228, 248.

35. *OR,* 8:751, 10(2):354, 362; Connelly, *Army of the Heartland,* 140; Hartje, *Van Dorn,* 105–6, 166–67; Arthur B. Carter, *The Tarnished Cavalier: Major General Earl Van Dorn, C.S.A.* (Knoxville: University of Tennessee Press, 1999), 69; Roland, *Johnston: General,* 52; Roland, *Johnston: Soldier,* 343; Maury, *Recollections,* 167; Beauregard to planters, March 8, 1862, RG 109, E 97, NARA.

36. Smith, *Shiloh,* 59, 64; Timothy B. Smith, *Corinth 1862: Siege, Battle, Occupation* (Lawrence: University Press of Kansas, 2012), 9.

37. *OR,* 10(2):354, 361; Breckinridge to Colonel Brewster, March 27, 1862, RG 109, chap. 2, vol. 311, NARA; Beauregard to ASJ, March 23, 1862; and ASJ Notes, March 24, 1862, Johnston Papers, TU.

38. Johnston, *Life,* 549–50; Roman, *Military Operations of General Beauregard,* 1:266; George Johnston to ASJ, March 26, 1862; and WP to WPJ, April 18, 1862, Johnston Papers, TU; Beauregard to WPJ, March 9, 1877, P. G. T. Beauregard Papers, MDAH; Jeremy Gilmer to wife, March 29, 1862, Jeremy F. Gilmer Papers, UNC.

39. Johnston, *Life,* 551–52; Lee to ASJ, March 26, 1862, Johnston Papers, TU.

40. *OR,* 10(1):775, 10(2):367, 375, 384; Johnston, *Life,* 548; George Garner to James Chalmers, March 31, 1862, RG 109, chap. 2, vol. 296, NARA.

41. *OR,* 10(2):370–73.

42. *OR,* 10(2):371, 373, 378–79; Davis, *Breckinridge,* 301; Beauregard to ASJ, March 23, 1862, Johnston Papers, TU; H. P. Brewster to Van Dorn, March 23, 1862, RG 109, chap. 2, vol. 218, NARA.

43. *OR,* 10(2):365, 367, 378; Johnston, *Life,* 526.

44. *OR,* 10(2):378; Woodworth, *Davis and His Generals,* 85.

45. *OR,* 10(2):381; Thomas Jordan and J. P. Pryor, *The Campaigns of Lieut.-Gen. N. B. Forrest, and of Forrest's Cavalry, with Portraits, Maps, and Illustrations* (New Orleans: Blelock, 1868), 109; Special Orders No. 5, April 1, 1862, Johnston Papers, TU; Special Orders No. 5, April 1, 1862, RG 109, E 97, NARA.

46. Roland, *Johnston: General,* 59–60.

47. *OR,* 10(2):389, 393; Parks, *Polk,* 224.

48. *OR,* 10(2):383, 387–89; Crist, *Davis Papers,* 8:132; ASJ to Davis, April 3, 1862, Johnston Papers, TU.

49. *OR,* 8:804, 10(1):392–95, 397, 51(2):727; Johnston, *Life,* 553; Crist, *Davis Papers,* 8:143; Roland, *Johnston: General,* 62, 66; Woodworth, *Davis and His Generals,* 96; Woodworth, "When Merit Was Not Enough," 24; Special Orders No. 8, April 3, 1862, ALPL; Benjamin to ASJ, November 5, 1861, ASJ Papers, Duke University, Durham, NC; Beauregard to WPJ, March 9, 1877, P. G. T. Beauregard Papers, MDAH; Special Orders No. 8 and Memorandum, April 3, 1862, Johnston Papers, TU; Special Orders No. 9, March 17, 1862, RG 109, chap. 2, vol. 220, NARA; Jeremy Gilmer to wife, March 9, 1862, Jeremy F. Gilmer Papers, UNC.

50. *OR,* 10(1):392–95, 10(2):387; Special Orders No. 465, March 28, 1862, RG 109, chap. 2, vol. 15, NARA.

51. *OR,* 10(2):388; Smith, *Shiloh,* 64; Bragg to Hardee, April 3, 1862, RG 109, E 103, NARA.

52. *OR,* 10(2):384, 390–91; ASJ to Breckinridge, April 4, 1862, Johnston Papers, TU.

53. *OR,* 10(1):400, 405, 10(2):387, 391–92, 51(2):727; WP Diary, April 4, 1862, RG 94, E 286, NARA, copy at SNMP; Johnston, *Life,* 562.

54. *OR,* 10(1):400, 405, 10(2):387, 391–92, 51(2):727; Johnston, *Life,* 553; Smith, *Shiloh,* 64.

55. *OR,* 10(1):390; Johnston, *Life,* 563; Daniel, *Conquered,* 21; David Yandell to WPJ, November 11, 1877, Johnston Papers, TU.

56. *OR,* 10(1):400, 403, 406, 10(2):391; Johnston, *Life,* 563, 565; David Yandell to WPJ, November 11, 1877, Johnston Papers, TU.

57. Johnston, *Life,* 565–66.

58. *OR,* 10(1):407, 10(2):384, 387–88, 51(2):727; Johnston, *Life,* 567; WP to WPJ, April 18, 1862, Johnston Papers, TU.

59. Johnston, *Life,* 568–70; Elliott, *Harris,* 108; Woodworth, "When Merit Was Not Enough," 26; Connelly, *Army of the Heartland,* 157; David Yandell to WPJ, November 11, 1877, Johnston Papers, TU.

60. Johnston, *Life,* 570–71; WP to WPJ, April 18, 1862, Johnston Papers, TU.

61. *OR,* 10(1):409; Dabney Maury to T. Churchill, March 28, 1862, RG 109, chap. 2, vol. 271, NARA.

62. Thomas Jordan, "Notes of a Confederate Staff-Officer at Shiloh," in *Battles and Leaders of the Civil War,* 1:599.

63. *OR,* 10(2):394; David Yandell to WPJ, November 11, 1877, Johnston Papers, TU.

6. WE MUST THIS DAY CONQUER OR PERISH

Much of this chapter has been previously published in Timothy B. Smith, "To Conquer or Perish: The Last Hours of Albert Sidney Johnston," in *Confederate Generals in the Western Theater: An Anthology, Volume 3,* ed. Larry Hewitt and Art Bergeron (Knoxville: University of Tennessee Press, 2011), 21–37; reprinted as Smith, "To Conquer or Perish: The Last Hours of Albert Sidney Johnston," in *Rethinking Shiloh: Myth and Memory* (Knoxville: University of Tennessee Press, 2013), 27–43.

1. *OR,* 10(1):403; Johnston, *Life,* 569, 582, 585; WP to Beauregard, April 20, 1862; David Yandell to WPJ, November 11, 1877, Johnston Papers, TU.

2. *OR,* 10(1):401, 403; Johnston, *Life,* 572, 580, 584; Daniel, *Conquered,* 23; Connelly, *Army of the Heartland,* 161; WP to Beauregard, April 20, 1862, Johnston Papers, TU.

3. *OR,* 10(1):403; J. B. Ulmer, "A Glimpse of Albert Sidney Johnston through the Smoke of Shiloh," *Southwestern Historical Quarterly* 10, no. 4, 285–96; Johnston, *Life,* 589; WP to WPJ, April 18, 1862; and WP to Beauregard, April 20, 1862, Johnston Papers, TU.

4. *OR,* 10(1):403; WP to Beauregard, April 20, 1862, Johnston Papers, TU; WP Diary, April 6, 1862, RG 94, E 286, NARA.

5. *OR,* 10(1):401; Johnston, *Life,* 594, 598; Jefferson Davis to WPJ, January 11, 1877, Johnston Papers, TU.

6. *OR,* 10(1):454; Johnston, *Life,* 730.

7. *OR,* 10(1):454; Johnston, *Life,* 730; A. S. Horsely, "Reminiscences of Shiloh," *Confederate Veteran* 2, no. 8 (August 1894): 234.

8. *OR,* 10(1):407, 414–15, 427; David W. Reed, *The Battle of Shiloh and the Organizations Engaged* (Washington, DC: Government Printing Office, 1909), 81.

9. *OR,* 10(1):427; Marshall Wingfield, *General A. P. Stewart: His Life and Letters* (Memphis: West Tennessee Historical Society, 1954), 55.

10. *OR,* 10(1):427; Reed, *Shiloh,* 73; Ulmer, "Glimpse," 285–96; Johnston, *Life,* 595; David Yandell to WPJ, November 11, 1877, Johnston Papers, TU.

11. Smith, *Shiloh,* 115–35.

12. Johnston, *Life,* 590.

13. *OR,* 10(1):404, 569; Johnston, *Life,* 597, 608; WP to Beauregard, April 20, 1862, Johnston Papers, TU.

14. Smith, *Shiloh,* 133–34.

15. Johnston, *Life,* 248, 597, 608; *OR,* 10(1):404, 532, 548–49, 554; Samuel Lockett, "Surprise and Withdrawal at Shiloh," in *Battles and Leaders of the Civil War,* 1:604; WP to Beauregard, April 20, 1862, Johnston Papers, TU.

16. *OR,* 10(1):407, 414, 427, 454, 532, 548, 554, 558, 621, 624; Johnston, *Life,* 584, 718.

17. Johnston, *Life,* 612.

18. Johnston, *Life,* 615; David Yandell to WPJ, November 11, 1877, Johnston Papers, TU.

19. D. W. Reed to Basil W. Duke, July 20, 1906, Ser. 1, Box 13, Folder 140, SNMP.

20. *OR,* 10(1):558; Johnston, *Life,* 608.

21. Smith, *Shiloh,* 186–88.

22. *OR* 10(1):404; Johnston, *Life,* 608–9, 611; Woodworth, *Davis and His Generals,* 99; WP to Beauregard, April 20, 1862, Johnston Papers, TU.

23. *OR,* 10(1):404, 621, 624; Smith, *Shiloh,* 188; Johnston, *Life,* 611–13.

24. *OR,* 10(1):404, 621, 624; Johnston, *Life,* 611–13; Smith, *Shiloh,* 188.

25. *OR,* 10(1):409; Connelly, *Army of the Heartland,* 158; Roland, *Johnston: Soldier,* 344; Johnston, *Life,* 566, 569; Daniel, *Conquered,* 22; WP to WPJ, April 7, 1862; and WP to Beauregard, April 20, 1862, Johnston Papers, TU.

26. *Johnston, Life,* 613–15, 718.

27. Isham G. Harris to WP, April 6, 1862, Ser. 1, Box 13, Folder 140, SNMP; Johnston, *Life,* 614.

28. Johnston, *Life,* 614; Isham G. Harris to WP, April 6, 1862, Ser. 1, Box 13, Folder 140, SNMP.

29. *OR,* 10(1):404; Johnston, *Life,* 614–16; Isham G. Harris to WP, April 6, 1862, SNMP; WP Diary, April 6, 1862, RG 94, E 286, NARA, copy at SNMP; WP to Beauregard, April 20, 1862; and David Yandell to WPJ, November 11, 1877, Johnston Papers, TU.

30. *OR,* 51(2):727; Johnston, *Life,* 614–15, 688, 691–93, 699; Connelly, *Army of the Heartland,* 160; Elliott, *Harris,* 111; Castel, "Dead on Arrival," 37; David Yandell to WPJ, November 11, 1877, Johnston Papers, TU. Wiley Sword has speculated that the location of Johnston's death currently marked at SNMP is in error. See Sword, *Shiloh: Bloody April,* rev. ed. (Dayton, OH: Morningside, 2001), 461–71.

31. Smith, *Shiloh,* 186–94.

32. Castel, "Dead on Arrival," 37.

33. Johnston, *Life,* 569, 583–84, 613; *OR,* 10(1):396; Engle, "Thank God, He Has Rescued His Character," 152–53; McPherson, *Battle Cry of Freedom,* 501, 524, 584–85, 639.

34. *OR,* 10(1):114, 117, 252, 303, 379, 12(3):65; *OR,* Ser. 2, 3:848; Johnston, *Life,* 659–60.

35. *OR,* 10(1):384, 390, 52(2):298–99, 302–3; Johnston, *Life,* 688; WP Diary, April 6, 1862, RG 94, E 286, NARA.

36. O. Edward Cunningham, *Shiloh and the Western Campaign of 1862,* ed. Gary D. Joiner and Timothy B. Smith (New York: Savas Beatie, 2007), 329; Mrs. F. A. Inge, "Corinth, Miss. in Early War Days," *Confederate Veteran* 17, no. 9 (September 1909): 442–44; Inge, "Corinth, Miss. in War Times," *Confederate Veteran* 23, no. 9 (September 1915): 412–13; Voucher for Coffin, April 16, 1862, RG 109, E 101/193, NARA.

37. Bills, February–April 17, 1862; Financial Documents and Estate, February–April 1862; WP to WPJ, April 7, 18, 1862; Inventory of Items, April 17, 1862; HPH to William Matthews, April 15, 1862; and Sam Tate to WPJ, April 28, 1862, Johnston Papers, TU; Jackson Smith to Colonel Taylor, undated; Pay Statements, May 20, 1862; and Court Documents, May 19, 1862, RG 109, E 101/193, NARA.

38. Davis, *Jefferson Davis,* 404; Crist, *Davis Papers,* 8:135; WP to Davis, April 7, 1862, Johnston Papers, TU.

39. *OR,* 52(2):298–99, 302–3.

40. *OR,* 52(2):298–99, 302–3; Johnston, *Life,* 691–93; "The Latest News," *New Orleans Weekly Delta,* April 12, 1862.

41. *OR,* 10(2):408–9, 414; *OR,* Ser. 2, 3:446.

42. Johnston, *Life*, 688–89, 695; Henry Quitman to wife, April 21, 1862, F. Henry Quitman Letter, Louisiana State University, Baton Rouge.

43. Davis, *Jefferson Davis*, 405; Crist, *Davis Papers*, 8:170; WPJ to Rosa Johnston, May 13, 1862, ASJ Papers, FHS; "Lines on the Death of Confederate Gen. ASJ"; and "Gen. Johnston," 1862, Confederate Broadsides, Wake Forest University, Winston-Salem, NC.

CONCLUSION. WE HAD NO OTHER HAND TO TAKE UP HIS WORK IN THE WEST

1. "The Confederate Monument," Ser. 1, Box 26, Folder 373, SNMP.

2. Timothy B. Smith, *This Great Battlefield of Shiloh: History, Memory, and the Establishment of a Civil War National Military Park* (Knoxville: University of Tennessee Press, 2004), 89–90. For the Lost Cause, see Gaines M. Foster, *Ghosts of the Confederacy: Defeat, the Lost Cause, and the Emergence of the New South* (New York: Oxford University Press, 1987).

3. William Preston Johnston, "Albert Sidney Johnston at Shiloh," in *Battles and Leaders of the Civil War*, 1:540–68; P. G. T. Beauregard, "The Campaign of Shiloh," ibid., 569–93; "The Confederate Dead," *New Orleans Daily Picayune*, April 11, 1862.

4. Timothy B. Smith, *Rethinking Shiloh: Myth and Memory* (Knoxville: University of Tennessee Press, 2013), 28; Wyatt-Brown, *Southern Honor* (1982), 360, 373. For detail on the consequences of Johnston's death, see Chris Mackowski and Brian Matthew Jordan, eds., *The Great "What Ifs" of the American Civil War: Historians Tackle the Conflict's Most Intriguing Possibilities* (El Dorado Hills, CA: Savas Beatie, 2021), 1–17 (upon which most of the preceding is based); and Smith, *Shiloh*, 217–35.

5. Johnston, *Life*, 658; Roland, *Johnston: Soldier*, 349; Albert Castel, "Savior of the South?," *Civil War Times Illustrated* 36, no. 1 (March 1997): 40. The following appeared in earlier form as Timothy B. Smith, "Lasting Void," *America's Civil War* 34, no. 2 (May 2021): 20–27.

6. *The Centennial of the United States Military Academy at West Point, New York. 1802–1902*, 2 vols. (Washington, DC: Government Printing Office, 1904), 1:681; Woodworth, *Davis and His Generals*, 308.

7. *OR*, 17(2): 403, 640; Davis, *Jefferson Davis*, 691; Crist, *Davis Papers*, 8:147–48.

8. Davis, *Jefferson Davis*, 360–61; Craig L. Symonds, *Joseph E. Johnston: A Civil War Biography* (New York: Norton, 1992), 187–335; Thomas, *Lee*, 225.

9. Crist, *Davis Papers*, 8:574; McWhiney, *Bragg*, 327.

10. McWhiney, *Bragg*, 327; Ezra J. Warner, *Generals in Gray: Lives of the Confederate Commanders* (Baton Rouge: Louisiana State University Press, 1959), 30, 34, 124, 242–43, 247, 314–15; Johnston, *Life*, 633; Crist, *Davis Papers*, 8:132; WP to WPJ, May 30, 1862, ASJ Papers, FHS.

11. Daniel, *Conquered*, 32–246.

12. *OR*, 20(1):683, 23(1):623, 52(2):407, 818; Woodworth, *Davis and His Generals*, 302; Hess, *Bragg*, 123; Davis, *Breckinridge*, 358, 361; Horn, *Polk*, 250, 349; Parks, *Polk*, 349; Daniel, *Conquered*, 32–246.

13. Johnston, *Life*, 635, 658.

14. Johnston, *Life*, 699, 700–701, 717.

15. Johnston, *Life*, 703–6, 708, 711, 714; "Albert Sidney Johnston," *Galveston Daily Bulletin*, January 26, 1867; "Honor to the Glorious Dead," *Houston Telegraph*, January 28, 1867.

16. Davis, *Jefferson Davis,* 496, 540, 681; Eliza Johnston to unknown, November 10, 1895, Eliza Johnston Letter, Louisiana State University, Baton Rouge; WPJ to H. F. Campbell, January 19, 1878, WPJ Letter, University of California, Santa Barbara; David Burnet to P. W. Gray, April 23, 1863, ASJ Collection, UTA.

17. Henri de Jomini, *The Art of War* (Philadelphia: J. B. Lippincott, 1862), 50–53, 298–313.

18. Carl Von Clausewitz, *On War,* ed. Michael Howard and Peter Paret (New York: Knopf, 1993), 115–31; Jeremy Gilmer to wife, March 29, 1862, Jeremy F. Gilmer Papers, UNC.

19. Johnston, *Life,* 164; ASJ to George Hancock, November 1, 1847, Johnston Papers, TU.

20. Jeremy Gilmer to wife, October 23, 1862, Jeremy F. Gilmer Papers, UNC; Ulysses S. Grant, *The Personal Memoirs of Ulysses S. Grant: The Complete Annotated Edition,* ed. John F. Marszalek, David F. Nolen, and Louie P. Gallo (Cambridge, MA: Harvard University Press, 2017), 246; Woodworth, "When Merit Was Not Enough," 26; Connelly, *Army of the Heartland,* 62.

21. ASJ to William Bickley, October 10, 1827, Johnston Papers, TU; Connelly, *Army of the Heartland,* 63.

22. Williams, *Beauregard,* 119; Connelly, "Johnston Mystique," 14–23; Connelly, *Army of the Heartland,* 62; Hughes and Stonesifer, *Pillow,* 242; Woodworth, "When Merit Was Not Enough," 17; Engle, "Thank God, He Has Rescued His Character," 144.

23. Johnston, *Life,* 154.

24. McMurry, *Two Great Rebel Armies,* 139.

25. Roland, *Johnston: Soldier,* 351; Lundberg, "I Must Save This Army," 25; Williams, *Beauregard,* 116; Albert Castel, *Decision in the West: The Atlanta Campaign of 1864* (Lawrence: University Press of Kansas, 1992), 28.

BIBLIOGRAPHY

—•—

MANUSCRIPTS

Abraham Lincoln Presidential Library, Springfield, Illinois
  Special Orders No. 8, April 3, 1862
Brigham Young University, Provo, Utah
  Albert Sidney Johnston Military Pay Record
Chicago History Museum, Chicago, Illinois
  Albert Sidney Johnston Letter
  W. W. Mackall Letter
Duke University, Durham, North Carolina
  Alfred Cumming Papers
  Albert Sidney Johnston Papers
  Pope-Carter Family Papers
Filson Historical Society, Louisville, Kentucky
  Albert Sidney Johnston Papers
Historical Society of Pennsylvania, Philadelphia
  Josiah Stoddard Johnston Papers
Huntington Library, San Marino, California
  Albert Sidney Johnston Letter
Kentucky Historical Society, Frankfort
  Albert Sidney Johnston Genealogy Letter
Library of Congress, Washington, DC
  Albert Sidney Johnston Papers
  George W. Morgan Papers
Louisiana State University, Baton Rouge

Eliza Johnston Letter

F. Henry Quitman Letter

Mississippi Department of Archives and History, Jackson

P. G. T. Beauregard Papers

Felix Huston Papers

Robert A. Smith Papers

National Archives and Records Administration, Washington, DC

RG 94—Records of the Adjutant General's Office, 1762–1984

E 243—U.S. Military Academy Cadet Application Papers, 1805–66

E 286—William Preston Diary

RG 109—War Department Collection of Confederate Records, 1825–1900

Chap. 2, Vol. 15—Special Orders, Commands of Generals Leonidas Polk, D. H. Maury, S. D. Lee, and Richard Taylor, 1862–64

Chap. 2, Vol. 217—Letters and Telegrams Sent, September 1861–April 1862

Chap. 2, Vol. 218—Letters and Telegrams Sent, October 1861–April 1862

Chap. 2, Vol. 220—Special Orders, Western Department, October 1861–March 1862

Chap. 2, Vol. 271—Letters and Telegrams Sent, Trans-Mississippi District, February–April 1862

Chap. 2, Vol. 296—Letters, Telegrams, Orders, and Circulars Received, Brig. Gen. James R. Chalmers, February–August 1862

Chap. 2, Vol. 311—Letters, Telegrams, and Orders Received and Sent, General Breckinridge's Command, December 1861–November 1863

Chap. 3, Vol. 8—Engineer Department, Letters Sent by the Chief Engineer of the Western Department, 1861–62

E 97—Orders and Circulars of the Army of the Mississippi, 1861–65

E 101—Western Department, Telegrams Received and Sent, 1861–62

E 101/193—General and Staff Officers Compiled Service Records

E 103—Correspondence of the Eastern Department and the Army of the Mississippi, 1861–62

E 119—John B. Floyd Papers

E 132—Gideon Pillow Papers

New-York Historical Society, New York

Fisher Hannum Letter

Rice University, Houston, Texas

Sam Houston Papers

Shiloh National Military Park, Shiloh, Tennessee

"The Confederate Monument"

Isham G. Harris Letter

William Preston Diary

D. W. Reed Letter

Tennessee State Library and Archives, Nashville

Gustavus A. Henry Papers

William H. Jackson Papers

Tulane University, New Orleans, Louisiana

Albert Sidney and William Preston Johnston Papers

University of California, Berkeley

Alfred Cumming Papers

University of California, Santa Barbara

William Preston Johnston Letter

University of Georgia, Athens

E. Merton Coulter Collection

University of Kentucky, Lexington

Albert Sidney Johnston Letter

University of New Mexico, Albuquerque

Albert Sidney Johnston Letter

University of North Carolina, Chapel Hill

Jeremy F. Gilmer Papers

David Urquhart Letter Book

University of Southern Mississippi, Hattiesburg

Albert Sidney Johnston Letter

University of Texas at Arlington

Albert Sidney Johnston Collection

University of Texas, Austin

Sam Houston Papers

Albert Sidney Johnston Letter

University of Utah, Salt Lake City

Albert Sidney Johnston Letters

Wake Forrest University, Winston-Salem, North Carolina

Confederate Broadsides

"Gen. Johnston"

"Lines on the Death of Confederate Gen. Albert Sidney Johnston"

Yale University, New Haven, Connecticut

Albert Sidney Johnston Letters

NEWSPAPERS

Buffalo (NY) Daily Courier

Galveston Daily Bulletin

Houston Telegraph

Louisville Courier

New Orleans Daily Picayune

New Orleans Weekly Delta

New York Herald

Southern Watchman (Athens, GA)

Texas Republican (Marshall)

PUBLISHED PRIMARY AND SECONDARY SOURCES

Ambrose, Stephen E. *Duty, Honor, Country: A History of West Point.* Baltimore: Johns Hopkins University Press, 1966.

Annual Report of the Secretary of War—1912. Washington, DC: Government Printing Office, 1913.

Beauregard, P. G. T. "The Campaign of Shiloh." In Johnson and Buel, *Battles and Leaders of the Civil War,* 1:569–93.

Berry, Stephen W. *All That Makes a Man: Love and Ambition in the Civil War South.* New York: Oxford University Press, 2004.

Bigler, David L., and Will Bagley. *The Mormon Rebellion: America's First Civil War, 1857–1858.* Norman: University of Oklahoma Press, 2011.

Billingsley, Carolyn Earle. *Communities of Kinship: Antebellum Families and the Settlement of the Cotton Frontier.* Athens: University of Georgia Press, 2004.

Biographical Directory of the United States Congress. Washington, DC: Government Printing Office, 1989.

Brands, H. W. *Lone Star Nation: The Epic Story of the Battle for Texas Independence.* New York: Anchor, 2005.

Broomall, James J. *Private Confederacies: The Emotional Worlds of Southern Men as Citizens and Soldiers.* Chapel Hill: University of North Carolina Press, 2019.

———. "Wartime Masculinities." In *The Cambridge History of the American Civil War,* 3 vols., edited by Aaron Sheehan-Dean, 3:3–24. Cambridge: Cambridge University Press, 2019.

Bruce, Dickson D., Jr. *Violence and Culture in the Antebellum South.* Austin: University of Texas Press, 1979.

Buell, Don Carlos. "Shiloh Reviewed." In Johnson and Buel, *Battles and Leaders of the Civil War,* 1:487–536.

Carter, Arthur B. *The Tarnished Cavalier: Major General Earl Van Dorn, C.S.A.* Knoxville: University of Tennessee Press, 1999.

Castel, Albert. "Dead on Arrival." *Civil War Times Illustrated* 36, no. 1 (March 1997): 30–37.

———. *Decision in the West: The Atlanta Campaign of 1864.* Lawrence: University Press of Kansas, 1992.

———. "Savior of the South?" *Civil War Times Illustrated* 36, no. 1 (March 1997): 38–40.

The Centennial of the United States Military Academy at West Point, New York. 1802–1902. 2 vols. Washington, DC: Government Printing Office, 1904.

Chisolm, Alexander R. "The Shiloh Battle-Order and the Withdrawal Sunday Evening." In Johnson and Buel, *Battles and Leaders of the Civil War,* 1:606.

Clausewitz, Carl Von. *On War.* Edited by Michael Howard and Peter Paret. New York: Knopf, 1993.

Crist, Linda Lasswell, et al., eds. *The Papers of Jefferson Davis.* 14 vols. Baton Rouge: Louisiana State University Press, 1971–2015.

Connelly, Thomas L. *Army of the Heartland.* Baton Rouge: Louisiana State University Press, 1967.

———. "The Johnston Mystique." *Civil War Times Illustrated,* no. 5 (October 1967): 14–23.

Cooling, Benjamin Franklin. *Forts Henry and Donelson: The Key to the Confederate Heartland.* Knoxville: University of Tennessee Press, 1987.

Cullum, George W. *Biographical Register of the Officers and Graduates of the U.S. Military Academy at West Point, N.Y., from Its Establishment, in 1802, to 1890, with the Early History of the United States Military Academy.* 10 vols. Boston: Houghton, Mifflin, 1891.

Cunningham, O. Edward. *Shiloh and the Western Campaign of 1862.* Edited by Gary D. Joiner and Timothy B. Smith. New York: Savas Beatie, 2007.

Daniel, Larry J. "'The Assaults of the Demagogues in Congress': General Albert Sidney Johnston and the Politics of Command." *Civil War History* 37, no. 4 (1991): 328–35.

———. *Conquered: Why the Army of the Tennessee Failed.* Chapel Hill: University of North Carolina Press, 2019.

———. *Engineering in the Confederate Heartland.* Baton Rouge: Louisiana State University Press, 2022.

———. *Shiloh: The Battle That Changed the Civil War.* New York: Simon and Shuster, 1997.

Davis, Jefferson. *The Rise and Fall of the Confederate Government.* 2 vols. New York: D. Appleton, 1881.

Davis, William C. *Breckinridge: Statesman, Soldier, Symbol.* Baton Rouge: Louisiana State University Press, 1974.

———. *Jefferson Davis: The Man and His Hour.* New York: HarperCollins, 1991.

Dick, Everett. *The Dixie Frontier: A Social History.* New York: Knopf, 1948.

Elder, Robert. *The Sacred Mirror: Evangelicalism, Honor, and Identity in the Deep South, 1790–1860.* Chapel Hill: University of North Carolina Press, 2016.

Elliott, Sam Davis. *Isham G. Harris of Tennessee: Confederate Governor and United States Senator.* Baton Rouge: Louisiana State University Press, 2010.

Engle, Stephen D. *Don Carlos Buell: Most Promising of All.* Chapel Hill: University of North Carolina Press, 1999.

————. *Struggle for the Heartland: The Campaign from Fort Henry to Corinth*. Lincoln: University of Nebraska Press, 2001.

————. "'Thank God, He Has Rescued His Character': Albert Sidney Johnston, Southern Hamlet of the Confederacy." In *Leaders of the Lost Cause: New Perspectives on the Confederate High Command*, edited by Gary W. Gallagher and Joseph T. Glatthaar, 133–63. Mechanicsburg, PA: Stackpole Books, 2004.

Foster, Gaines M. *Ghosts of the Confederacy: Defeat, the Lost Cause, and the Emergence of the New South*. New York: Oxford University Press, 1987.

Glover, Lorri. *Southern Sons: Becoming Men in the New Nation*. Baltimore: Johns Hopkins University Press, 2007.

Grant, Ulysses S. "The Battle of Shiloh." In Johnson and Buel, *Battles and Leaders of the Civil War*, 1:465–86.

————. *The Personal Memoirs of Ulysses S. Grant: The Complete Annotated Edition*. Edited by John F. Marszalek, David F. Nolen, and Louie P. Gallo. Cambridge, MA: Harvard University Press, 2017.

Greenberg, Kenneth S. *Honor and Slavery*. Princeton, NJ: Princeton University Press, 2020.

————. *Masters and Statesmen: The Political Culture of American Slavery*. Baltimore: Johns Hopkins University Press, 1988.

Hafendorfer, Kenneth A. *Mill Springs: Campaign and Battle of Mill Springs, Kentucky*. Louisville: KH Press, 2001.

Haley, James L. *Sam Houston*. Norman: University of Oklahoma Press, 2002.

Hardee, William J. *Rifle and Light Infantry Tactics; for the Exercise and Manoeuvres of Troops when Acting as Light Infantry or Riflemen*. Philadelphia: Lippincott, Grambo, 1855.

Hartje, Robert G. *Van Dorn: The Life and Times of a Confederate General*. Nashville: Vanderbilt University Press, 1967.

Hess, Earl J. *Braxton Bragg: The Most Hated Man in the Confederacy*. Chapel Hill: University of North Carolina Press, 2016.

Horn, Huston. *Leonidas Polk: Warrior Bishop of the Confederacy*. Lawrence: University Press of Kansas, 2019.

Horsely, A. S. "Reminiscences of Shiloh." *Confederate Veteran* 2, no. 8 (August 1894): 234.

Hughes, Nathaniel Cheairs, Jr. *The Battle of Belmont: Grant Strikes South*. Chapel Hill: University of North Carolina Press, 1991.

————. *General William J. Hardee: Old Reliable*. Baton Rouge: Louisiana State University Press, 1965.

Hughes, Nathaniel Cheairs, Jr., and Roy P. Stonesifer Jr. *The Life and Wars of Gideon J. Pillow*. Chapel Hill: University of North Carolina Press, 1993.

Inge, Mrs. F. A. "Corinth, Miss. in Early War Days." *Confederate Veteran* 17, no. 9 (September 1909): 442–44.

———. "Corinth, Miss. in War Times." *Confederate Veteran* 23, no. 9 (September 1915): 412–13.

Isaac, Rhys. *The Transformation of Virginia: 1740–1790*. Chapel Hill: University of North Carolina Press, 1980.

Johnson, Robert Underwood, and Clarence Clough Buel, eds. *Battles and Leaders of the Civil War, Being for the Most Part Contributions by Union and Confederate Officers: Based upon "The Century" War Series*. 4 vols. New York, 1884–87.

Johnston, William Preston. "Albert Sidney Johnston at Shiloh." In Johnson and Buel, *Battles and Leaders of the Civil War*, 1:540–68.

———. *The Life of Gen. Albert Sidney Johnston: His Service in the Armies of the United States, the Republic of Texas, and the Confederate States*. New York: D. Appleton, 1879.

Jomini, Henri de. *The Art of War*. Philadelphia: J. B. Lippincott, 1862.

Jones, J. B. *A Rebel War Clerk's Diary: At the Confederate States Capital*. 2 vols. Edited by James I. Robertson Jr. Lawrence: University Press of Kansas, 2015.

Jordan, Thomas. "Notes of a Confederate Staff-Officer at Shiloh." In Johnson and Buel, *Battles and Leaders of the Civil War*, 1:594–603.

Jordan, Thomas, and J. P. Pryor. *The Campaigns of Lieut.-Gen. N. B. Forrest, and of Forrest's Cavalry, With Portraits, Maps, and Illustrations*. New Orleans: Blelock, 1868.

Lockett, Samuel. "Surprise and Withdrawal at Shiloh." In Johnson and Buel, *Battles and Leaders of the Civil War*, 1:604–6.

Lundberg, John R. "'I Must Save This Army': Albert Sidney Johnston and the Shiloh Campaign." In *The Shiloh Campaign*, edited by Steven E. Woodworth, 8–28. Carbondale: Southern Illinois University Press, 2009.

Mackowski, Chris, and Brian Matthew Jordan, eds. *The Great "What Ifs" of the American Civil War: Historians Tackle the Conflict's Most Intriguing Possibilities*. El Dorado Hills, CA: Savas Beatie, 2021.

Marszalek, John F. *Sherman: A Soldier's Passion for Order*. New York: Free Press, 1993.

Maury, Dabney H. *Recollections of a Virginian in the Mexican, Indian, and Civil Wars*. New York: Charles Scribner's Sons, 1894.

McDonough, James Lee. *Shiloh: In Hell before Night*. Knoxville: University of Tennessee Press, 1977.

———. *William Tecumseh Sherman: In the Service of My Country: A Life*. New York: Norton, 2016.

McMurry, Richard M. *Two Great Rebel Armies: An Essay in Confederate Military History*. Chapel Hill: University of North Carolina Press, 1989.

McPherson, James B. *Battle Cry of Freedom: The Civil War Era*. New York: Oxford University Press, 1988.

———. *For Cause & Comrades: Why Men Fought in the Civil War*. New York: Oxford University Press, 1997.

McWhiney, Grady. *Braxton Bragg and Confederate Defeat. Volume 1: Field Command.* New York: Columbia University Press, 1969.

Nevins, Allen, ed. *Diary of the Civil War.* New York: Macmillan, 1962.

Parks, Joseph H. *General Leonidas Polk, C.S.A.: The Fighting Bishop.* Baton Rouge: Louisiana State University Press, 1962.

Potter, E. B. *Nimitz.* Annapolis: Naval Institute Press, 1976.

Reed, David W. *The Battle of Shiloh and the Organizations Engaged.* Washington, DC: Government Printing Office, 1909.

Register of the Officers and Cadets of the U.S. Military Academy, June, 1823. New York: U.S. Military Academy Printing Office, 1823.

Register of the Officers and Cadets of the U.S. Military Academy, June, 1824. New York: U.S. Military Academy Printing Office, 1824.

Register of the Officers and Cadets of the U.S. Military Academy, June, 1825. New York: U.S. Military Academy Printing Office, 1825.

Register of the Officers and Cadets of the U.S. Military Academy, June, 1826. New York: U.S. Military Academy Printing Office, 1826.

Roland, Charles P. *Albert Sidney Johnston: Jefferson Davis' Greatest General.* Abilene, TX: McWhiney Foundation Press, 2000.

———. *Albert Sidney Johnston: Soldier of Three Republics.* Austin: University of Texas Press, 1964.

Roll of the Cadets Arranged According to Merit in Conduct for the Year Ending 30th June, 1826. New York: U.S. Military Academy Printing Office, 1826.

Roman, Alfred. *The Military Operations of General Beauregard.* 2 vols. New York: Harper and Brothers, 1884.

Sehlinger, Peter J. *Kentucky's Last Cavalier: General William Preston, 1816–1887.* Lexington: University Press of Kentucky, 2004.

Shaw, Arthur Marvin, Jr. "General Albert Sidney Johnston's Horses at Shiloh." *Arkansas Historical Quarterly* 8, no. 3 (Autumn 1949): 206–10.

Sherman, William T. *Memoirs of General William T. Sherman: Written by Himself.* 2 vols. New York: D. Appleton, 1875.

Shoup, F. A. "How We Went to Shiloh." *Confederate Veteran* 2, no. 5 (May 1894): 137–40.

Smith, Timothy B. *Corinth 1862: Siege, Battle, Occupation.* Lawrence: University Press of Kansas, 2012.

———. "A Frolic Up the Tennessee." *America's Civil War* (March 2017): 44–49.

———. *Grant Invades Tennessee: The 1862 Battles for Forts Henry and Donelson.* Lawrence: University Press of Kansas, 2016.

———. "Historians and the Battle of Shiloh: One Hundred and Forty Years of Controversy." *Tennessee Historical Quarterly* 62, no. 4 (2003): 332–53.

———. "Lasting Void." *America's Civil War* 34, no. 2 (May 2021): 20–27.

———. "Myths of Shiloh." *America's Civil War* (May 2006): 30–36, 71.

———. *Rethinking Shiloh: Myth and Memory*. Knoxville: University of Tennessee Press, 2013.

———. *Shiloh: Conquer or Perish*. Lawrence: University Press of Kansas, 2014.

———. *This Great Battlefield of Shiloh: History, Memory, and the Establishment of a Civil War National Military Park*. Knoxville: University of Tennessee Press, 2004.

———. "To Conquer or Perish: The Last Hours of Albert Sidney Johnston." In *Confederate Generals in the Western Theater: An Anthology, Volume 3*, edited by Larry Hewitt and Art Bergeron, 21–37. Knoxville: University of Tennessee Press, 2011.

Stahr, Walter. *Seward: Lincoln's Indispensable Man*. New York: Simon and Schuster, 2013.

Stowe, Steven M. *Intimacy and Power in the Old South: Ritual in the Lives of Planters*. Baltimore: Johns Hopkins University Press, 1987.

Sword, Wiley. *Shiloh: Bloody April*. Rev. ed. Dayton, OH: Morningside, 2001.

Symonds, Craig L. *Joseph E. Johnston: A Civil War Biography*. New York: Norton, 1992.

———. *Nimitz at War: Command Leadership from Pearl Harbor to Tokyo Bay*. New York: Oxford University Press, 2022.

Thomas, Emory M. *Robert E. Lee: A Biography*. New York: Norton, 1995.

Trask, Kerry A. *Black Hawk: The Battle for the Heart of America*. New York: Henry Holt, 2005.

Ulmer, J. B. "A Glimpse of Albert Sidney Johnston through the Smoke of Shiloh." *Southwestern Historical Quarterly* 10, no. 4 (April 1907): 285–96.

Warner, Ezra J. *Generals in Gray: Lives of the Confederate Commanders*. Baton Rouge: Louisiana State University Press, 1959.

War of the Rebellion: A Compilation of the Official Records of the Union and Confederate Armies. 128 vols. Washington, DC: Government Printing Office, 1880–1901.

Watson, Samuel J. *Peacekeepers and Conquerors: The Army Officer Corps on the American Frontier, 1821–1846*. Lawrence: University Press of Kansas, 2013.

Williams, T. Harry. *P. G. T. Beauregard: Napoleon in Gray*. Baton Rouge: Louisiana State University Press, 1954.

Wills, Brian Steel. *George Henry Thomas: As True as Steel*. Lawrence: University Press of Kansas, 2012.

Wingfield, Marshall. *General A. P. Stewart: His Life and Letters*. Memphis: West Tennessee Historical Society, 1954.

Wood, Gordon S. *Empire of Liberty: A History of the Early Republic, 1789–1815*. New York: Oxford University Press, 2009.

Woodworth, Steven E. *Jefferson Davis and His Generals: The Failure of Confederate Command in the West*. Lawrence: University Press of Kansas, 1990.

———. "When Merit Was Not Enough: Albert Sidney Johnston and Confederate Defeat in the West, 1862." In *Civil War Generals in Defeat*, edited by Steven E. Woodworth, 9–27. Lawrence: University Press of Kansas, 1999.

Wooster, Robert. *The United States Army and the Making of America: From Confederation to Empire, 1775–1903*. Lawrence: University Press of Kansas, 2021.

Wyatt-Brown, Bertram. *Southern Honor: Ethics and Behavior in the Old South*. New York: Oxford University Press, 1982.

———. *Southern Honor: Ethics and Behavior in the Old South*. 25th anniv. ed. New York: Oxford University Press, 2007.

INDEX

———•———

Henderson, Kentucky, 60
Henderson Station, Tennessee, 78
Henry, Gustavus A., 60–62, 81
Hindman, Thomas, 84, 120, 128–129, 134, 149
Hobbs, Edward, 14
Hood, John B., 34, 175
Hooker, Joseph, 30, 163
Houston, Sam, 18, 20, 23–25, 29, 38
Houston, Texas, 26, 175
Hughes, Nathaniel C., 93
Humboldt, Tennessee, 60, 62, 90
Hunt, R. P., 58
Huntsville, Alabama, 120
Hurlbut, Stephen A., 155, 160
Huston, Felix, xv, 21–22

Illinois, 11, 36, 65, 80
Indians, 11, 13, 17, 24, 36, 39–40, 63
Indian Removal Policy, 11
Indian Territory, 35, 47, 49–50, 53, 69
Inge, Augusta, 131, 141, 165
Inge, William, 131, 141
Ingram's Barr, Tennessee, 71
Iowa, xvii
Island No. 10, 90, 137
Isaac, Rhys, xiii
Iuka, Mississippi, 128, 130, 133–134

Jack, Thomas M., 125, 141, 156, 167, 175
Jackson, Andrew, 4, 11, 23, 29
Jackson, Mississippi, 90, 134
Jackson, Tennessee, 117–118, 128–129, 132, 135
John K. Jackson, 155, 157
Jackson, Thomas K., 58
Jefferson Barracks, Missouri, 9–11, 34
Jefferson, Thomas, 6
John (slave), 32–33
Johnson, Andrew, 57
Johnson, Bushrod, 75, 87, 93, 102–103, 126
Johnson, George W., 90, 132
Johnson, Robert W., 58
Johnston, Abigail Harris, 1

Johnston, Albert Sidney: ancestry, 1–2; early life, 2–13; crisis, 13–17; in Texas, 18–31; as paymaster, 31–33; as colonel of 2nd U.S. Cavalry, 33–36; and Utah Expedition, 36–39; as commander Department of the Pacific, 39–42; in early western Confederate command, 43–73; and forts Henry and Donelson, 74–104; and retreat to Corinth, 115–134; and Shiloh, xi, 135–168; legacy, 169–183
Johnston, Albert Sidney, Jr., 26, 44
Johnston, Archibald, 1
Johnston, Darius, 4, 19
Johnston, Eliza, 26, 28–33, 35–36, 39–40, 57–58, 75, 121, 166, 176
Johnston, Harris, 4
Johnston, Henrietta Preston (wife), 10–12, 14–16, 26
Johnston, Henrietta Preston (daughter), 12, 14–15
Johnston, John (father), 1, 4
Johnston, John (brother), 4, 14
Johnston, Joseph E., xiv, 1, 8, 46, 172
Johnston, Josiah Stoddard, 4–8, 13–17, 19, 26, 36
Johnston, Lucius, 4
Johnston, Maria Preston, 14, 16
Johnston, Mary Stoddard, 1
Johnston, Mary (daughter), 32
Johnston, Orramel, 4, 19
Johnston, Rosa, 57
Johnston, William Preston, xv, xvii, 8, 11, 14–15, 27, 31–33, 36, 40, 44–45, 49, 50, 57, 76, 121, 163–166, 168, 173, 176
Johnston, William Stoddard, 14
Jordan, Thomas, 137, 145

Kansas, 47, 69
Kentucky, xi, xix, xxi, 1, 3–4, 7, 10, 12, 15, 18, 22–23, 25–28, 32–34, 39, 44, 47, 50–53, 56, 60, 64–66, 69, 72, 76–77, 79–81, 83–85, 91, 93, 95, 102, 117–118, 122–123, 131–132, 164, 173–174; Legislature, 52
Kentucky Campaign, 174
Knoxville, Tennessee, 47, 91, 118